Contents

List of contributors   v
Acknowledgements   vii

Introduction: The meaning of mass imprisonment   1
David Garland

1   The causes and consequences of prison growth in the
    United States   4
    Marc Mauer

2   Fear and loathing in late modernity: Reflections on the
    cultural sources of mass imprisonment in the United States 15
    Jonathan Simon

3   Television, public space and prison population: A commentary
    on Mauer and Simon   28
    Thomas Mathiesen

4   Governing social marginality: Welfare, incarceration, and
    the transformation of state policy   35
    Katherine Beckett and Bruce Western

5   The *macho* penal economy: Mass incarceration in the United
    States – a European perspective   51
    David Downes

6   *Novus ordo saeclorum*?: A commentary on Downes, and on
    Beckett and Western   70
    David F. Greenberg

7   Deadly symbiosis: When ghetto and prison meet and mesh   82
    Loïc Wacquant

8   Going straight: The story of a young inner-city ex-convict 121
    Elijah Anderson

9   Bringing the individual back in: A commentary on Wacquant
    and Anderson   138
    Jerome Miller

10   Imprisonment rates and the new politics of criminal
      punishment   145
      Franklin E. Zimring

11   Unthought thoughts: The influence of changing sensibilities
      on penal policies   150
      Michael Tonry

12   Facts, values and prison policies: A commentary on
      Zimring and Tonry   165
      James B. Jacobs

13   The private and the public in penal history: A commentary
      on Zimring and Tonry   171
      Alex Lichtenstein

      Epilogue: The new iron cage   179
      David Garland

      Index   182

List of contributors

ELIJAH ANDERSON is the Charles and William L. Day Professor of the Social Sciences and Professor of Sociology at the University of Pennsylvania.

KATHERINE BECKETT is Associate professor in the Department of Sociology at the University of Washington. Her research focuses on the political and cultural dynamics of crime and punishment.

DAVID DOWNES is Professor of Social Administration and Director of the Mannheim Centre for Criminology and Criminal Justice at the London School of Economics. His books include *The delinquent solution* (1966), *Contrasts in tolerance* (1988) and, with Paul Rock, *Understanding deviance* (3rd edn 1998).

DAVID GARLAND is Professor of Law and Sociology at New York University and editor-in-chief of *Punishment & Society*. His most recent book is *The Culture of Control* (2001) co-published by Oxford University Press and University of Chicago Press.

DAVID F. GREENBERG is Professor of Sociology at New York University. A former prisoners' rights activist, he has published books and articles on physics, crime, criminal justice, law, homosexuality, statistics and mathematical modeling.

JAMES B. JACOBS is Professor of Law and Director, Center for Research in Crime and Justice, NYU School of Law. He has been a visiting professor at Columbia Law School and a Fulbright scholar at the University of Cape Town. His publications include *The pursuit of absolute integrity: how corruption control makes government ineffective* (with Frank Anechiarico, 1996), *Hate crimes: criminal law and identity politics* (with Kimberly Potter, 1998) and *Gotham unbound: the liberation of NYC from the grip of organized crime* (with Colleen Friel and Robert Raddick, 1999).

ALEX LICHTENSTEIN is the author of *Twice the Work of Free Labor: The Political Economy of Convict Labor in the New South* (Verso), and Associate Professor of History at Florida International University in Miami. He is currently a Fulbright Scholar at the University of the Western Cape, South Africa.

THOMAS MATHIESEN, born 1933, since 1972 professor of sociology of law at the University of Oslo, Norway. The author of a number of books in sociology of law, criminology, political sociology and sociology of the media. He was one of the founders of the Scandinavian prison movement.

MARC MAUER is Assistant Director of the Sentencing Project and the author of *Race to incarcerate* (The New Press). His areas of research include sentencing policy, racial disparity in the criminal justice system, and the unintended consequences of incarceration.

JEROME MILLER is President of the National Center on Institutions and Alternatives, Virginia, USA – a non-profit making agency involved in criminal justice and juvenile justice issues. He previously headed the Massachusetts Department of Youth Services. He is the author of *Search and destroy: American African males in the criminal justice system* (Cambridge University Press, 1998).

JONATHAN SIMON is Professor of Law at the University of Miami and has also taught at the University of Michigan, New York University, and Yale University. His current research deals with the transformation of regulatory and crime control strategies in advanced liberal societies.

MICHAEL TONRY is Director, Institute of Criminology, University of Cambridge and Sonosky Professor of Law and Public Policy, University of Minnesota.

LOÏC WACQUANT is Researcher at the Centre de sociologie européenne du Collège de France and an Associate Professor of Sociology and Research Fellow at the Earl Warren Legal Institute, University of California-Berkeley. He is the author of *Les Prisons de la misère, Corps et âme. Carnet ethnographique d'un apprenti-boxeur*, and of the forthcoming *In the Zone: Life in the Dark Ghetto at Century's End*. Aside from racial domination and the role of carceral institutions in the regulation of social misery in neoliberal society, his interests include comparative urban marginality, social theory, violence and the body.

BRUCE WESTERN is a Professor of Sociology at Princeton University. His interests include labour market dynamics and comparative social policy.

FRANKLIN E. ZIMRING is William G. Simon Professor of Law and Director of the Earl Warren Legal Institute at the University of California at Berkeley. He is co-author with Gordon Hawkins, of *The scale of imprisonment* (1991) and *Democracy and punishment: three strikes and you're out in California* (also with Sam Kanin).

Acknowledgements

The chapters published here were first published as a Special Issue of *Punishment & Society: The International Journal of Penology* in January 2001. Prior to that, they were presented as papers at a conference on 'The Causes and Consequences of Mass Imprisonment in the USA' that was held at New York University School of Law on 26 February 2000. The Institute of Law and Society at NYU sponsored the conference, with support from the School of Law and the Faculty of Arts and Sciences. As conference organizer, and editor of the present book, I would like to record my thanks to all conference participants as well as to the authors of the chapters published here. I would also like to record my gratitude to Dean John Sexton for his support, to Gina Diaz for her administrative assistance, and to Bobbie Glover for her help and advice. Finally, I would like to thank the editors and production staff at Sage publications, particularly Gillian Stern, Miranda Nunhofer and Anthony Green, who have been remarkably helpful and supportive throughout.

David Garland

Introduction

The meaning of mass imprisonment

DAVID GARLAND

The contributors to this volume have used the term 'mass imprisonment' to describe the institution that has emerged in the United States over the past two decades. Current government estimates suggest that, in the course of the present year, the total number of inmates incarcerated in America's jails and prisons will exceed 2,000,000 for the first time ever. This is an unprecedented event in the history of the USA and, more generally, in the history of liberal democracy.

For most of the 20th century, America's imprisonment rate fluctuated around a stable mean of about 110 per 100,000. In 1973 the rate began to increase and it has continued to increase in every single year since. During the 1990s – the decade of widespread and sustained reductions in American crime rates – prison growth accelerated and the already high prison population was doubled. Today's imprisonment rate (the number in custody as a proportion of the general population) is over 450 per 100,000 or 680 per 100,000 if one includes inmates in local jails. This rate is five times as large as it was in 1972. Compared to European and Scandinavian countries, the American rate is six to 10 times higher.

This is a phenomenon – Emile Durkheim (1933) would say a pathological phenomenon – that has no parallel in the western world. One has to look to China and Russia to get comparable incarceration patterns, and the news from Russia is that the government is doing everything it can to decarcerate. Because it is so extraordinary, this phenomenon should be differentiated from imprisonment as it occurs in other comparable nations. An extraordinary phenomenon of this kind deserves a name of its own. The 17th century had its 'Great Confinement', when the poor and the mad all over Europe were moved into houses of correction and asylums for the first time – a process memorably described by Michel Foucault in *Madness and civilization* (1967). The Soviet Union had its gulag archipelago, vividly portrayed by Alexander Solzhenitsyn (1997) and countless other survivors of the labour camps. America now has 'mass imprisonment' – a new name to describe an altogether new phenomenon.

What are the defining features of mass imprisonment? There are, I think, two that are essential. One is sheer numbers. Mass imprisonment implies a rate of imprisonment and a size of prison population that is markedly above the historical and comparative norm for societies of this type. The US prison system clearly meets these criteria. The other feature is the social concentration of imprisonment's effects. Imprisonment becomes *mass imprisonment* when it ceases to be the incarceration of individual offenders and becomes the systematic imprisonment of whole groups of the population. In the case of the USA, the group concerned is, of course, young black males in large urban centres. For these sections of the population imprisonment has become normalized. It has come to be a regular, predictable part of experience, rather than a rare and infrequent event.

As Mauer and Huling (1995) and others have shown, 1 in 3 black men aged 20 to 29 years of age is currently in penal custody or under penal supervision. If current trends continue, 30 percent of all black males born today will spend some of their lives in prison. (The comparative figure for white males is 4 percent and for Hispanics 14 percent.) This means that imprisonment has become one of the social institutions that structure this group's experience. It becomes part of the socialization process. Every family, every household, every individual in these neighbourhoods has direct personal knowledge of the prison – through a spouse, a child, a parent, a neighbour, a friend. Imprisonment ceases to be the fate of a few criminal individuals and becomes a shaping institution for whole sectors of the population.

We do not currently know what 'mass imprisonment' will mean for the society in which it develops, or for the groups who are most directly affected. As Frank Zimring and Gordon Hawkins (1991) have pointed out, we do not have a jurisprudence of the scale of imprisonment. For all of our philosophizing about the *purpose* of imprisonment, we have scarcely begun to address the question of its *extent*. We have libraries of criminological research about the impact of imprisonment upon the individual offender, but scarcely anything on its *social* impact upon communities and neighbourhoods.

Mass imprisonment was not a policy that was proposed, researched, costed, debated and democratically agreed. America did not collectively decide to get into the business of mass imprisonment in the way that it decided to build the institutions of the New Deal, or the Great Society, or even the low-tax, low-spending, free-market institutions of Reaganomics. Instead, mass imprisonment emerged as the overdetermined outcome of a converging series of policies and decisions. Determinate sentence structures; the war against drugs; mandatory sentencing; truth in sentencing; the emergence of private corrections; the political events and calculations that made everyone tough on crime – these developments built upon one another and produced the flow of prisoners into custody. These developments may have been part of a general realignment of politics and culture – part of the same process that has transformed the welfare state and 'ended welfare as we know it' – but they did not take the form of a coherent programme. They were never presented and debated as a package that voters could take or leave. Instead America has drifted into this situation, with voters and politicians and judges and corporations willing the specific means without anyone pausing to assess the overall outcome.

We are only now beginning to glimpse the social and financial costs of this institution in terms of: reduced state budgets for other spending; the alienation of whole sectors of the population; the normalization of the prison experience and the transfer of prison culture into the community; the criminogenic consequences of custody for inmates and their families and their children; and the disenfranchisement of whole sectors of the community. Particularly troubling is the way in which penal exclusion has been layered on top of economic and racial exclusion, ensuring that social divisions are deepened, and that a criminalized underclass is brought into existence and systematically perpetuated.

We are just beginning to reflect upon the political and cultural meanings of this new institution, upon what it means for America to be a mass imprisonment society – a process of reflection that has begun somewhat late in the day. What does it say about this society that, in a matter of 30 years, the prison has gone from being a failed correctional facility, destined for abolition, to being a major and apparently indispensable element of modern social order? What are the limits to which this process can be taken? What are its implications for penal politics and policies elsewhere? How could we reverse these processes, assuming that we wanted to, and assuming that the demand for safety, security and protection against crime is not going to lessen any time soon? The articles in this volume seek to further this process of reflection, and to deepen our understanding of this new social institution – an overdue task that is now more urgent than ever.

References

Durkheim, E. (1933) *The division of labor in society*. New York: Free Press.

Foucault, M. (1967) *Madness and civilization: a history of insanity in the age of reason*. London: Tavistock.

Mauer, M. and Huling, T. (1995) *Young black Americans and the criminal justice system*. Washington, DC: The Sentencing Project.

Solzhenitsyn, A.I. (1997) *The gulag archipelago*. New York: Westview.

Zimring, F.E. and Hawkins, G. (1991) *The scale of imprisonment*. Chicago, IL: University of Chicago Press.

1 The causes and consequences of prison growth in the United States

MARC MAUER

Imagine that we are back in 1972 and Richard Nixon is President. In recent years rising rates of crime and urban unrest have become significant sources of concern for the nation. The President makes a televised address to the nation to announce an initiative to respond to the crime problem. He declares a bold program – he will lead the nation in building enough prison cells to house an additional 1 million inmates over the current population of 200,000. Further, since street crime is disproportionately concentrated in black and Hispanic communities, two-thirds of the new prison cells will be reserved for minorities. And, with the death penalty having just been declared unconstitutional, he will spearhead a drive to enact new laws and fill the nation's Death Rows with more than 3000 inmates.

What would have been the reaction to such a proposal? One can certainly imagine massive protests led by civil rights organizations and their allies. Editorial boards at leading newspapers – many of which already viewed Nixon with distrust – would have written scathing editorials decrying the abandonment of more positive solutions to inner-city problems. And, leading criminologists would have bemoaned the failure to address the underlying societal factors leading to crime.

Nixon never proposed such an audacious plan, of course, yet these are precisely the outcomes that national policy has produced in the ensuing quarter century. Seemingly oblivious to fluctuations in crime rates, the scale of incarceration has risen inexorably to the point where an inmate population of 2 million Americans seems likely by year-end 2001.

Political analysts in 1972 would have had to be particularly prescient to have anticipated such developments. Indeed, one could have argued at the time that a *reduction* in the use of incarceration was a more likely development. In 1971, the Attica prison rebellion had led to the tragic loss of lives of 43 inmates and guards, while symbolizing for the nation a politically conscious prisoner population raising a fundamental critique of the penal system. That same year, David Rothman published his highly acclaimed, *The discovery of the asylum,* closing with these words: '. . . we have been gradually escaping from institutional responses and one can foresee the period when incarceration will be used *still more rarely* than it is today' (Rothman, 1971: 295, emphasis added). By 1973, the final report of the National Advisory Commission on Criminal Justice Standards and Goals recommended that 'no new institutions for adults should be built and exist-ing institutions for juveniles should be closed' and concluded that 'the prison, the refor-matory, and the jail have achieved only a shocking record of failure' (National Advisory Commission on Criminal Justice Standards and Goals, 1973: 358, 597).

What is most striking about these calls for a reduction in the use of incarceration is that they were voiced at a time when the inmate population in prisons and jails totaled just over 300,000, a rate of incarceration about one-fifth of that today. Not only is that level of incarceration unimaginable in the current political climate, but even a mora-torium on the construction of new institutions hardly seems possible.

This article will explore the criminal justice policy changes that have substantially con-tributed to this unprecedented prison-building frenzy, as well as the political climate under-lying these developments. It will also assess the efforts of reformers and suggest that many of their cherished arguments in support of reduced incarceration may be unpersuasive.

POLICY CHANGES AND INCARCERATION

In tracing the landscape of change in criminal justice policy that has contributed to the growing use of imprisonment the most significant area of examination is sentencing policy. Beginning in the 1970s we see a shift toward the use of determinate sentencing in a variety of forms and its attendant consequences on power relationships within the court system and, perhaps more significantly, on public perceptions of issues of crime and punishment.

Prior to this, American sentencing policy had been characterized by indeterminate sentencing, accompanied by an emphasis on rehabilitation as a major objective (whether reasonably implemented or not). That model came under attack in the 1960s from both the political left and right. Liberals came to view the broad range of discretion available to sentencing judges and parole boards as too fraught with potential for discrimination based on race, gender, and other factors, while conservatives felt that criminals were not being treated harshly enough. Both camps came to embrace sentencing structures that were far more fixed, or determinate, than the prevailing models.

Early proposals designed to implement these changes are illustrative of the sometimes competing goals offered by proponents. New York's 'Rockefeller Drug Laws,' adopted in 1973 and still among the nation's harshest drug policies, called for a 15-year prison term for anyone convicted of selling 2 ounces or possessing 4 ounces of narcotics, regard-less of the offender's criminal history. Sentencing guidelines systems, advocated promi-nently by Marvin Frankel in his 1972 book, *Criminal sentences: law without order*, envisioned a more rational sentencing structure in which judicial discretion was con-strained to varying degrees and sentences were largely determined by a grid system emphasizing the severity of the offense and the offender's prior record (Frankel, 1972). Of the structured sentencing systems in place today in the federal courts and one-third of the states, the federal guidelines stand at one extreme in placing severe constraints on the consideration of individual offender characteristics, while systems such as those in Minnesota and North Carolina grant judges greater latitude in considering relevant vari-ables (see generally Tonry, 1996).

The movement toward determinate sentencing quickened in the 1980s and continues through the present, with much of it intimately intertwined with the 'war on drugs.'

Political leaders and law enforcement officials at the state and local level quickly embraced the launching of this new 'war' by the Reagan Administration in the early 1980s. In Washington, both budget allocations and political attention gave prominence to drug issues throughout the decade. Federal funding for the drug war soared from $1.5 billion in 1981 to $6.6 billion by 1989 (The White House, 1992) (and continued to rise to $17 billion by 1999). As a public policy concern, political attention heightened regarding the drug 'scourge' by the Bush Administration and its drug 'czar' William Bennett. As Katherine Beckett has documented, public concern about the drug problem followed, rather than instigated, policymaker initiatives in this area (Beckett, 1997).

Law enforcement attention to drug offenses increased dramatically, with a doubling of drug arrests in the 1980s and a record 1.6 million arrests by 1998. Those offenders convicted on drug charges often were faced with the new generation of mandatory sentencing penalties enacted throughout the country. The federal drug penalties enacted in the Anti-Drug Abuse Act of 1986 and the Anti-Drug Abuse Act of 1988 impose five-year mandatory prison terms for possession of as little as 5 grams of crack cocaine. Harsh penalties, most often imposed for drug offenses, were adopted at the state level as well. In Michigan, for example, a 1978 law ('Public Act 368 of 1978' – sometimes referred to as the '650 Lifer Law') required that the sale of 650 grams of heroin or cocaine, even for a first offender, be punished by a mandatory sentence of life without parole, the same penalty as for first degree murder. (The legislation was eventually scaled back in 1998.) A 1996 survey published by the Bureau of Justice Assistance indicated that every state had adopted some form of mandatory sentencing (Bureau of Justice Assistance, 1996).

The impact of these sentencing changes on prison populations has been dramatic, and far outweighs any change in crime rates as a contributing factor. Criminologists Alfred Blumstein and Allen Beck have documented that 88 percent of the tripling of the national prison population from 1980 to 1996 is explained by changes in the imposition of punishment (51 percent a greater likelihood of incarceration upon conviction and 37 percent longer prison terms), while changes in crime rates explain only 12 percent of the rise (Blumstein and Beck, 1999).

By the year 2000, not only are mandatory prison terms employed across the nation, but 'three strikes and you're out' policies exist in half the states (Clark et al., 1997) (although only used extensively in California and Georgia), as do 'truth in sentencing' statutes, which generally lengthen time served in prison by offenders. Despite the fact that crime rates have declined for much of the 1990s, prison populations have continued their seemingly inexorable climb. While harsh sentencing policies are clearly a key factor in this regard, in recent years higher rates of probation and parole revocation have played an increasing role in prison admissions (Caplow and Simon, 1999). This trend is most likely a result of a combination of factors: high caseloads that result in limited services to offenders; untreated substance abuse leading to new crimes or violations; and the failure to develop a broader range of non-incarcerative options for responding to violations.

INCARCERATION AND CRIME

Public policy discourse has all too often assumed an overly simplistic relationship between incarceration and crime, ignoring the complex set of factors that influence individual behavior. While it is not inappropriate to examine the impact of incarceration on crime, in doing so one would also want to explore two additional key questions: (1) to the extent that incarceration has an impact on crime, how does this compare with other potential investments in crime control? And (2) what are the social costs of the investment in incarceration and how are they borne in society? The advent of mass imprisonment is now creating some discussion of these questions. This section will focus only on providing an overview of what we know about incarceration and crime control.

From the vantage point of the late 1990s one might (and many politicians have) become rather smug about the results achieved by the rising levels of imprisonment. While the number of inmates rose by 58 percent from 1991 to 1998, crime rates declined by 22 percent and rates of violent crime by 25 percent. Murder rates in 1998 were at a 30-year low. For some observers, this confirmed the 'prison works' theory of crime control.

But examining complex relationships such as these over a short time span is not terribly helpful. In fact, the prison–crime correlation for the 1990s is precisely the opposite of that which prevailed in the late 1980s. From 1984 to 1991, the number of inmates nationally rose by 79 percent, while crime rates also increased, by 17 percent, and violent crime by 41 percent. Further, the low homicide rate of the late 1990s, while quite welcome, is all the result of substantial declines in just the past several years. Over a 20-year period of steadily rising incarceration, homicide rates fluctuated within the range of 8–10 per 100,000, not falling below this level until 1996.

Yet homicide is down, and quite substantially. Why is this so? Several factors seem most relevant here. First, the national declines are influenced disproportionately by the dramatic changes in New York City, accounting for 32 percent of the total decline for 1993–4 and 22 percent for 1994–5 (Blumstein and Rosenfeld, 1998). Whether one believes that homicide is down in New York because of aggressive policing or other factors, the one certainty is that the decline is *not* a result of more offenders being incarcerated than in other cities. In fact, the 47 percent drop in homicide in New York from 1990 to 1995 occurred during a time when the state prison population (a majority of whose inmates are from New York City) rose at a significantly lower rate than the national average and the city's jail population actually declined.

Second, changes in homicide (both the rise of the late 1980s and the decline of the 1990s) have disproportionately occurred among juveniles, who are generally not subject to adult incarceration (although this is changing in recent years as states permit more juveniles to be tried as adults). To the extent that general deterrence is a factor in crime control, juveniles have historically been viewed as being less influenced by this than adults.

A more compelling assessment of the decline in homicides (and violence overall) is provided by the mix of factors addressed by Blumstein and Beck (1999), who point to the youth-drugs-guns nexus of causation. As crack cocaine entered urban areas in the mid-1980s new drug markets emerged. These markets primarily employed young men who increasingly resorted to protecting their 'turf' with illegal guns. A surge of violence then ensued, often engulfing neighborhood residents who were not themselves involved in the drug trade.

By the 1990s this picture had changed substantially. Law enforcement strategies in cities such as Boston aimed to stem the supply of guns into communities. As young people witnessed the devastation caused by crack, fewer of them began using the drug themselves. Research by Richard Curtis (1998) also indicates that individuals and communities changed their behavior in ways that provided more protection. Teenagers stopped 'hanging out' in dangerous neighborhoods and drug dealers moved their operations off the streets.

A key issue in the change in crime rates is that the bulk of the recent decline has been in property offenses, and burglary in particular, with a 27 percent decline from 1980 to 1990. But two factors should give us pause in regard to the efficacy of prison in this regard. First, it is quite possible that much of the burglary decline of the 1980s may have been displaced to drug offenses. As a means of making money drug selling is hardly without its risks, but these may be viewed as preferable compared to the risk involved in breaking into a home or business and the often cumbersome process of 'fencing' stolen goods. Second, to the extent that incarceration may have had an impact on burglary rates, imprisoning convicted burglars at a cost of $20,000 a year is a substantial investment that might be more effectively used to address the problems of substance abuse and low-wage jobs that lead to many of these offenses.

To question the value of incarceration in achieving crime control is not to suggest that prison has no impact on these matters. But in the year 2000 we are not discussing whether or not the United States should maintain a prison system at all. Rather, the public policy question is whether, with an already world record-sized prison population, we should continue to expand prison capacity indefinitely. From a crime control perspective, continued expansion is likely to lead to diminishing returns, as successively less serious offenders are incarcerated on average. From a societal standpoint, mass imprisonment results in fundamental concerns of human rights and racial polarization becoming more prominent each day (see Wacquant, this volume).

UNDERSTANDING THE 'TOUGH ON CRIME' MOVEMENT

While the contours of change in criminal justice policy are not difficult to discern, the more intriguing issue regards how and why this particular policy direction was selected. In the early 1970s the nation was confronted with a rising rate of crime. To what extent crime was actually increasing is a matter of some dispute since rates of reporting became more inclusive in the 1970s as a result of funding through the Law Enforcement Assistance Administration and the upgrading of police technology. But the coming of age of the 'baby boom' generation, increasing urbanization and other factors clearly contributed to a certain rise, and clearly a strong *perception*, that crime was increasing.

Given this situation, it was hardly preordained that mass incarceration was the only, or the most effective, approach possible to respond to the problem. Certainly a national commitment to address the 'root causes' of crime would have been an alternative policy approach. Indeed, efforts in this direction were already underway, albeit modestly funded. The 'War on Poverty' of the 1960s, the development of the Head Start program, and the orientation toward drug treatment encouraged by the Nixon administration all contained elements of an approach with a greater social welfare orientation. Further, other industrialized nations were experiencing similar demographic trends, yet chose not to pursue the 'get tough' policies of the USA (although aspects of these trends as well as rising rates of incarceration can be seen in a number of these nations in the 1990s).

Several factors contributed to the 'get tough' climate that began in the 1970s and then was exacerbated in the following decades. These include the following:

- *Politicization of crime.* Prior to the 1960s crime had primarily been addressed as a local issue, rarely surfacing in national political discussions. In 1964, though, Barry Goldwater's presidential campaign clearly proclaimed the problem of 'crime in the streets,' followed by Richard Nixon's 1968 appeal for 'law and order.' These messages resonated with a substantial portion of the population concerned with crime and the social unrest of the period.
- *American culture of individualism.* In comparison to other industrialized nations, the much greater American emphasis on individual as opposed to collective approaches to social welfare created a receptive climate for harsh prison policies. As exemplified by being the only industrialized nation without universal health care, the promotion of more collective approaches to social problems is far less ingrained in the American political culture. This makes it simpler to conceptualize 'solutions' that punish individual behavior rather than addressing underlying contributors to crime. On a broad scale, the consequences of such approaches can be seen in the much-vaunted low unemployment rates of the USA in comparison with western Europe. As the work of Bruce Western and Katherine Beckett (1999) has demonstrated, though, the US rates are substantially tempered by the massive American prison system. If one factors in the prison population as part of the unemployed group, the labor force participation rate in the US declines substantially (Western and Beckett, 1999).
- *Growing conservative political climate.* Changes in criminal justice policy can hardly be divorced from the growing conservative tide that was particularly evidenced with the election of Ronald Reagan in 1980. 'Getting tough' on criminals is consistent with increasingly harsh attitudes and policies toward welfare recipients, immigrants, and other politically unpopular and marginalized groups. In recent years the 'get tough' approach is increasingly being expanded to school expulsion policies, homeless 'removal,' and other areas as well.

Once the tough on crime movement was underway, social and economic developments contributed to its strengthened hold on political and popular discourse. As the manufacturing economies of the Rust Belt cities in the Midwest began to be eclipsed in the 1970s by the emerging high-tech economies, the disparity of wealth between the rich and the poor created an increasingly polarized society, often overlapping with racial divisions (see Wilson, 1997). As the work of Leslie Wilkins (quoted in Young and Brown, 1993) demonstrates, a correlation can be found between national income disparity and rates of incarceration. Wilkins theorizes this relationship as a type of 'negative reward' for those who are not successful in a competitive social structure. But one can also discern the practical aspects of how these developments would emerge under such conditions.

The key variable in this area is the ease with which a society imposes punishment. As Nils Christie (1981) views the relationship, it is easier to impose pain (or punishment) on those with whom we have little in common or do not know in any personal sense (Cayley, 1998). Thus, the more stratified a society, the easier it becomes for the well-off to advocate greater pain for those less fortunate. Two extreme divisions within the USA exacerbate this dynamic. First, due to patterns of racial segregation in housing and employment, low-income African-American communities, which are disproportionately the recipients of criminal punishments, are in many ways spatially and otherwise isolated from the larger society. Second, over the past two decades, American society has become more stratified, and not only by income levels. The rise of gated housing communities, the increasing flight of the middle class from the public school system, and the technological divide in regard to computers and high technology all serve to heighten class and race differences and to reduce interaction. The cumulative impact of these trends can be seen in the mix of social and criminal justice policies that have resulted in a situation whereby 29 percent of black males born today can expect to serve time in prison in their lifetimes (Bonczar and Beck, 1997). These are the very same policies described by political leaders as 'successes' in the war against crime.

Problems with the reform strategy

Criminal justice reform efforts of the past 20 years have achieved greater success than is often acknowledged. In the realm of sentencing alternatives and community corrections, concepts that were once viewed as intriguing but untested are now standard practice in most jurisdictions. Community service and restitution as sanctions are common throughout the country, as are the more complex programmatic responses such as day reporting centers, drug courts, and the use of graduated sanctions for probation and parole violators. And, while political rhetoric on crime policy remains woefully constrained, political leaders ranging from President Clinton to local officials have joined in the growing chorus that recognizes that 'we can't jail our way out of the problem.'

Despite these successes, the prison system continues its relentless rise, seemingly unrelated to crime rates or any rational calculation of its benefits to society. It would be uncharitable to blame this situation on the failings of the relative handful of reformers, but an assessment of reform tactics and strategies over this period may shed some light on the prospects for change in the new century.

Misplaced emphasis on rational analysis and fiscal arguments

Much of the work that has been done to advance the reform agenda has focused on the development of factual analyses that argue that the cost-benefits of mass imprisonment are quite modest, particularly in comparison with other policy options. Without belittling these efforts (I have authored many such analyses myself) their limitations in the policy arena stem from the fact that instrumental considerations such as cost-benefit are but one component in the development of criminal justice policy.

We can see this most clearly on the issue of the death penalty. Where once the question of deterrence was hotly debated, the vast literature demonstrating the absence of any deterrent effect has effectively eliminated this argument from the proponents of capital punishment. Vengeance and retribution – the misunderstanding of the Biblical limitation of 'an eye for an eye' – have since emerged as the primary rationale for continuation of this barbaric policy. Any type of rationality-based cost-effectiveness argument is therefore of little consequence.

Outside the criminal justice arena, one can see parallels with military spending. Arms control analysts spent many frustrating years during the Cold War churning out well-researched arguments decrying the wasteful and unnecessary spending on a bloated military system. These arguments were of little consequence, though, when competing with the popular resonance and emotional force of policies directed at the 'Soviet menace' and the 'threat' of communism.

Misunderstanding of public opinion dynamics

Reformers have also placed their faith in a series of public opinion studies of the past decade showing substantial public support for alternatives to incarceration. Typically, these studies (Doble and Klein, 1989) engage in a two-step polling process. First, respondents are asked to choose a sentence of either prison or probation for a series of hypothetical offenders. Respondents are then offered an additional non-incarcerative sentencing option that incorporates some elements of community service, restitution, and/or treatment. Support for imprisonment generally declines substantially when a broader range of sentencing options are considered. Reformers have taken great comfort in these results and have interpreted them as demonstrating that the public is receptive to reasonable sentencing alternatives when a more robust discussion takes place.

The limitation of this approach, though, is that there is little room in the political arena for such a wide-ranging presentation of alternatives. While alternative options may be significant in a local courtroom looking at real offenders and real sentencing options, they are generally too complex to fit into the political 'sound bite' debate, which rarely allows for more than competing 'get tough' proposals.

Misunderstanding media dynamics

A third, and related, problem regards the media. In this area as well, the problem is more complex than is often presented in the more simplistic versions of blaming 'the media' for all our problems. Despite the failings one can find with all media, there is, after all, a significant difference between the *New York Times* and *America's Most Wanted*. The former, like many other print media, has published many useful analyses of crime trends and the impact of mandatory sentencing policies, as well as editorializing against the death penalty and in favor of expanded treatment as an alternative to current drug policies. Yet while these pronouncements have helped to broaden discussion of criminal justice policy, they have had relatively little impact on actual legislative action.

The primary cause of this failure relates to the powerful imagery of television. With local news broadcasts throughout the nation still composed substantially of crime stories with little context, the nation continues to be flooded with a relentless assault of nightly crime stories, regardless of whether crime is rising or falling. The visual and emotional impact of television is on a different order than the more contained messages of the print media (although many of the print tabloids have clearly emulated TV's style). Further, many of television's drama shows contribute to the portrayal of violence that reinforces these images. Consider the much-acclaimed *NYPD Blue*, winner of many awards for its high-quality scripts and acting. Of the several crimes portrayed in each episode, one or more almost invariably feature a murder or armed robbery. These clearly make for more drama than would a stolen car vignette, but since car theft accounts for 70 times more crime than homicide, their inclusion also distorts our perception of the relative mix of offenses in real life. These images, rather than the more sober editorial one might read in the morning paper, are what linger in the mind as policymakers enact legislation and citizens consider which candidate will have the most impact on crime.)

While each of these factors have been critical in thwarting the reform agenda, the more overriding problem is that our societal framework for considering issues of crime and justice has been changed in very profound ways. It will be exceedingly difficult to reverse course unless this paradigm is addressed.

The most significant change within the criminal justice system is the loss of the individual in the sentencing process, as determinate sentencing and other 'reforms' have taken us from an offender-based to an offense-based system. Without overlooking the abuses that arose in the past within the indeterminate sentencing structure, the primary virtue of that system was its ability to incorporate the individual characteristics and circumstances of the offender into the sentencing process. The movement toward determinate sentencing, particularly in its most extreme forms of mandatory sentencing, 'three strikes' laws, and the federal sentencing guidelines, has largely eliminated any consideration of these unique factors from the court process.

This dehumanization contributes to a vicious cycle in which power is increasingly concentrated in legislative hands at the expense of judges and corrections officials who once had greater input into individual decisionmaking. This is also an area to which reformers have often unwittingly contributed. For example, many advocates (correctly) argue that incarceration at $20,000 per inmate is not terribly cost-effective for non-violent offenders. But the practical corollary of this in the policy arena has been that virtually *no* amount of imprisonment for violent offenders is considered to be too long. 'Three strikes' laws and 'truth in sentencing' statutes exemplify this practice. Public policy has now all but obliterated the distinction between a violent *offender* and a violent *offense*, with Charles Manson emblematic of the former and a battered wife who attacks her abuser the latter. For purposes of incarceration policy, many persons who commit a violent offense do *not* in fact need to be incarcerated for long periods of time for public safety reasons, but the terms of political debate increasingly make this an irrelevant issue.

It is difficult to quantify to what extent this process of dehumanization is tied in with perceptions of race and ethnicity, but the data on prison populations and the political imagery of recent years strongly suggest that these issues are intimately connected. The notion of offenders as 'predators,' not to mention the 'superpredator' mythology with its pernicious political impact, is hard to imagine were we not speaking of a prison system comprised of two-thirds racial and ethnic minorities. The same is true when policymakers talk of the need to remove 'weeds' from our neighborhoods through federally funded Weed and Seed programs. These images certainly do not portray the life history of anyone that we might know or care about, at least enough to investigate whether a prison cell is the most effective response to their offending behavior.

Implications for policy change

The foregoing assessment may be a bit harsh in that, despite being woefully underfunded, reformers have in fact made considerable progress in recent years. This is evidenced both in the proliferation of new programmatic approaches within the criminal justice system as well as increasing recognition of the need for drug treatment and other services. Clearly, these research and advocacy efforts need to continue and be expanded. But if we are to see more overarching change in the landscape, two types of strategic approaches need to be considered. First, reform efforts need to include broader constituencies. These might include education leaders concerned about the diversion of funding to prisons, religious leaders raising moral concerns, and family members in communities heavily impacted by incarceration.

Second, it will be necessary to convey an overarching vision of how to move from a punitive response to crime to a problem-solving orientation. In this regard, consider the strategy of the early civil rights movement. African-Americans were demanding a practical reform – a seat at the front of the bus – but also presented a broad call for freedom in all its manifestations. Some observers would argue that in a time of political conservatism such an approach is foolhardy. But unless such a vision is created, reformers run the risk of continuing to be identified as not tough enough on crime.

How, then, can a more effective public policy picture be presented? The first step involves expanding the discussion of crime policy beyond the day-to-day debates on the relationship between prison and crime to more fundamental concerns about the type of society we wish to create. Is it one where three of every 10 African-American males born today can expect to spend time in prison in their lifetime, most of whom will lose the right to vote for at least part of their adult lives? One in which one-quarter million mentally ill persons are behind bars? Or one in which 11-year-olds can be sentenced to terms of life without parole? These questions are not just idle speculation, but rather the concrete outcomes of the 'get tough' policies that have been promoted over the past quarter century.

The second component of a strategy involves the articulation of a more positive vision of public safety. Contrary to popular wisdom, this is one that is actually intuitively understood by most people. A 'safe' neighborhood is not one with the most police or most frequent use of the death penalty, but rather one with adequate resources to build strong families and communities. Policies of the past 25 years that have invested in prisons at the expense of low-income communities have in effect created less safe neighborhoods.

Within the field of criminal justice the concept of restorative justice has made substantial headway in recent years. Once the province of religious-based reformers the idea is now the subject of conferences and publications produced by the Department of Justice and other official bodies. It is too early to assess the actual impact of restorative justice on common perceptions of crime and justice, but much of its potential rests on the non-adversarial approach to conflict that it promotes. One does not need to 'favor' victims or offenders to endorse its precepts, and therefore it holds the possibility of moving us away from a zero-sum game that pits the supposed interests of one against the interests of the other.

We should not underestimate the difficulty of enacting such a dual-pronged strategy. But unless we are able to do so it is unlikely that we will see any significant change in our national commitment to mass incarceration.

References

Beckett, K. (1997) *Making crime pay*. Oxford: Oxford University Press.

Blumstein, A. and Beck, A.J. (1999) 'Population growth in US prisons, 1980–1996', in M. Tonry and J. Petersilia (eds) *Prisons, crime and justice: a review of research, vol. 26.* Chicago, IL: University of Chicago Press.

Blumstein, A. and Rosenfeld, R. (1998) 'Explaining recent trends in US homicide rates', *Journal of Criminal Law and Criminology* 88(4): 1175–216.

Bonczar, T.P. and Beck, A.J. (1997) *Lifetime likelihood of going to state or federal prison.* Washington, DC: Bureau of Justice Statistics, March.

Bureau of Justice Assistance (1996) *National survey of state sentencing structures.* Washington, DC: Department of Justice.

Caplow, T. and Simon, J. (1999) 'Understanding prison policy and population trends', in M. Tonry and J. Petersilia (eds) *Prisons: crime and justice: a review of research, vol. 26.* Chicago, IL: University of Chicago Press.

Cayley, D. (1998) *The expanding prison.* Cleveland, OH: Pilgrim Press.

Christie, N. (1981) *Limits to pain.* New York: Oxford University Press.

Clark, J., Austin, J. and Henry, D.A. (1997) *'Three strikes and you're out', a review of state legislation.* Washington, DC: National Institute of Justice, September.

Curtis, R. (1998) 'The improbable transformation of inner-city neighborhoods: crime, violence, drugs, and youth in the 1990s', *Journal of Criminal Law and Criminology* 88(4): 1233–76.

Doble, J. and Klein, J. (1989) *Punishing criminals: the public's view – an Alabama survey.* New York: The Edna McConnell Clark Foundation.

Frankel, M. (1972) *Criminal sentences: law without order.* New York: Hill & Wang.

National Advisory Commission on Criminal Justice Standards and Goals (1973) *Task force report on corrections.* Washington, DC: Government Printing Office.

Rothman, D.J. (1971) *The discovery of the asylum: social order and disorder in the new republic.* Boston, MA: Little, Brown & Co.

Tonry, M. (1996) *Sentencing matters.* New York: Oxford University Press.

Western, B. and Beckett, K. (1999) 'How unregulated is the US labor market? The penal system as labor market institution', *American Journal of Sociology* 104(4): 1030–60.

White House, the (1992) *National drug control strategy.*

Wiliam, W.J. (1997) *When work disappears: the world of the new urban poor.* New York: Knopf.

Young, W. and Brown, M. (1993) 'Cross national comparisons of imprisonment', in M. Tonry (ed.) *Crime and justice: a review of research, vol. 17.* Chicago, IL: University of Chicago Press.

2 Fear and loathing in late modernity

Reflections on the cultural sources of mass imprisonment in the United States

JONATHAN SIMON

In recent work, Theodore Caplow and I (Caplow and Simon, 1999) have argued that there is no singular cause of the unprecedented growth of imprisonment in the United States. We point to three different factors whose interrelationship has driven incarceration rates in ways quite different than might have been expected for each independently. First, we argue that changes in the political culture of the United States have made fear of crime a priority issue for politics. Second, the 'war on drugs,' largely a product of this political priority of crime, produced an almost limitless supply of arrestable and imprisonable offenders. Third, the growing integration of criminal justice agencies into a more transparent and interactive system has introduced a strong element of reflexivity into the system, which in turn produces strong internal pressures for growth.

In this article I want to focus more closely on the first factor. Most observers agree that fear of crime is a major predicate to incarceration growth in the United States. Mainstream politicians and criminal justice experts treat this as an understandable product of real increases in crime (Wilson, 1996). Criminologists also point to how crime fear is privileged by American political culture (Scheingold, 1991) as well as mobilized and manipulated by politicians and the media (Miller, 1996; Beckett, 1997). Scholars, however, have only begun to focus on what features of contemporary culture increase and sustain crime fear (Garland, 2001). What follows offers a preliminary framework for the comparative analysis of this phenomenon drawn from the pioneering study of risk selection and social organization by Mary Douglas and Aaron Wildavsky (Douglas and Wildavsky, 1982).

CRIME, RISK, AND CULTURE

We begin with the observations that the residents of the United States are not alone in being haunted by the specter of terrible personal and collective disaster in late modernity.

While Americans fret about crime, publics in Western Europe have become increasingly agitated around the question of threats borne by food, especially food produced through genetic or other high-technology forms of manipulation. Members of both publics can point to real events that crystallize the kind of risks they fear that have been well publicized in the media. Professional risk assessors in both places are often skeptical of these public fears, pointing to objective indicators of actual damages that are ambiguous at best.

In fact, crime and the purity of food are part of a set of 'problems' that have obsessed modern societies, beginning along with industrial accidents, pollution, unemployment and poverty, just to name a few. Why do certain problems come to occupy our attention at a particular time even though the others have not gone away? While the culture of public problems (as Joseph Gusfield usefully denominated this inquiry some years ago) requires specificity, it also requires a more general theoretical framework. In the next section, I outline the analysis of risk and culture developed some years ago by the anthropologist Mary Douglas and the late political scientist Aaron Wildavsky, which will form the starting point for my analysis.

RISK SELECTION AND SOCIAL ORGANIZATION

Douglas and Wildavsky (1982) set out to understand why America in the 1970s and early 1980s was so captivated by specters of environmental pollution and high-technology disasters. They noted that this was a surprising turn in the culture of modernism that was supposed to have accepted risk as a normal part of life and abandoned the primitive obsession with explaining all unfortunate results as a product of moral forces. Moderns had long embraced both science and industry as sources of optimism and comfort, but since the 1960s both had increasingly come to be mistrusted and feared.

Douglas and Wildavsky posited that risk selection and the intensity of concern are both functions of social organization. Individuals rarely confront questions of risk selection in isolation (the mistake of economic and psychological approaches). Instead a framework of institutional structures and institutional values pre-screens dangers. The institutions in which people are embedded provide them with signals as to which kinds of risks to worry about. At the level of the individual, the goal is not to maximize security in an abstract sense, but to avoid 'dishonorable' risks.

According to Douglas and Wildavsky, institutions identify risk based largely on their values. They select those risks that allow them to valorize certain people and behavior while mobilizing disdain for other people and behaviors. In short, a particular risk is attractive because of who or what it allows people to blame. The point is not that such dangers are totally socially constructed. Nuclear power plants, air pollution, and crime create certain very real dangers. Indeed, if risk serves institutions mainly as a vehicle for directing blame in certain directions then the more plausible and visible such risks are the easier they can fulfill this blaming role. Institutions differ not only in their preferred objects of risk, but also in the intensity with which fears are mobilized. Not all institutions have the same internal need for projecting blameworthy enemies. Douglas and Wildavsky argued that blaming is most useful to institutions with weak incentives or internal controls. Such institutions retain loyalty by intensifying the boundaries between those in and out of the institution. The relative intensity with which concern is mobilized thus varies with the strength of internal mechanisms of loyalty and control.

Douglas and Wildavsky described three ideal-type institutional frameworks: hierarchical (or bureaucratic),[1] individualist (or market), and sectarian. Each has a particular structure of social organization, which directs members to highlight certain kinds of dangers. Each has different pressures to promote blaming of others. The history of just which risks have become fashionable, then, is a genealogy of institutional dominance. Douglas and Wildavsky described the political culture of the United States as dominated by bureaucracies and markets who occupy the center of society in the Shilsian sense that lines of media, political, and social influence converge and concentrate there (Shils, 1982).

The social organization of bureaucracies generally provides incentives for people to participate through a system of ranks and rules which distribute prestige, wealth, and power to those who fulfill their roles loyally. They also rely on the control of information through secrecy and censorship, which allows the bureaucracy to prevent efforts to sidestep its authority structure. The prestige of rules and ranks leads bureaucratic institutions to prioritize the risks of betrayal and disloyalty (foreign invasion and civil war or the civil society analogs of these, for example, hostile takeovers and challenges to authority). It also leads to a tendency to underestimate or even create other risks. For example, valuing loyalty and stability raises the risks of impeding the free flow of goods, services, and information, and thus ultimately of both economic and political disaster. Likewise, the mandate to deter foreign enemies through weapons of mass destruction raises the risk of significant environmental damage as the USA experienced throughout the Cold War. Ironically the same features make them vulnerable to military problems because they discourage innovative thinking about what the enemy may be up to (Douglas and Wildavsky offer the example of American lack of preparedness for Pearl Harbor).

Market mechanisms rely on direct incentives, most commonly financial rewards, to assure cooperation and coordination. Markets value equality but not in a consistent and thoroughgoing way. They must tolerate temporary divisions of winners and losers but they tend to discount the possibility that such divisions will harden. Market institutions are likely to foreground economic stagnation and decline as the primary risks (Douglas and Wildavsky, 1982: 179). They value loyalty (creating common ground with bureaucracies), but only to a point. They tend to hide and create other risks. For example, in their drive to eliminate barriers to pure competition mechanisms for decision making, markets create the risk that persistent losers may fall altogether out of market participation. Markets are also likely to ignore threats to the environment out of the belief that anything worthwhile will be protected by self-interested market activity and thus they oppose regulatory controls.

According to Douglas and Wildavsky both institutions of the center are relatively complacent. Their values select certain dominant risks, but their organizational structures provide sufficient incentives for participation that they have little need to mobilize fear of the outside to generate loyalty. Given Douglas and Wildavsky's most important insight, that it is not loss, but dishonorable loss that must be avoided, both markets and bureaucracies are well adopted to shelter individuals. Markets tend to keep people focused on present performance demands rather than distant risks of the future while individuals within bureaucracies have little incentive to focus on dishonorable risks at all because the structure of rules and ranks protects them from blame so long as they follow the correct procedures.

The third organizational type in Douglas and Wildavsky's typology, sectarian groups, have always occupied the peripheries of American society. Sectarians include a broad variety of religious and social movements. Lacking strong internal incentives to participate, sectarians are particularly likely to generate consensus based on pervasive threats. While their specific ideologies vary, sectarians tend to value moral sanctity, purity of thought and behavior, and an egalitarianism that emphasizes a direct relationship between each individual and the moral forces of the universe. The preferred risks are those that can be painted as wholly evil, conspiratorial and avaricious. The ideal enemies are large organizations motivated by wealth and power, i.e. those ones that dominate the center.

Douglas and Wildavsky analyzed the modern environmental movement as a paradigm of sectarian risk selection. Nature is an ideal subject of concern for a post-religious sectarianism looking to celebrate values of purity, goodness, and equality. Conceived as an independent and harmonious order, in which human beings can find a proper place, nature offers a perfect repository for the positive values of the border. Portrayed as incredibly vulnerable and in need of constant protection against corrupting forces seeking to exploit it, nature is also a vehicle for mobilizing outrage at the 'pollution' produced and tolerated by the bureaucracies and markets of the center. Pollution is trope found in many cultures where it often serves to enforce norms of separation. Those sectarians most threatened by larger and stronger neighbors capable of absorbing its membership are most likely to bind themselves with fears of pollution in contact with others (the laws of Kosher diet set out in the Torah's Book of Leviticus is only the most famous example of this – see Douglas, 1966).

Douglas and Wildavsky argue that contemporary fears of environmental pollution reproduce the same basic structure of sectarian risk (p. 128). Like witchcraft and communism, environmental pollution proceeds invisibly through the corrupt workings of avaricious enemies, and threatens to cause irreversible damage. Its patent evil clarifies both the vulnerabilities of nature and the impossibility of any compromise with the forces of the center. The political success of environmentalism in the United States, according to Douglas and Wildavsky represented a triumph of sectarian values over those of markets and bureaucracies. That does not mean that all environmental policy is inevitably a pollution cult but rather that issues of pollution are attractive vehicles for other values that are being served. Consider, for example, the now controversial superfund program that for years has mandated massive expenditure not simply to limit the risk of industrial wastes, but to restore industrially damaged lands to near pristine condition. Such policies arguably reflect a vision of purified nature and an imperative to remove every trace of evil industrial activity.

While sectarians occupy the border, they have frequently influenced the center of American politics. The New Deal, for example (in which the character of the center shifted from being completely dominated by market institutions to allowing an increasing role for bureaucracies) was inspired in part by the threats and visions of sectarian groups (left and right) responding to the crisis of the Depression. The Cold War period, in which the center became both more market affirming and more bureaucratic, was also driven in part by sectarian energies mobilized by Senator McCarthy and the emerging new right of the 1950s. In the 1960s sectarian movements from the left challenged the center to expand access to both markets and bureaucracies to previously excluded groups like blacks and women. Thus while sectarian groups rarely if ever govern directly, they have at times had profound influence on the shape of the center.

Douglas and Wildavsky argued that the growth of environmentalism in the 1970s reflected an expanded role for sectarianism in American politics. An expanded population of young and highly educated activists had developed through the civil rights and opposition to the war in Vietnam. While many of these activist would have been attractive candidates for upper-level positions in both bureaucracies and markets, the experiences of that period, especially the war in Vietnam, left the center discredited in the eyes of many. This population in the early 1970s found themselves increasingly rebels without causes. The environment provided a ready target for the same ideological narratives and organizational strategies that they had developed in these earlier movements. Their claims and demands drew support in an American society itself becoming less rooted in center institutions and with many of its previous loyalties to the center undermined. Politicians quickly jumped on board. The growth in federal regulation to protect the environment offers evidence of the successful capture of the center.[2]

THE BORDER COMES TO THE CENTER

Douglas and Wildavsky argue that American politics since the 1960s have seen an increased merging of the border and the center (p. 152). While earlier sectarian groups influenced the center, or stimulated change in the power struggles at the center, contemporary politics is marked by changes in the very nature of how the center governs which suggests the model of the border. Perhaps the most significant manifestation of this is the rise of single-issue politics and the decline of solidaristic class-based politics and parties. In recent years such new social movements, on the left and right, have come to dominate the traditional political parties. The anti-war and environmental movements reshaped the Democrats in the 1970s, and the Christian right has come to dominate the Republican Party in the 1980s and 1990s. In a sense, both major parties have become sec-tarian in style even as they seek to moderate the content of their politics.

Douglas and Wildavsky point to a number of structural and conjunctural forces in American history that have facilitated this shift. Perhaps the most important change is the shift to a postindustrial economy. Industrial capitalism required a fair amount of coordination between firms and with labor. The growth of service and information industries – which produce knowledge and manipulate symbolic systems such as law firms, software producers, and the entertainment industry – has empowered a new class far more loosely coupled to the fate of other parts of the economy than in the manufacturing past. These firms and their participants act with little concern for the fate of the traditional pillars of the center such as large cities, unions, and the political parties. Likewise, the very nature of these information and service industries, which tend to market identity and life-style as much as instrumental values, makes it possible for participants to operate without the same bureaucratic or market values of the past. Indeed, the character of innovation in these fields may select people with more sectarian leanings.

Another important change is in the structure of American politics. The emergence of television and courts as pivotal institutions of social change has increased the potential for sectarians by dramatically lowering the costs of getting attention and of imposing reform. So long as important changes were dependent on capturing legislative majorities, few sectarian groups could hope to have much of a role. Indeed to the extent that these groups' ideas were popular enough to attract interest in the general public, centrist[3] parties could easily move to the left or right enough to capture the appeal of these ideas while leaving the groups themselves still out on the border. With the rise of courts as policy makers in American politics this changed. Courts are designed to make decisions in answer to the best argument not the largest voting block. Thus, access to court decision making is open to virtually any group that can attract lawyers sympathetic to their cause. Success can be achieved by attracting the intellectual curiosity of a few judges rather than the self-interest of legions of mid-level politicians. Even if full implementation of reform ultimately requires support from legislative and executive branches of government (Rosenberg, 1991), courts can hand down decisions that force the center to negotiate with sectarian groups.

Ironically the late 1970s when Douglas and Wildavsky published their book may have been the high-water mark of the environmental movement in the United States. The 1980s and 1990s saw a considerable backlash against environmentalism as traditional centrist fears for foreign invasion and economic decline made a comeback. At the same time a new populist punitiveness gained rapid momentum since the late 1970s and early 1980s, just as environmentalism was peaking. I will argue that these penal developments bear the mark of sectarian values and sectarian social organization that Douglas and Wildavsky ascribed to environmentalism.[4] There is an important difference, however. While environmentalism genuinely arose from the border and eventually captured the center, the anti-crime juggernaut represents an effort from the center to borrow the symbolic logic of the border in order to legitimate government at a time of massive mistrust.

Crime as pollution

Crime fear evidences many of the features that make pollution an attractive risk to mobilize against. These common features are often distortions of crime as seen by criminologists, but the same holds for pollution, which is seen very differently by scientists than the general public. Indeed seeing crime fear as a sectarian value helps identify precisely those distortions in public discourse about crime that criminologists have long suggested. Pollution is invisible so that there is little that the ordinary person can do to avoid it until it does damage. It is involuntary in the sense that unlike automobile accidents or smoking-related cancer it strikes people regardless of whether they have chosen to expose themselves to it. It is irreversible. Once the body is exposed to certain pollutants, like asbestos or radiation, the damage cannot be undone; cancer will either form or not but there is no remedy after the fact.

Crime is also seen as invisible, involuntary, and irreversible. Crime is by nature stealthy. It operates through deception, absence, or surprise. Crime is seen as involuntary. Indeed while criminologists note that most victims of violent crime actually know their assailants and thus could choose to avoid them, the public discourse greatly overvalues incidents of random violence which strike people while driving or walking through a presumably safe neighborhood. Likewise stranger rapes have long dominated the image of rape even though studies all show that rape is predominantly a crime among family and friends. Crime is often depicted as irreversible. While the damage of most property offenses can be reversed by insurance, the public is much more concerned with violent crime precisely because it poses risks of death and permanent injury, which cannot be undone or effectively remedied by definition.

The features of invisibility, involuntariness, and irreversibility, are especially salient to drugs, which have become the major focus of crime fear in the 1990s.[5] Drugs operate invisibly to those around the user. Parents and employers have been encouraged to fear that their children and employees may be using drugs with dire consequences that only emerge when a crime or accident takes place. This has in turn led to a major new industry of drug testing. Drug use may begin by choice but a major part of the lore of drugs is that addiction follows which makes continued use involuntary. For the same reason drug use is often viewed as irreversible. A popular anti-drug advertising campaign of the 1980s featured vials of crack attached to a fishhook.

Douglas and Wildavsky argue that the key to understanding the selection of any particular danger for mobilization is analyzing the sources of blame and valorization it facilitates. Pollution fears target blame at large companies, which exploit the environment, the scientific and educational establishments, which produce new environment endangering technologies, and the government bureaucracies, which both promote these technologies and fail to regulate exploitation of the environment. These are, of course, the classic representatives of center institutions. Pollution also allows the valorization of nature perceived as a spiritual order as well as traditions and groups of individuals who seek to live in harmony with nature like Native Americans, organic farmers, and voluntaristic communes. These are classic representatives of sectarian organizations.

Crime fear evidences some of the same sectarian virtues with the added feature that it is not the center in general but certain aspects of it that are targeted i.e. those associated with the liberal post-New Deal state of the 1960s. Perhaps the most important blame targets of crime fear are minorities, and programmes that benefit minorities particularly African-Americans. Katherine Beckett (1997) has traced the route by which segregationists in the American south translated their resistance to integration by characterizing civil rights groups as criminal. Northern opponents of integration who focused on the crime threat of desegregated schools and from scattered site housing projects picked up the same theme. Politicians such as Richard Nixon and Ronald Reagan, who sought to mobilize support from these groups, made crime a major focus of their campaign rhetoric. In the 1990s immigrants have also become the targets of blame for crime.

Crime fear also points back at the alleged permissiveness of liberal government itself. Government is blamed for failing to adequately punish criminals and thus deter future crime. This does not strike all of government. Police, for example, are generally viewed as doing a good job. It is certain aspects of government, particularly the courts, which are painted as undermining social control. Government social programs have been special targets of this fear-based outrage. Welfare in particular has been blamed as a source of crime since at least the Goldwater campaign of 1964 (Beckett, 1997). A closely related target has been the so-called liberal establishment. Liberals have been blamed for weakening the resolve of government to fight crime. Academics, and sociologists in particular, have been seen as corrupting both government and society by spreading the idea that crimes are the fault of societal failures and that individual criminals should be coddled rather than scorned and punished. Large cities have also emerged as a central target of crime criticism. While cities, which have tended to have higher crime rates, might be seen as victims of crime, contemporary rhetoric tends to portray the city as a source of crime. Cities are blamed for providing a corrupting mixture of people and for facilitating the spread of demoralizing commodities like pornography and drugs. City government has been particularly castigated. Since they have been associated in recent years with both minority groups and liberals this also channels the previously noted blaming preferences.[6]

Crime fear is also important for what and whom it allows to be valorized. The logic of media panics about crime points to the children of white suburban families as the ideal-type victim. Although these families are statistically unlikely to suffer from violent crime they are clearly the preferred models of virtue held up by the mirror of crime fear. The murders in the 1990s of Megan Kanka in New Jersey and Polly Klass in California led to major mobilization of public concern and important legislative changes making criminal punishment more severe. Crime fear valorizes personal responsibility. Anti-crime rhetoric since the early 1960s has emphasized the importance of individual moral integrity as the key to crime. Violent criminals are taken as examples of how crime reflects not social pathologies but failures of individuals to hold their desires in check. The mirror images of these monsters are people who practice moral discipline and do not expose themselves to drugs and pornography. The popularity of the 'just say no' slogan in the 1980s captures this moral valence perfectly.

Analyzing crime fear as a sectarian value system also helps explain the predominance of imprisonment as the institutional response of choice. Crime fear does not inevitably lead to punitive policies (Beckett, 1997). For example, juvenile delinquency was emphasized early in the Kennedy administration, as a vehicle for building support for a war on poverty. Earlier in the century fear of crime was mobilized to develop alternatives to prison such as juvenile justice, parole and probation (Simon, 1993). The centrality of imprisonment to the current crime panic reflects its attraction to the sectarian political culture. If crime is a kind of pollution then the prison with its capacity to isolate and contain is the ideal punishment (with the death penalty close behind as recourse for the most dangerous). If crime is a kind of witchcraft then no lesser sanctions can be nearly enough to deter and incapacitate. Not surprisingly it is in the area of drug trafficking that we have seen the most severe escalation of sentences. So high are many mandatory drug sentences that murderers, rapists, and robbers will almost invariably do less time in prison. As with 'super-fund' expenditures to clean up industrial contamination, there is no point asking whether the costs of imprisoning these offenders can be justified by the reduction in risk. When the moral survival of a society is threatened there can be no cost-benefit analysis.

The new sectarian center

Douglas and Wildavsky saw the major sectarian tendency in contemporary American society as coming from the left. This perception was understandable after the 1960s and 1970s but in the decades since it has become clear that the left has no monopoly on sectarian values. After all sectarians are often traditionalists who castigate the libertine features of center institutions. The movement behind the contemporary anti-crime panic is thus a clear successor to such earlier sectarian movements as McCarthyism and Prohibition. Like the environmental movement, however, crime panic depicts a Manichean universe where evil is pitted against good. The image of virtue that is endangered by the selected risk is one of moral righteousness and purity (thus the popularity of pre-sexual females as the poster children of crime victimization). There is also a kind of egalitarianism in the focus of this movement on individual moral choices to give in to crime. Crime as a moral choice portrays each individual as equally susceptible to the temptation to give in to evil.

Perhaps the most important difference between the left sectarianism of the environmental movement and the right sectarianism of the crime panic is the relationship to the center. Demands for fighting pollution clearly emerged from the border. Politicians looking for new sources of support as the traditional sources of political power were dissolving quickly recognized the environment as potent. As early as 1970 President Nixon recognized the importance of this movement and sought to harness it by declaring a national 'Earth Day' and proposing the creation of a federal Environmental Protection Agency. Right from the start politicians have promoted the crime panic (Beckett, 1997). Polling data from the 1960s and the 1980s show that crime surfaced as a major focus of public concern only after politicians emphasized it. Richard Nixon again emerges as a savvy innovator. By running on a law and order platform in 1968 he was able to merge surging arrest rates, major urban riots, and violent political protests into one potent stew. After Watergate, however, the crime image became confused with questions of political corruption and white-collar avarice. Polling data show little interest in crime after 1973. The issue was revived with Ronald Reagan's successful campaign for President in 1980. Reagan invoked an image of crime that linked violent street crime to welfare, to liberal social policies, and to declining respect for traditional moral values.

Reagan's presidency can be seen as a period of center backlash. Environmental concerns were down-played and dismissed while the risks of war and economic decline, the classic center risks according to Douglas and Wildavsky, enjoyed a renaissance. But it became clear by the election of 1988 that these issues were not sufficient to sustain political mobilization any more. Reagan's Vice President George Bush looked to be in trouble when the major campaign issue was seen as economic decline. Turning the issue to crime salvaged his campaign. Democratic candidate Michael Dukakis suffered an irreversible wound when Bush's campaign linked him to African-American murderer Willie Horton.[7]

The continuing failure of economic and foreign policy issues to form the basis for successful consensus formation in American democracy is evidenced by the course of the Clinton administration as well. Right from the start, candidate Clinton sought to avoid the vulnerabilities of earlier Democratic candidates on the crime issues. As governor of a southern state he could point to a tough-on-crime record and he was aided by the opportunity to carry out an execution just before the crucial New Hampshire primary.[8] But Clinton's election at the bottom of the recession cycle was perceived as about economic issues. His early initiatives emphasized the economy and health care. But when these proved incapable of attracting sufficient support, Clinton shifted to crime just before the 1994 congressional elections. The Crime Bill of that year among other things added over 60 new capital crimes to the federal code and mandated that states receiving federal prison funds revise their codes to provide that felons serve 85 percent of their nominal sentence.

While the impetus for the crime panic has come from the center it has developed a popular anti-crime movement that closely matches Douglas and Wildavsky's description of the environmental movement. Organizations like Mothers Against Drunk Driving and the loosely structured Victims Rights Movement are voluntaristic. They draw on individuals who belong to market and bureaucratic institutions but whose values are not necessarily defined by them, particularly suburban women ambivalent about feminism. The Government has promoted these groups starting with funding of victim advocacy programs in the early 1970s. Correctional officers' unions, prison suppliers, and other center organizations have also subsidized them with strong self-interest in the promotion of incarceration.

THE TRIUMPH OF THE BORDER

The forces that Douglas and Wildavsky described as pushing America in a sectarian direction have only increased during the last two decades. Forty years ago southern segregationists grumbled about impeaching Earl Warren. In 1996 Republican presidential candidate Robert Dole openly called for the impeachment of a federal judge who suppressed evidence of cocaine possession on the grounds that the evidence was illegally obtained. When President Clinton implied that he might ask the judge to step down the judge buckled and ultimately reversed his opinion. Seventy years ago rightwing clergy threatened to enter the campaign for President. Today presidential candidates willingly travel to pay homage to the Christian Coalition. America has become even more of a border nation than it was when Douglas and Wildavsky studied environmentalism. Douglas and Wildavsky assumed that the shift away from the center was largely a cultural one, leaving the capacities of markets and bureaucracies fundamentally intact if less capable of sustaining loyalty. In this final section I want to consider some factors that have become more visible since Douglas and Wildavsky's path-breaking study.

Globalization

Douglas and Wildavsky focused on the post-industrial economy as an important source of culture shift from center to border. The global nature of this economy, already visible in the early 1980s, produces effects that were not considered by Douglas and Wildavsky. These effects undermine the traditional capacities of both forms of center institutions – markets and bureaucracies – to govern without undue reliance on risk. The strong form of bureaucracy once present in both business and government, with its lifetime employment, steady and uniform wage increases, generous retirement and medical benefits, has increasingly been dismantled in the name of fiscal order and competitiveness, both defined by the global economy. The ability of governmental organizations to regulate and stimulate the economy to protect the wellbeing of the population is increasingly discredited. The market economy, once framed by national circumstances, domestic competitors, unions and customers, increasingly operates on a global basis in a manner that raises the costs of negotiating agreements and that inevitably increases insecurity for all these groups.

Government and politicians have responded by mobilizing a more sectarian risk dynamic with crime as the preferred risk. The degree to which the state sheds power and responsibility for managing the economy (a tenet of sound statecraft under globalization) has been rather strikingly paralleled by the rise of its penal vigor (Garland, 1996). Business has also been aided by the association of poverty and joblessness with exposure to the intertwined terrors of crime and imprisonment. Indeed, economic experts generally believe today that fear of unemployment has continued to keep wage inflation down even after an extended period of economic growth and despite a currently favorable job picture for most Americans.[9]

Hyper-individualization or the postmodern condition

Douglas and Wildavsky recognized that the post-industrial economy and the suburban community were creating a new space of individualism resistant to the appeals of center institutions. In the succeeding two decades it has become apparent how truly radical this individualization process has become. German sociologist Ulrich Beck (Beck, 1991) has used the term 'hyper-individualization' to describe the way that institutions like nuclear families, unions, and traditional neighborhoods that once limited the relentless individualization of capitalism and modernity have been undermined and themselves 'individualized.'

Douglas and Wildavsky saw the individualism of the Baby-Boom generation as playing into that generation's readiness to valorize the environment at the expense of traditional left concerns for equality and economic security. In retrospect the individualism of what was once called the 'me generation' seems to have been superceded by the powerful economic and cultural forces toward disaggregation associated with neoliberalism and the information revolution. In retrospect one can see a great deal of communitarianism in the environmentalist movement. It may have ignored the pain faced by real communities experiencing de-industrialization, but it did so in the name of a kind of collective utopian project.

This suggests another departure with the sectarian politics of crime control. While traditional sectarianism appealed to a strong communitarian sentiment reflective of precisely these kinds of boundaries to individualization, crime fear as sectarianism reflects a kind of individualism that finds little anchor other than strictly personal security. In this regard crime fear shares with the food fears of affluent Europeans a form of 'solidarity' that has trouble extending much beyond the boundaries of the self.

CONCLUSION

Crime in the USA and genetically altered foods in Europe function as two of the preferred risks of the global/postmodern societies. Both reflect the profound transformations of center institutions. The cultural analysis of risk introduced by Douglas and Wildavsky suggests that efforts to characterize this fear as either a natural response to threat or as the result of elite strategies of manipulation are both inadequate. Instead we must return to middle-range questions of social organization, and we must reflect upon the differential selection of risks by different cultures. Why food in Europe and crime in the USA? Such research might begin by focusing upon the cultural traditions, the ideological influence (left in Europe, right in the USA), and the differences in social organization that remain despite common tendencies toward both globalization and postmodernization.

Notes

1 Douglas and Wildavsky use the term hierarchy. I use the more conventional term 'bureaucracy.'

2 Douglas and Wildavsky offer a fascinating account of internecine battles between groups with different organizational styles within the environmental movement ranging from the relatively center-oriented Sierra Club, to the more purist direct-action movements like Friends of the Earth. They show parallels between this conflict and that between sectarian religious orders in the 19th century.

3 Here we use the term centrist not to describe an ideological center, but an organizational orientation toward the center.

4 At the outset of their book Douglas and Wildavsky argue that major risks which the public pays attention to are foreign affairs, crime, pollution, and economic failure (1982: 2). While they later identify foreign affairs with bureaucracies, economic failure with markets, and pollution with sectarians, they never take up the issue of crime. Pollution and crime both represent variations of sectarian values inversely projected as danger. The left has tended to emphasize environmental concerns while the right has tended to emphasize crime.

5 Indeed, the anti-drug campaign has been emphasized to intensify public concern at times when the generally flat overall crime rate has not provided a plausible enough source of danger to mobilize the public.

6 It will be interesting to see whether the recent election of white Republican mayors with a tough on crime stance, like Rudy Giuliani of New York, will reverse this particular vector of blame.

7 Interestingly, Bush also attacked Dukakis on the environment, but few attribute the latter's loss to commercials about pollution in Boston Harbor.

8 More ethical governors tend to suspend executions for the period of an election they are involved in so as to be able to exercise the commutation power with something like disinterest.

9 Unemployment is a classic center risk (Douglas and Wildavsky, 1982). What is distinct about the new climate of job fear, however, is how much it assimilates the pollution elements associated with crime. The 1980s introduced America to homelessness and the underclass, both conditions heavily laden with stigma. What might seem like classic center economic fear today, then, is actually far closer to crime fear than earlier periods of economic challenge.

References

Beck, U. (1992) *Risk society: towards a new modernity*. London: Sage.

Beckett, K. (1997) *Making crime pay: law and order in contemporary American politics*. New York: Oxford University Press.

Caplow, T. and Simon, J. (1999) 'Understanding prison policy and population trends', in M. Tonry and J. Petersilia (eds) *Crime & justice, vol. 26: prisons*. Chicago, IL: University of Chicago Press.

Douglas, M. (1966) *Purity and danger*. London: Routledge & Kegan Paul.

Douglas, M. and Wildavsky, A. (1982) *Risk and culture*. Berkeley, CA: University of California Press.

Garland, D. (1996) 'The limits of the sovereign state: strategies of crime control in contemporary society', *British Journal of Criminology* 36(4): 445–71.

Garland, D. (2001) *The culture of control: crime and social order in contemporary society*. Chicago, IL: University of Chicago Press.

Miller, J. (1996) *Search and destroy: African-American males in the criminal justice system.* Cambridge: Cambridge University Press.

Osborne, D. and Gaebler, T. (1992) *Reinventing government: how the entrepreneurial spirit is transforming the public sector.* Reading, MA: Addison-Wesley.

Rosenberg, G.N. (1991) *The hollow hope: can courts bring about social change?* Chicago, IL: University of Chicago Press.

Scheingold, S. (1991) *The politics of street crime.* Philadelphia: Temple University Press.

Shils, E. (1982) 'Centre and periphery', in E. Shils *The constitution of society.* Chicago, IL: University of Chicago Press.

Wilson, J.Q. (1996) 'Interview with James Q. Wilson', *Criminal Justice Matters* 25(1).

3 Television, public space and prison population

A commentary on Mauer and Simon

THOMAS MATHIESEN

The two articles under discussion have one significant feature in common: they are both interesting and useful contributions. They are different in that they analyse the question of causes of mass imprisonment on different levels: Marc Mauer on the relatively concrete level of criminal justice policy changes contributing to the current prison-building frenzy and the political climate underlying these developments, and Jonathan Simon on the somewhat more abstract and complex level of organizational analysis, making the fear of crime – if you compare different societies or one society over time – just one of several possible fears. Both perspectives seem very useful.

Certainly, Simon is right when arguing that fears can vary and change. I studied sociology at the University of Wisconsin in the early 1950s, and vividly remember the presumed 'communist threat' in the McCarthy era. I live in a country close to the Soviet/Russian border, and the 'communist threat' has been extremely strong there. Moreover, in my country there has been a kind of sequence of threats, partly overlapping and partly succeeding each other, very broadly speaking from the 'communist threat' via the 'drug threat' to the 'organized, internationalized crime threat'. Presumably, and partly contradicting what we know on the basis of empirical research and police reports, the 'organized crime threat' emanates from Russia. The Russian 'mafia', an undefined term indeed, is presumed to be behind everything (Christie, 1999). The 'organized crime threat' is presently all over Western Europe, much more pervasive, incidentally, than the fear of genetically altered foods which Simon refers to, permeating the very structure of the European Union, leading to drastic developments and changes in the policing of the new Europe, including the vast systems of data registration and surveillance known as Schengen, Europol, Eurodac, Enfopol and so on (see Fijnaut, 1995; Mathiesen, 1999).

Though threats and enemy images may differ and change, depending on underlying social forces such as the ones that Simon refers to, I venture the hypothesis that the 'crime threat', including the 'organized crime threat', which has appeared during the last years, has a certain stability and overarching character, existing not only in the USA but in most western societies, though it may of course exist alongside other perceived threats. The rise, permanence and pivotal importance of the 'crime threat' crossing Europe and North America may, I think, be traced to what Mauer calls 'the powerful imagery of television'. Mauer is right in saying that 'blaming the media' for all our problems becomes all too simplistic. But the advent of television implied not an extention of the old media, but an entirely new medium, with its own logic and criteria of news, requiring its own sociological analysis. Its advent constituted a fundamental break with the past, and its development coincided with the rise of the crime fear and with mass incarceration more or less throughout the western world. In what follows, I wish to elaborate on that.

TELEVISION: THE NEW RELIGION

My main concern is with the influence of television in and on public space. Very roughly, you can equate 'public space' with 'public opinion', but for reasons that I will explain later, I prefer the former term. The former term also introduces a 'spatial' or 'room-like' element, implying that it is not only a question of 'flat opinion', but of public communication, debate and discourse.

The point is that with the entry and development of *television*, we have entered something that is equivalent to a new religion. When the automobile arrived around the turn of the century, many people believed it was a horse and buggy, only without the horse. Reminiscient of that, we still speak of 'horse power'. But it was not a horse and buggy without a horse, it was something entirely new, which contained the seeds of an entirely different society. So with television. When television arrived after the Second World War, some people believed that it was just a newspaper in pictures. But it was not just that, it was an entirely new medium, and one that fundamentally influenced the shape and content of the old media – newspapers, film and radio. In doing so, it helped create a completely new society. The American media researcher George Gerbner has put it succinctly, as follows:

> [The point is a concept of] broad enculturation rather than of narrow changes in opinion or behavior. Instead of asking what communication 'variables' might propagate what kinds of individual behavior changes, we want to know what types of common consciousness whole systems of messages might cultivate. This is less like asking about preconceived fears and hopes and more like asking about the 'effects' of Christianity on one's views of the world or – as the Chinese *had* asked – of Confucianism on public morality. (Gerbner and Gross, 1976: 180)

The parallel drawn to religion should be taken as more than a metaphor. Our relationship to television has several of the characteristics of the relationship of the faithful to the Church. We worship television. The British media researcher James Curran has put it this way, in functional terms:

> The modern mass media in Britain now perform many of the integrative functions of the Church in the middle ages. Like the medieval Church, the media link together different groups and provide a shared experience that promotes social solidarity. The media also emphasize collective values that bind people closer together, in a way that is comparable to the influence of the medieval Church: the communality of the Christian faith celebrated by Christian rites is

now replaced by the communalities of consumerism and nationalism celebrated in the media 'rites' such as international sporting contests (that affirm national identities) and consumer features (that celebrate a collective identity of consumers). Indeed, the two institutions have engaged in some ways in very similar ideological 'work' despite the difference in time that separate them . . . The modern mass media have [for example] given, at different times, massive and disproportionate attention to a series of 'outsiders' . . . comparable to the hunting down and parading of witches allegedly possessed by the devil by the medieval and early modern Church . . . (Curran, 1982: 227)

Curran may to some extent be right in saying that such are the functions of the media in general. He seems definitely right if the reference is television. He ends with the following words:

The medieval Church masked the sources of inequality by ascribing social injustice to the sin of the individual; the modern mass media [read television] tend, in more complex and sophisticated ways, to misdirect their audiences by the ways in which they define and explain structural inequalities . . . The Church . . . offered the chiliastic consolation of eternal salvation to 'the meek (who) shall inherit the earth'; the media similarly give prominence to show-business personalities and football stars who, as 'a powerless elite', afford easily identifiable symbols for vicarious fulfilment . . . The new pristhood of the modern media has supplanted the old as the principal ideological agents building consent for the social system. (1982: 227–8)

The transformation may be described in more precise terms. As Neil Postman (1985) has emphasized, in terms of media *form* we are in the midst of a crucial transformation from an emphasis on the written message towards an emphasis on the picture. The emphasis on the picture, and on the picture as that which defines what is true and false, as that which defines what actually happened as if staging did not exist, implies a fundamental cultural change in the West. The change also includes the modern press, for example through the 'tabloidization' of the newspapers, with large 'on the scene' pictures, large punchy headlines and brief texts, but it pertains particularly to television. Foucault's notion of a 'panoptical' development, in which the few see and survey the many, is parallelled by an enormous contrasting but functionally related 'synoptical' development, in which the many see, survey and admire the few (Mathiesen, 1987, 1997).

In terms of media *content*, we are in the midst of a parallel change towards entertainment. We need not agree with Postman that the transformation of form from the word to the picture *necessarily* changes the content into entertainment, to agree with him that we are, in fact, 'amusing ourselves to death'. Even the most serious news and even the most violent of reported events, are given an 'entertaining slant'. Information and entertainment are fused into 'infotainment'. Writing is still with us, to be sure, as are serious analyses. But in terms of tendency, public news space is predominantly filled with pictures which 'entertain'. There is no space here to analyse the forces which in turn shape these tendencies. Suffice it to say that a new technological era, with new production as well as communication systems in the mass media area, and with countless satellites filling the sky, has enabled market forces to enter public space in a way unthinkable three or four decades ago.

Crime fits perfectly with the demand for entertainment, and with the criteria of entertaining news selection. But more than that, you have television as depicting the truth about crime. How can you doubt your own eyes? We realize, of course, that a thriller is fantasy. But the thriller rings true because you see those acting it out with your own eyes; you see that people are molested, tortured or killed by terrorists, wife beaters, incestuous fathers and organized criminals. A generalized consciousness emanates: such is crime; such is, in fact, the world. Even more forceful are the so-called news pro-grammes. You actually see what is happening, in movement and colour. How can you doubt that? You do not see the staging, you do not see the selection and the cuttings, the drama-tugical techniques, you think you see people in the round. It is far more con-vincing than any newspaper commentary or novel. This is not a question of conscious manipulation to create a particular image of crime on the part of television personnel, but a question of their adherence to the standard criteria of what is newsworthy in tele-vision public space and the market. The truth-like character of television is like the religious revelation of the faithful. To be sure, if you had competing information, you might begin to doubt, even become a heretic. We have plenty of research showing that when competing information is available, television heresy abounds. But, and this is fundamental: in the area of crime, large masses of the population do not have compet-ing information. They are in much the same position as those who had to take for granted the Ptolemaic understanding of the world, with Earth and not the Sun as the centre, as promulgated by the Catholic Church before Galileo.

PRISON GROWTH

Now, what has this to do with the theme of mass imprisonment and prison growth? Quite a bit, I think. I am *not* suggesting that the development of modern television is a factor operating with equal strength in all regions of the world which have seen prison growth. My hunch is that the forces behind prison growth vary internationally. To repeat, I am restricting myself to something which I feel I know a little about – the western world, though I must add that information from such different societies as Argentina, Brazil, Russia and Lithuania suggests that television is of fundamental cross-cultural importance. And I am *not* suggesting that the development of television is the only factor behind prison growth in the West. This would be much too simple an expla-nation, though I should add that there seems to be at least a rough correlation in the West between television consumption in terms of number of hours and symbolic importance and degree of rise in prison populations, with the USA in the lead on both counts. More modestly I *am* suggesting that the development of television which I have sketched, *facilitates prison growth in the sense that it opens up for growth, it dismantles the defences which otherwise might be mustered against escalation and for de-escalation.* These defences are of a cultural kind: they are *values* – civil rights, the rule of law, humanity – emphasizing a restraint in the use of our harshest mass punishment, prison, and conse-quently restraint in escalation of the prison population. Television corrodes these values.

Let me be more precise. Three major and related developments inextricably inter-woven in modern television, corrode the cultural defences – the values – which might otherwise hinder and halt major escalations of prison systems.

First, penal policy has become much more of a 'commodity' than was the case a few decades ago. In the 1950s, penal policy was at least to some limited extent governed by general theoretical, philosophical and even scientific concerns. The treatment philosophy of the 1950s and 1960s is an example. That philosophy, and other philosophies as well, came to be discredited. This, however, does not detract from the sociological significance of the change which has occurred. Penal policy today is governed much more by the kind of news that is news-worthy and thereby saleable for television and by what is marketable political opinion in the media.

Second, in parallel with the first change, a change has also occurred in the type of legitimation sought by those who make penal policy decisions. Some decades ago, one could say that legitimation at least to some extent was principled: it was at least to some extent grounded in principles about the rule of law and similar values. These principles could open the way for many kinds of policies but they were principles nevertheless. Today, legitimation seems to be almost purely opportunistic: it is grounded in concerns about what 'goes' on television and consequently among the voters. The kind of principled reductionist penal reform initiated by Winston Churchill during his brief tenure as British Home Secretary in 1910–11, described so eloquently by Andrew Rutherford (1986), which was followed by a major drop in the British prison population, is therefore much more difficult to imagine today. So, too, is the principled reductionist policy of the then Swedish Minister of Justice, Lennart Geijer, as late as the 1970s.

Third, as a parallel to the first two changes, a change has also occurred in the nature of public debate over penal policy. As a result of the more theoretical or philosophical concerns underlying penal policy some decades ago, and the search that did exist for principled legitimation, what may be called communicative rationality – to use the German sociologist Jürgen Habermas' term (Habermas, 1981) – was at least to some extent present in that debate. Communicative rationality implies an emphasis on truthfulness, relevance and sincerity in argumentation. It was, in other words, possible to argue in a truthful manner, with relevance and with sincerity, and such argumentation was given at least some hearing at the decision-making level. The best example of this is the fall of the treatment philosophy. That fall occurred at least partly as a consequence of research into the effects of treatment, and it followed a relatively informed debate where research results were an important part of the argument (Mathiesen, 1990). Today, communicative rationality seems to be in retreat. Systematic and principled argumentation is given less of a hearing. One might say that even more than before, communicative rationality lives its life in the secluded corners of the professional journals and meetings, while the public debate, flooded as it is with dire warnings by the police and sensational crime stories and, most significantly, by opportunistic political initiatives in the context of burlesque television shows called 'debates', is predominantly characterized by the rationality of the market place.

AN ALTERNATIVE PUBLIC SPACE

What I have said here points to a rather bleak immediate future. I think this is realistic. But the fact that penal policy is developing for the worse, is not a good reason for not mustering resistance against it. Rather the other way around: it *is* a reason for mustering resistance.

The key word is, in Norwegian, 'alternativ offentlighet', in German 'Alternative Öffentlichkeit', in English the much more cumbersome phrase 'alternative public space'.

The point is to contribute to the creation of an alternative public space in penal policy, where argumentation and principled thinking represent the dominant values. I envisage the development of an alternative public space in the area of penal policy as containing three ingredients.

First, liberation from what I would call the absorbent power of the mass media, especially television. There is widespread definition of the situation in the age of television show business that our very existence as a politically active person is dependent on media interest and 'media coverage'. Without media coverage, with silence in the media, I do not exist, my organization does not exist, the meeting has not taken place. This is a part of the truth-like character of television. In western society, it is probably impossible to refrain completely from media participation. But it is certainly possible to say 'no!' to the many talk shows and entertainment-like 'debates' referred to earlier which flood our various television channels, and, most importantly, it is certainly possible not to let the definition of our success and very existence be dependent on the media.

Second, a restoration of the self-esteem and feeling of worth on the part of the grass-roots movements. It is not true that the grass-roots movements, emphasizing network organization and solidarity at the bottom, have died out.[1] What has happened is that with the development of television which I have outlined, these movements have lost faith in themselves.

Third, a restoration of the feeling of responsibility on the part of intellectuals. I am thinking of artists, writers, scientists – and certainly social scientists. That responsibility should partly be directed towards a refusal to participate in television show business. Partly it should be directed towards revitalization of research taking the interests of common people as a point of departure. This point is not new, but goes, of course, several decades back in western intellectual history. The area is full of conflicts and problems, but they are not unsolvable.

We have tried to do some of this in Norway, in the organization KROM, the Norwegian Association for Penal Reform, which is a strange hybrid of an organization, with intellectuals and many prisoners, with a common cause (Mathiesen, 1974, 1995). By organizing large conferences on penal policy every year (to create a tradition, organizing them in the same place, in a mountain resort outside Oslo) with wide participation from the whole range of professions and agencies relevant to penal policy, and many prisoners, by organizing public meetings in cooperation with a large number of related organizations, and so on, we try to create *a network of of opinion and information* crossing the formal and informal borders between segments of the relevant administrative and political systems. The point is precisely that of trying to create an alternative public space where argumentation and principled thinking are dominant values, a public space that in the end may compete with the superficial public space of the mass media.[2]

This is one line of thinking and working. There are obviously others. The limitation of the growth of prisons, and perhaps even the turning of escalation into reduction, requires them all.

Notes

1 An important example from recent Norwegian history of the actual vitality of grass-roots movements: in 1993, thousands of ordinary Norwegians participated in a widespread movement to give refugees from Kosovo-Albania long-term refuge in

Norwegian churches throughout the country. The movement ended in a partial victory, in that all of the cases concerning Kosovo-Albanian refugees were reviewed again by the Ministry of Justice. The example suggests that grass-roots solidarity even with 'distant' groups like refugees did not die out with the Vietnam war.

2 Our attempt has the advantage, over against what goes on in the mass media, of being based on the actual and organized relationships between people. The public space of the mass media, and especially of television, is in that sense weak: it is a public space that is disorganized, segmented, splintered into millions of unconnected individuals – this is its truly mass character – and equally segmented into thousands of individual media stars on the media sky. This is the Achilles' heel of the public space of television, which we try to turn to our advantage.

References

Christie, N. (1999) *En høyst nødvendig mafia (A highly necessary mafia)*. Nordisk: Øst-forum.

Curran, J. (1982) 'Communications, power and social order', in M. Gurevitsch et al. (eds) *Culture, society and the media*. London: Methuen.

Fijnaut, C. (ed.) (1995) *The internationalization of police cooperation in Western Europe*. Deventer: Kluwer.

Gerbner, G. and Gross, L. (1976) 'Living with television: the violence profile', *Journal of Communication*.

Habermas, J. (1981) *Theorie des Kommunikativen Handelns*. Suhrkamp.

Mathiesen, T. (1974) *The politics of abolition. essays in political action theory.* Scandinavian Studies in Criminology No. 4. Martin Robertson/Norwegian Universities Press.

Mathiesen, T. (1987) *Seersamfundet. Om medier og kontroll i det moderne samfund (The viewer society. On media and control in modern society)*. Socpol.

Mathiesen, T. (1990) *Prison on trial. A critical assessment.* London: Sage.

Mathiesen, T. (1995) *About KROM. Past – present – future*. Oslo: Institute for Sociology of Law.

Mathiesen, T. (1997) 'The viewer society: Michel Foucault's "Panopticon" revisited', *Theoretical Criminology* 1(2): 215–34.

Mathiesen, T. (1999) *On globalisation of control: towards an integrated surveillance system in Europe*. London: Statewatch Publication.

Postman, N. (1985) *Amusing ourselves to death*. London: Viking Penguin.

Rutherford, A. (1986) *Prisons and the process of justice*. Oxford: Oxford University Press.

4 Governing social marginality

Welfare, incarceration, and the transformation of state policy

KATHERINE BECKETT AND BRUCE WESTERN

The US criminal justice system has grown at a spectacular pace in recent decades. Between 1980 and 2000, the number of people incarcerated in the United States increased by 300 percent, from 500,000 to nearly 2 million (Sentencing Project, 2000). The share of the population behind bars has also grown rapidly, and the parole and probation populations now include 3.8 million persons. By 1998, nearly 6 million people – almost 3 percent of the adult population – were under some form of correctional supervision (BJS, 1998; Butterfield, 1998). The impact of these developments has fallen disproportionately on young African-Americans and Latinos. By 1994, one of every three black males between the ages of 18–34 was under some form of correctional supervision, and the number of Hispanic prisoners has more than quintupled since 1980 (Currie, 1998: 14). These developments are not primarily the consequence of rising crime rates, but rather of the 'get-tough' policies of the wars on crime and drugs (Tonry, 1995; Donziger, 1996; Beckett and Sasson, 2000).

Like penal policy, social policy has become more punitive. Several decades ago, the civil and welfare rights movements sought to expand the war on poverty programs. As a result, the 'welfare rolls' grew dramatically: while fewer than 600,000 families applied for AFDC benefits in 1960, more than 3 million Americans received such benefits by 1972 (Piven and Cloward, 1979). After the election of Ronald Reagan to the presidency in 1980, however, policy efforts to support and integrate the poor were sharply curtailed. The 1981 Omnibus Budget Reconciliation Act (OBRA) reduced real spending on employment assistance and training, unemployment compensation, and Aid to Families with Dependent Children, the main welfare program for poor families with children. Driven by a philosophy of self-reliance and justified by claims of 'welfare fraud,' OBRA removed nearly half a million working families from AFDC rolls between 1981 and 1983 alone (Danziger and Gottshcalk, 1995: 25). Recent welfare reform measures have further reduced welfare caseloads: the number of families receiving AFDC declined by 44 percent between 1993 and 1998 (Administration for Children and Families, 1999). The average benefit payment to families entitled to AFDC has also declined considerably, from $376 in 1975 to $220 in 1995 (measured in 1983 dollars). In short, both penal and social policy have become harsher and more exclusionary.

In this article we explore the idea that the simultaneity of these developments is not coincidental, but reflects a larger shift in the governance of social marginality.[1] Specifically, we borrow the concept of 'policy regimes' to explore the hypothesis that penal and social welfare institutions comprise a single policy regime aimed at the problems associated with deviance and marginality. In his analysis of variation in types of modern capitalist societies, Esping-Anderson (1990) uses the term 'policy regime' to describe the clustering of particular kinds of social and economic policies in 20th-century welfare states. According to Esping-Anderson, each cluster is characteristic of a particular kind of welfare state policy regime. For example, liberal welfare states are characterized by means-tested assistance programs offering minimal benefits, modest universal transfers and social insurance programs, and strict eligibility rules (1990: 26). By contrast, social-democratic regimes offer more generous benefits and services, the aim of which is to bestow upon workers rights and services commensurate with those enjoyed by the middle classes (1990: 27). According to Esping-Anderson, these policy regimes, once formed, are stable and enduring over time.

Drawing on the concept of the 'policy-regime,' we suggest that welfare and penal institutions comprise a single policy regime aimed at the governance of social marginality. In the contemporary United States, these regimes vary according to their commitment to including or excluding marginal groups. Inclusive regimes emphasize the need to improve and integrate the socially marginal and tend to place more emphasis on the social causes of marginality. These regimes are therefore characterized by more generous welfare programs and less punitive anti-crime policies. By contrast, exclusionary regimes emphasize the undeserving and unreformable nature of deviants, tend to stigmatize and separate the socially marginal, and are hence more likely to feature less generous welfare benefits and more punitive anti-crime policies.[2] On the basis of this formulation, we hypothesize that governments that provide more generous welfare benefits have lower incarceration rates, controlling for other relevant factors, while governments that spend less on welfare incarcerate a larger share of their residents.[3]

State-level data provide a unique opportunity to assess this argument. As striking as the general increase in incarceration rates and decrease in welfare spending have been, substantial inter-state variation in levels of incarceration and welfare spending persists (and may actually be growing). In 1995, for example, the state prison incarceration rate was 677 per 100,000 residents in Texas but just 95 in North Dakota and 105 in Minnesota (BJS, 1999). Similarly, in 1975, the average AFDC payment (in 1983 dollars) ranged from $91 a month in Mississippi to $604 in Hawaii. This variation persists, but average benefits have fallen. By 1995, Mississippi continued to provide the lowest average benefit of $78 a month, while Alaska was most generous at $475 (also 1983 dollars).

In what follows, we analyze state-level incarceration rates to assess our argument that as components of a single policy-regime, welfare spending and incarceration rates will be systematically (negatively) related. However, we also want to know whether this relationship, if it exists, is a stable one. We therefore specify a model that allows us to see if the relationship between these policy sectors changes over time. The results of this analysis provide partial support for our argument, indicating that by 1995, but not in 1975 or 1985, welfare and incarceration were strongly negatively related; states with less generous welfare programs incarcerated at a significantly higher level, while those with more generous welfare programs imprisoned a smaller share of their residents. Our results also show that in the 1990s, states with larger minority populations incarcerated a larger share of their population. We conclude with a discussion of these findings and their implications for our conceptual framework.

SOCIAL AND PENAL POLICY: HISTORICAL AND CONTEMPORARY DEVELOPMENTS

The idea that both social and penal policy are components of a government's response to social marginality has a rich sociological pedigree. Rusch and Kircheimer were among the first to treat penal institutions as connected to non-penal social policy and institutions[4] (Rusch and Kircheimer, 1939; see also Garland, 1990: 91). In *Punishment and Welfare* (1985), David Garland developed this argument much more explicitly, showing that the transformation of social and penal policy in late 19th and early 20th-century Britain was part of a larger shift in the regulation of social marginality. Garland argues that Victorian penal policies reflected the individualistic laissez-faire philosophy of free-market capitalism. At the turn of the century, however, a 'crisis of social regulation' triggered by the growth of the 'disreputable' classes shattered consensus around this approach and created widespread support among elites for large-scale state intervention in the administration of poverty. As the century progressed, penal and social policy increasingly reflected the idea that this government intervention could and should reform and integrate the socially marginal. According to this new philosophy (which Garland terms 'penal-welfarism' or, sometimes, 'penological modernism,' deviant behavior is at least partially caused (rather than freely chosen), although the nature of these causes was thought to vary from case to case. Penological modernists therefore identified rehabilitation – operationally defined as the use of 'individualized, corrective measures adapted to the specific case' – as the most appropriate response to deviant behavior (Garland, 1985: 187). The ability of penological modernists to inscribe these beliefs in British criminal justice policy and institutions reflected their compatibility with the philosophy of the welfare state, as well as growing support among elites for welfarist government intervention (Garland, 1985; see also Rose, 1996).

Accounts of the transformation of US social and penal policy in the early 20th century also provide evidence for the idea that these policy sectors comprise a single policy-regime aimed at social marginality (see especially Sutton, 1997a; Rothman, 1980). Like Garland, these analysts document a shift in the early 20th century from a liberal, 'free market' to a welfarist approach to social marginality characterized by faith in the ability of government agents and professionals to reform and integrate the socially marginal. This new welfarist philosophy, they suggest, served as the foundation of both criminal justice and social welfare practices in most western countries, although it has co-existed somewhat uneasily with on-going concern about deterrence (Sparks, 1996; Vaughan, 2000). As Sutton concludes, 'criminal justice and welfare policies in modern democracies are historically intertwined – that they are, in effect, sub-discourses within a larger policy discourse about the management of social marginality' (1997a: 3).

Beginning in the 1960s, the goals and suppositions of the welfarist paradigm came under attack. In the penal sphere, conservatives opposed rehabilitation on the grounds that punishment must be harsh and painful if it is to deter crime. Liberals also criticized policies associated with rehabilitation, arguing that the open-ended ('indeterminate') sentences that ostensibly rewarded 'rehabilitated' offenders also created the potential for the intrusive, discriminatory, and arbitrary exercise of power. Under the weight of these critiques, the rehabilitative project was called into question. Since that time, the goals of incapacitation, deterrence and retribution have enjoyed something of a renaissance, and the US penal system has expanded dramatically.

As we have seen, this development coincided with efforts to scale back the welfare state. Indeed, over the past several decades, the proper role of government in economic and social life has become the subject of intense controversy. Social policies based on Keynesian economic theory such as redistributive tax schemes, labor support measures, and especially welfare programs aimed at the poor have come under attack. In response to these cuts in state assistance to the poor, child poverty rates in the 1980s and 1990s have been about one-third higher than in the 1970s (Danziger and Gottschalk, 1995: 67). The severity of poverty has also increased: the average payment required to lift the poor above the poverty line was more than 20 percent higher in the 1980s and early 1990s than in the 1970s (Danziger and Weinberg, 1995: 33). As Garland concludes: 'One might say that we are developing an official criminology that fits our social and cultural configuration – one in which amorality, generalized insecurity and enforced exclusion are coming to prevail over the traditions of welfarism and social citizenship' (1996: 462).

Like the historical research just described, analyses of contemporary political discourse document a close connection between policy debates over poverty and discussions of crime and punishment (Katz, 1989; Morris, 1994; Gans, 1995; Schram, 1995; Beckett, 1997). According to this research, the reconceptualization of the nature and causes of the problems associated with social marginality has legitimated the shift away from welfarism in both the penal and social spheres. Contemporary political discourse tends to frame discussions of problems such as homelessness as security issues rather than social problems, is quite pessimistic about the possibility of integrating the socially marginal, and places more emphasis upon the dangerous and undeserving nature of the poor than was the case earlier in the century. This discourse also emphasizes individual responsibility for social problems, although it simultaneously identifies welfare programs and the 'culture of welfare' as important causes of crime (Beckett, 1997), and stresses the need to exclude those who fail to conduct themselves 'responsibly'. To the extent that such rhetoric and images become pervasive, they may have important consequences. As Michael Katz (1989: 185–6) suggests, 'when the poor seemed menacing, they became the underclass' (see also Morris, 1994; Schram, 1995). In short, these studies suggest that there has been an assault on the modernist paradigm, in which the logic of welfarism and rehabilitation predominated in both the penal and welfare sectors. Politicians have made a concerted effort to promote conceptions of social marginality that imply the need for more exclusionary and security-minded responses to marginal groups and individuals. As a result, discussions of social marginality are increasingly framed in terms of the need for heightened security, and the logic of social control and social exclusion permeates both penal and welfare institutions.

DATA AND ANALYSIS

It appears, then, that the social and penal spheres are components of a policy-regime concerned with the governance of social marginality. We have argued that in the contemporary United States, these regimes vary according to their commitment to including or excluding marginal groups. As was discussed earlier, inclusive regimes emphasize the social causes of marginality and are more optimistic about the capacity of the government to reform and integrate those seen as marginal. As a result, these regimes are characterized by more generous welfare programs and less punitive anti-crime policies. By contrast, exclusive regimes have a more pessimistic theory of deviance, one that emphasizes the undeserving and unreformable nature of deviants. These regimes see exclusion and separation as the best that government can accomplish, and are therefore characterized by less generous welfare benefits and more punitive anti-crime policies. We therefore hypothesize that state governments that provide more generous welfare benefits will also have lower incarceration rates, while those with less generous welfare programs will have higher incarceration rates (controlling for other relevant factors).

Ranking the states from most to least punitive and comparing the average welfare payments of each of these groups provides preliminary support for our hypothesis that welfare generosity and incarceration rates are negatively related (see Table 1).

In what follows, regression analysis is used to determine whether this apparent correlation is a spurious one. We also want to know whether the negative relationship between welfare and incarceration, if it exists, is consistent over time. The literature discussed above leads to somewhat contradictory hypotheses on this question. On the one hand, the policy regimes described and analyzed by Esping-Anderson are quite stable and enduring over time. On the other hand, the historical research and analyses of contemporary political discourse discussed earlier show that social and penal policy became interconnected at particular historical moments. Welfare and penal policy respond to changing political and cultural conditions, as well as to political efforts to alter prevailing conceptions of social marginality. For example, the analyses of political discourse discussed above suggest that social and penal policy became more ideologically coherent in response to the Reagan and Bush administrations' attempts to alter public perceptions of policy regarding social marginality. The implication of this analysis is that 'policy-regimeness,' if it exists, may be historically contingent, and therefore variable rather than constant. We therefore specify a model that allows us to see if the relationship between these sectors changes over time. To study the relationship between welfare and incarceration both before and after the 1980s (a time in which political leaders clearly attempted to legitimate and institutionalize the exclusionary approach to social marginality), we examine data from the 50 US states in 1975, 1985, and 1995.

Table 2 describes the variables used in our analysis. Because we are interested in state-level policy effects, the dependent variable is the state prison incarceration rate (i.e. the number of state prison inmates per 100,000 adult population). This figure does not include inmates housed in federal prisons or local jails. Although state policies do influence the size of the jail population, about half of all jail inmates are awaiting trial. The size of the jail population is thus significantly affected by prosecution and court practices, as well as by local police priorities. For example, some localities largely ignore marijuana offenders, while others vigorously pursue them. Six states have combined jail

TABLE 1 Incarceration rate, welfare spending, and demographic characteristics in the 10 most and 10 least punitive states

	INCARCERATION RATE	WELFARE SCORE	BLACK POPULATION (%)	MINORITY POPULATION (%)
Punitive states				
Texas	717	−4.1	12.1	42.3
Louisiana	672	−5.1	31.0	35.6
Oklahoma	617	−3.3	7.5	20.4
South Carolina	536	−4.5	30.6	32.7
Nevada	518	−0.5	6.7	23.1
Arizona	484	−4.8	3.0	30.8
California	475	−1.5	7.9	48.8
Georgia	472	−3.3	27.3	30.7
Michigan	457	2.7	14.6	19.3
Delaware	443	−2.7	18.1	23.2
Non-punitive states				
North Dakota	112	−1.9	.6	6.4
Minnesota	113	5.0	2.5	7.2
Maine	124	−1.1	.4	2.2
Vermont	140	2.7	.3	2.1
West Virginia	174	−2.2	3.2	4.3
New Hampshire	184	0.4	.6	3.1
Nebraska	200	−2.1	3.9	8.7
Utah	205	−1.3	.7	10.3
Rhode Island	213	5.9	4.2	12.7
Washington	233	3.3	3.1	15.6
Punitive state average	539	−2.7	15.8	30.7
Non-punitive state average	170	.9	2.2	7.1
National average	389	0	12.6	26.8

Note: Data for the incarceration rates are 1997 data and are taken from Proband (1998). Welfare scores measure state spending on Aid to Families with Dependent Children (AFDC), Supplemental Security Income (SSI), unemployment insurance, all non-tertiary education spending, food stamps, and Medicaid. Average welfare score and black and minority populations are 1995 data.

and prison systems. Omitting these states and a few observations with missing data yields a total sample size of 128 state-years.

Our key independent variable measures the generosity of the state welfare system. This welfare variable includes measures of state spending on Aid to Families with Dependent Children (AFDC), Supplemental Security Income (SSI), unemployment insurance, all non-tertiary education spending, food stamps, and Medicaid. All spending measures were converted to constant 1982 dollars. To obtain a comparable measure of welfare effort, we divided total spending in each program area by the estimated number of

TABLE 2 Description of variables

Variable name	Description
Dependent variable	
Incarceration rate	Sentenced and unsentenced prison inmates in state prison facilities per 100,000 state adult population
Independent variables	
Welfare	An additive scale that sums measures of state spending on AFDC, unemployment benefits, education, food stamps, supplemental security income, and Medicaid
Percent black	Percentage of the state population identified as African-American (includes black Hispanics)
Percent minority	Percentage of the state population identified as Asian, Native American, African-American, and/or Hispanic
Violent crime	Number of homicides, rapes, robberies, and aggravated assaults per 100,000 population known to the police and compiled in the FBI Uniform Crime Reports
Property crime	Number of burglaries, larcenies, and auto thefts per 100,000 population known to the police and compiled in the FBI Uniform Crime Reports
Unemployment	Percentage of the civilian adult population defined as unemployed
Poverty	Percentage of state residents falling below the poverty line
Urban	Percentage of state's population living in metropolitan areas
Republican	Percentage of state legislators who are Republican, lagged by two years

Note: Data on ethnicity ('Spanish origin') included in our estimate of the minority population in 1975 are from 1976. Estimates of the size of the urban (metropolitan) population included in the 1995 analysis are 1996 estimates. All other data are for 1975, 1985, and 1995.

recipients. For instance, education spending is scaled by the number of pupils in the state school system. These adjusted spending measures were then standardized and summed, yielding an index that measures the generosity of the state welfare system. (We experimented with a variety of different welfare measures, including AFDC benefit levels and several combinations of programs. All measures provided substantively similar results.)

Previous research indicates that the size of the African-American population has a pronounced effect on criminal justice outcomes (Jackson and Carroll, 1981; Bridges et al., 1987; Bridges and Crutchfield, 1988; McGarrell et al., 1992; McGarrell, 1993; Yates, 1997). This finding is typically interpreted as evidence that minorities are subject to a greater degree of surveillance than are whites, although it is also possible that non-whites are more likely to engage in illegal behaviors not captured by the crime data included in the analysis. In one model, we also use the size of the black population as our measure of racial heterogeneity to estimate the effect of the black population on incarceration rates. In a second model, we experimented with a broader category – racial minority – to assess the influence of the size of the non-white population on incarceration. The size of the minority population was estimated as the percentage of the state population identified as Asian, Native American, African-American, or Hispanic. There is also reason to suspect that poverty levels are related to incarceration rates: poor people in general and the urban poor in particular tend to be more vulnerable to state surveillance than their middle-class and suburban counterparts (Bridges and Crutchfield, 1988). The poor may also be more likely to engage in illegal behaviors that are not measured in the Uniform Crime Reports (UCR) crime data, such as selling drugs, engaging in prostitution, or pan-handling, that put them at higher risk of such control. We therefore included measures of a state's poverty rate in our analysis.

A number of researchers representing a broad spectrum of approaches argue that crime rates affect levels of incarceration (see Zimring and Hawkins, 1991). The evidence for this proposition is mixed. Crime rates are positively associated with incarceration rates in some national time-series analyses and cross-sectional studies of the US states (Taggart and Winn, 1993; Jacobs and Helms, 1996). Others have found that violent crime rates are more strongly related to incarceration than are property crime rates (Jankovic, 1980; Carroll and Doubet, 1983; Michalowski and Pearson, 1990). Still other studies report that crime and incarceration rates are largely unrelated (see Zimring and Hawkins, 1991; Davey, 1998). To control for the influence of crime on incarceration, we included state-level violent and property crime rates reported in the UCR. These crime rates are based on the number of crimes known to the police and reported by them to the FBI. In recent decades, heightened awareness of the problem of crime has increased people's willingness to report their crimes to the police (O'Brien, 1996; Boggess and Bound, 1997). There is also evidence that the police have become more likely to record these reports (Jenks, 1991; O'Brien, 1996; Rand et al., 1997). To the extent that the UCR data are measuring the increased willingness of the public and the police to report and record crimes, our results probably over-state the association of crime rates with (rising) incarceration rates.

To assess the impact of economic and demographic factors on imprisonment, we also included the state's gross product, unemployment and poverty rates, and the size of its urban population. The idea that incarceration rates and economic conditions are highly related finds its clearest expression in the work of Rusch and Kircheimer (1939), who argued that penal forms and institutions are shaped by their economic context, especially the size of the available labor pool. Support for this hypothesis is also uneven. Chircos and Delone's (1992) review of 44 analyses of the relationship between levels of unemployment and incarceration reports that 60 percent of these studies find a significant, independent, and positive unemployment effect. Since the pioneering work of Rusche and Kirscheimer, researchers have also explored the more general notion that social inequality and penal severity are related (see especially Melossi, 1993). A number of studies have found that economic inequality is positively related to penal severity (Killias, 1986; Wilkins and Pease, 1987: 21; Gottfredson and Clarke, 1990: 119–25; Wilkins, 1991: 97; Jacobs and Helms, 1996, 1997; Greenberg, 1999). However, because measures of income inequality are highly correlated with our measure of welfare generosity, they were not included in the analysis presented here.

Finally, because Republicans have historically campaigned on law and order platforms, researchers have estimated the effects of the legislative strength of the Republican party at both the state and national level (Jacobs and Helms, 1996), as well as the effect of Republican control of the presidency (Jacobs and Helms, 1999). In both cases, partisan politics were found to be significant determinants of incarceration rates. To measure the impact of partisan politics, we included Republican Party representation in state legislatures, lagged by two years.[5]

RESULTS AND DISCUSSION

Table 3 reports the regression results for models that include the size of the African-American population as the measure of racial heterogeneity. The results of analyses including main effects (i.e. effects for all years) of welfare spending and the size of the black population are reported in the first two columns. The results of interaction models that allow the effects of welfare and the black population to vary across the three time points are reported in the final two columns. The results of the main effects models

TABLE 3 Regression results for a model of state incarceration rates, 1975–95 (128 state-years)

	NORMAL	T-DISTRIBUTION	NORMAL	T-DISTRIBUTION
Intercept	−814.07	−574.71	266.44	187.15
	(3.69)	(4.3)	(1.34)	(2.21)
1975	–	–	−133.46	−103.2
			(5.84)	(11.03)
1985	–	–	−94.3	−84.68
			(5.35)	(11.21)
Welfare	−21.96	−20.71	−14.12	−6.81
	(3.45)	(5.93)	(3.18)	(3.64)
Welfare x 1975	–	–	9.01	5.96
			(1.8)	(3.22)
Welfare x 1985	–	–	7.05	5.9
			(1.87)	(4.07)
Percent black	393.16	376.59	63.55	106.76
	(3.52)	(5.35)	(.63)	(2.36)
Percent black x 1975	–	–	−81.59	−84.75
			(5.21)	(13.6)
Percent black x 1985	–	–	−54.1	−54.83
			(4.14)	(11.02)
Violent crime	.42	.42	.07	.08
	(5.09)	(9.81)	(1.18)	(3.48)
Property crime	−.02	−.03	−.04	−.05
	(1.3)	(3.31)	(3.85)	(11.14)
Unemployment	−9.6	−11.51	1.45	1.24
	(1.88)	(3.95)	(.4)	(.87)
Gross state product	.46	−.15	.30	.40
	(.43)	(.3)	(.45)	(1.89)
Poverty	4.43	2.02	6.79	7.04
	(.92)	(.71)	(1.96)	(5.25)
Republican	.42	.44	1.09	1.65
	(.57)	(1.11)	(2.23)	(9.33)
Urban	4.46	3.02	−1.22	−.18
	(2.58)	(3.23)	(.94)	(.39)
R^2	.85	.81	.95	.92
Log likelihood	−690.43	−684.46	−623.29	−594.05

Note: Numbers in parentheses are *t*-ratios. Percent black effects have been multiplied by 10. State-level fixed effects have been suppressed.

indicate that state social welfare effort is negatively related to incarceration when data from the three time points are analyzed together. A four-point rise in the welfare scale – approximately one standard deviation – is associated with a decline of 80 in the state incarceration rate. By this measure almost half the difference in incarceration rates between California and Washington is attributable to the relative generosity of the Washington state welfare system.

The addition of interactions allows the effects of welfare and the size of the African-American population to vary over time. In these models, the main effect of welfare describes the relationship between welfare spending and incarceration in 1995. The interaction terms describe departures from this benchmark in 1985 and in 1975. These results indicate that in 1995, incarceration rates were significantly lower in states with generous systems of social welfare (and vice versa). A standard deviation change in the welfare level (four points on the welfare scale) is associated with a difference in incarceration rates of between 16 and 52. If the true effect is midway between the OLS and robust estimates, differences in welfare policy account for more than one-third of the 300-point difference in incarceration between Texas and New York. These results indicate that the trade-off between welfare and incarceration, although still existent, was flatter in earlier years. (The OLS results suggest that the welfare effect was around –7 in 1985 and –5 in 1975.) Thus it appears that a strong negative relationship between welfare generosity and penal punitiveness did not come into existence until 1995. The penal-welfare regime thus appears to have crystallized relatively recently.

The interaction model also allows us to capture variation in the effects of the racial composition of state population over time. The robust model provides evidence of a strong and significant positive effect of the black population on incarceration in 1995. Indeed, the 1995 estimate attributes more than half the difference in incarceration between Illinois and Louisiana to differences in the racial composition of the population. These robust results show that the effect of the African-American population was positive but small in 1985 and essentially zero in 1975. In short, the association between race and incarceration has also grown substantially larger over the last three decades.

Several of our control variables also had a significant impact on incarceration rates. We estimated several significant crime effects, and although violent crime rates positively impacted levels of incarceration, property crime effects are negative. These uneven results underline the fact that incarceration rates are only loosely shaped by reported rates of criminal offending. By contrast, poverty rates were positively associated with incarceration, as expected, supporting the idea that poor populations are subject to greater surveillance (although it is also possible that the poor are more likely to engage in illegal behaviors other than those included in the UCR crime data). And consistent with research on incarceration trends at the national level, we also find that Republican Party representation in state legislatures has a significant positive impact on incarceration.

Table 4 shows the results of the analysis when the size of the minority (i.e. African-American, Hispanic, American Indian, and Asian) population is used as the measure of racial heterogeneity. The welfare results are similar to those reported in Table 3. The interaction model indicates that a strong negative relationship between welfare and the size of the penal system emerged by the 1990s. While the results provide evidence of negative effects of welfare on incarceration rates in the 1970s and 1980s, the magnitude of these effects is much smaller than in the 1990s. As in the previously reported model,

TABLE 4 Regression results for a model of state incarceration rates (128 state-years)

	Normal	T–Distribution	Normal	T–Distribution
Intercept	−310.8	−408.82	543.63	445.3
	(2.28)	(5.06)	(4.21)	(10.31)
1975	−	−	−142.53	−93.27
		(6.06)	(10.96)	
1985	−	−	−79.13	−78.35
		(3.69)	(10.55)	
Welfare	−13.32	−16.83	−10.24	−4.01
	(2.21)	(5.15)	(2.59)	(3.12)
Welfare x 1975	−	−	4.59	2.75
			(.97)	(1.73)
Welfare x 1985	−	−	6.76	6.28
			(1.9)	(5.67)
Minority	139.25	108.93	12.47	−4.68
	(3.62)	(4.43)	(.39)	(.47)
Minority x 1975	−	−	−68.03	−86.41
			(5.28)	(19.02)
Minority x 1985	−	−	−41.83	−48.09
			(4.27)	(13.73)
Violent crime	.32	.41	.08	−.03
	(3.41)	(7.16)	(1.18)	(1.64)
Property crime	−.01	.01	−.03	−.04
	(.30)	(.78)	(2.53)	(8.32)
Unemployment	−9.23	−6.54	1.80	2.77
	(1.80)	(2.36)	(.48)	(2.33)
Gross state product	.21	.20	−.15	.03
	(.20)	(.41)	(.22)	(.19)
Poverty	.60	.30	−3.00	1.70
	(.12)	(.10)	(.81)	(1.35)
Republican	−.11	.74	.86	1.13
	(.15)	(1.88)	(1.69)	(6.71)
Urban	4.09	3.73	−2.78	.83
	(2.36)	(3.98)	(2.07)	(1.97)
R²	.85	.80	.94	.91
Log likelihood	−689.9	−684.18	−626.08	−591.97

Note: Numbers in parentheses are *t*-ratios. Percent minority effects have been multiplied by 10. State-level fixed effects have been suppressed.

the negative impact of welfare generosity on levels of incarceration is quite strong by the 1990s.

Results regarding the impact of the minority population differ some from those for percentage black. The main effects estimates indicate that states with a large minority population have higher rates of incarceration. However, the interaction model suggests that minority effects were negative in the 1970s and 1980s. The period main effects and the intercept terms of the interaction model help us to interpret these results. Both

45

period effects are large and negative, while the intercept is large and positive. This suggests that over the three time periods, the minority population is positively associated with incarceration because minority populations were small in 1975 when incarceration was low but large in the 1990s when incarceration rates were comparatively high. Despite this gross positive relationship, within particular years the relationship between the size of the minority population and incarceration was either flat or negative. The absence of the expected positive relationship may also be due to the inclusion of Asians in the minority classification: low incarceration rates among Asians may be confounding what would otherwise be a positive relationship between incarceration and the size of the African-American, American Indian, and Hispanic populations.

These results thus suggest that the effects of both welfare and the size of the black population have become quite significant in the 1990s. This pattern of results is robust to a variety of other specifications. If the three time periods are analyzed separately, all coefficients are allowed to change over time, but we cannot control for unobserved state-specific effects. In this unpooled analysis, welfare effects are negative each year, becoming larger in absolute magnitude over time. These effects are statistically significant in 1985 and 1995. The black (and minority) effects show a similar pattern, being larger in the positive direction in 1985 and 1995 than in 1975. These effects are also significant in later years.

Our results thus suggest that beginning in the 1980s, states with larger black populations are states that spent less on social welfare and also incarcerated at higher levels. This negative relationship was quite significant by the mid-1990s. Unlike the policy-regimes analyzed by Esping-Andersen, then, the policy sectors we analyze here appear to be sometimes loosely coupled and at other times tightly coupled. When loosely coupled, policy incoherence prevails (that is, there is no consistent relationship between welfare and incarceration). But when efforts are made to alter prevailing approaches to social marginality, these sectors become more tightly coupled and policy more coherent (i.e. a negative relationship between welfare and incarceration develops). This interpretation is consistent with John Hagan's analysis of the criminal justice system, in which he shows that under normal conditions, criminal justice institutions are loosely coupled, but when crime-related problems are the target of political action, they become more tightly coupled (1998).

In sum, our findings suggest that in the wake of the Reagan revolution, penal and welfare institutions have come to form a single policy regime aimed at the governance of social marginality. In the 1990s, states with less generous welfare programs feature significantly higher incarceration rates, while those with more generous programs incarcerate a smaller share of their residents. Our results also suggest that states with larger poor and African-American populations and more Republican-dominated legislatures have been more inclined to adopt this approach to social marginality. Thus it appears that more exclusionary approaches to social marginality are especially likely to be adopted by states that house more of those defined in contemporary political discourse as 'troublemakers.' On the basis of this analysis, we conclude that the contraction of welfare programs aimed at the poor and the expansion of penal institutions in the 1980s and 1990s reflects the emergence of an alternative mode of governance that is replacing, to varying degrees, the modernist strategy based on rehabilitation and welfarism. Reduced welfare expenditures are not indicative of a shift toward reduced government intervention in social life (as is implied by the claim that welfare reform reflects the rise of 'neo-liberalism'), but rather a shift toward a more exclusionary and punitive approach to the regulation of social marginality.

Notes

1 Following Selznick, we use the term 'governance' rather than 'management' to suggest that these policies are not selected according to narrow instrumental criteria such as efficiency and cost-effectiveness, but rather according to complex political goals and considerations (Selznick, 1992; see also Garland, 1990).

2 Under most circumstances both inclusionary and exclusionary mechanisms for dealing with 'danger-carrying strangers' exist (Bauman, 1995; see also Vaughan, 2000). As Bauman points out, these alternative strategies depend upon one another for their efficacy: inclusionary measures 'are effective only as far as they are complemented by the sanctions of expulsion . . . but the latter may inspire conformity only as long as the hope of admission is kept alive' (1995: 181; see also Jamieson, 1999: 132). It is nonetheless the case that either end of this continuum may be more pronounced in specific historical moments.

3 Because our analysis will control for reported levels of crime, we refer to states with high rates of incarceration as more punitive than states with lower levels of incarceration.

4 According to Garland, Rusche and Kirchheimer's work suggests that 'penal institutions are to be viewed in their interrelationship with other institutions and with non-penal aspects of social policy. In effect, penal policy is taken to be one element within a wider strategy of controlling the poor . . .' (1990: 91).

5 The panel structure of the data allows us to control for state-specific effects, such as enduring variation in prison capacity, regional effects, or other factors not captured by the independent variables, by introducing a dummy variable for each state (Hsiao, 1986: 29–32). It is theoretically possible that this fixed effects model controls for enduring characteristics that are part of the very regime we wish to measure. However, because the rank-ordering of states by welfare level does not change very much over time, the welfare measure usefully captures cross-sectional variation. Because the average incarceration rate changes over time, we specified dummy variables to indicate the years 1975 and 1985. To assess whether the impact of welfare has become larger over time, we interacted these dummy variables with the welfare variable. Finally, diagnostics show that the incarceration rate variable has a heavy-tailed distribution. We therefore fit both an OLS model that assumes a normal distribution of the errors and a robust t-distribution (Western, 1995). In the analyses below, the robust regression has higher likelihood than the normal OLS model.

References

Administration for Children and Families, Health and Human Services (1999) *Change in welfare caseloads*. Washington, DC.

Baumann, Z. (1995) *Life in fragments*. Oxford: Blackwell.

Beckett, K. (1997) *Making crime pay: law and order in contemporary American politics*. New York: Oxford University Press.

Beckett, K. and Sasson, T. (2000) *The politics of injustice: crime and punishment in America*. Beverly Hills, CA: Pine Forge Press.

Boggess, S. and Bound, J. (1997) 'Did criminal activity increase during the 1980s? Comparisons across data sources', *Social Science Quarterly* 78: 725–36.

Bridges, G. and Crutchfield, R. (1988) 'Law, social standing and racial disparities in imprisonment', *Social Forces* 3: 699–724.

Bridges, G.S., Crutchfield, R.D. and Simpson, E.E. (1987) 'Crime, social structure and criminal punishment: white and nonwhite rates of imprisonment', *Social Problems* 34: 345–61.

Bureau of Justice Statistics (BJS) (1997, 1995) *Sourcebook of criminal justice statistics*. Washington, DC: Bureau of Justice Statistics.

Bureau of Justice Statistics (BJS) (1999) *Prison and jail inmates at midyear 1998*. Washington, DC: Bureau of Justice Statistics.

Burtless, G. (1994) 'Public spending on the poor: historical trends and economic limits', in S.H. Danziger, G.D. Sandefur and D.H. Weinberg (eds) *Confronting poverty: prescriptions for change*. New York: Russell Sage Foundation.

Butterfield, Fox (1998) 'Inmates serving more time, Justice Department reports', *New York Times* 11 January: A10.

Carroll, L. and Doubet, M.B. (1983) 'US social structure and imprisonment', *Criminology* 21: 449–56.

Chircos, T.G. and Delone, M.A. (1992) 'Labor surplus and punishment: a review and assessment of theory and evidence', *Social Problems* 39(4): 421–46.

Danziger, S. and Gotschalk, P. (1995) *America unequal*. New York: Russell Sage Foundation.

Davey, J.D. (1998) *The politics of prison expansion*. Westport, CT: Praeger.

Donziger, S.R. (ed.) (1996) *The real war on crime: the report of the National Criminal Justice Commission*. New York: HarperCollins.

Esping-Andersen, G. (1990) *The three worlds of welfare capitalism*. New Jersey: Princeton University Press.

Gans, H. (1995) *The war against the poor*. New York: Basic Books.

Garland, D. (1985) *Punishment and welfare: a history of penal strategies*. Aldershot: Gower.

Garland, D. (1990) *Punishment and modern society*. Chicago, IL: University of Chicago Press.

Garland, D. (1996) 'The limits of the sovereign state: strategies of crime control in contemporary society', *British Journal of Criminology* 36(4): 445–71.

Gottfredson, D.M. and Clarke, R.V. (1990) *Policy and theory in criminal justice*. Brookfield, VT: Gower.

Greenberg, D. (1999) 'Punishment, division of labor and social solidarity', *The Criminology of Criminal Law: Advances in Criminological Theory* 8: 283–361.

Greenberg, D. and West, V. (n.d.) 'Growth in state prison populations, 1971–1991' unpublished manuscript.

Hagan, J. (1998) 'The everyday and the not so exceptional in the social organization of criminal justice practices', in A. Sarat, M. Constable, D. Engel, V. Hans and S. Lawrence (eds) *Everyday practices and trouble cases*. Chicago, IL: Northwestern University Press.

Hsiao, C. (1986) *Analysis of panel data*. New York: Cambridge University Press.

Jackson, P.I. and Carroll, L. (1981) 'Race and the war on crime: the sociopolitical determinants of municipal police expenditures', *American Sociological Review* 46:
290–305.

Jacobs, D. and Helms, R.E. (1996) 'Towards a political model of incarceration', *American Journal of Sociology* 102(2): 323–57.

Jacobs, D. and Helms, R.E. (1997) 'Testing coercive explanations for order', *Social Forces*
75(4): 1361–92.

Jamieson, R. (1999) 'Genocide and the social production of immorality', *Theoretical
Criminology* 3(2): 131–46.

Katz, M.B. (1989) *The undeserving poor: from the war on poverty to the war on welfare.*
New York: Pantheon Books.

Killias, M. (1986) 'Power concentration, legitimation crisis and penal severity', in W.B.
Groves and G. Newman (eds) *Punishment and privilege.* New York: Harrow &
Heston.

McGarrell, E.F. (1993) 'Institutional theory and the stability of a conflict model of the
incarceration rate', *Justice Quarterly* 10(1): 7–27.

McGarrell, E.F., Duffy, D.E. and McDowall, D. (1992) 'Correctional resources and the
structure of the institutionalized environment: a cross-sectional study of the States',
unpublished paper.

Melossi, D. (1993) 'Gazette of morality and social whip: punishment, hegemony, and
the case of the USA, 1970–1992', *Social and Legal Studies* 2: 259–79.

O'Brien, R.M. (1996) 'Police productivity and crime rates: 1973–1992', *Criminology*
34(2): 183–207.

Piven, F.F. and Cloward, R. (1979) *Poor people's movements: why they succeed, how they
fail.* New York: Vintage Books.

Rand, M., Lynch, J.P. and Cantor, D. (1997) *Criminal victimization, 1973–1995.*
Washington, DC: Bureau of Justice Statistics.

Rose, N. (1996) 'Governing "advanced" liberal democracies', in A. Barry, T. Osborne
and N. Rose (eds) *Foucault and political reason: liberalism, neo-liberalism, and ratio-
nalities of government.* Chicago, IL: University of Chicago Press.

Rothman, D. (1980) *Conscience and convenience: the asylum and its alternatives in progressive America.* New York: HarperCollins.

Rusche, G. and Kirchheimer, O. (1939) *Punishment and social structure.* New York:
Russell & Russell.

Schram, S. (1995) *Words of welfare: the poverty of social science and the social science of
poverty.* Minneapolis, MN: University of Minnesota Press.

Sentencing Project (1997) *Facts about prisons and prisoners.* Washington, DC.

Sentencing Project (2000) 'U.S. Surpasses Russia as World Leader in Rate of Incarceration'. Posted at www.sentencingproject.org/news/news.htm

Simon, J. (1997) 'Governing through crime', in L. Friedman and G. Fisher (eds) *The
crime conundrum: essays in criminal justice.* Westview Press.

Sparks, R. (1996) 'Penal "austerity": the doctrine of less eligibility reborn?', in R.
Matthews and P. Francis (eds) *Prisons 2000: an international perspective on the current
state and future of imprisonment.* London: Macmillan.

Sutton, J. (1997a) 'Punishment, labor markets and welfare states: imprisonment trends
in five common law countries, 1955–1985', unpublished paper.

Sutton, J.R. (1997b) 'Rethinking social control', *Law and Social Inquiry* 22(4): 943–59.

Taggart, W.A. and Winn, R.G. (1993) 'Imprisonment in the American states', *Social Science Quarterly* 74: 736–49.

Tonry, M. (1995) *Malign neglect: race, crime, and punishment in America*. New York: Oxford University Press.

Vaughan, B. (2000) 'Punishment and conditional citizenship', *Punishment and Society* 2(1): 23–39.

Wacquant, L. (1999) 'Blairism: Trojan horse of Americanism?', paper presented at the Roundtable on 'Blairism: a beacon for Europe?', London, May.

Western, B. (1995) 'Concepts and suggestions for robust regression analysis', *American Journal of Political Science* 39: 786–817.

Western, B. and Beckett, K. (1999) 'How unregulated is the US labor market? The penal system as labor market institution', *American Journal of Sociology* 104(4): 1030–60.

Wilkins, L.T. (1991) *Punishment, crime and market forces*. Aldershot: Dartmouth Publishing Company.

Wilkins, L.T. and Pease, K. (1987) 'Public demand for punishment', *International Journal of Sociology and Social Policy* 7(3): 16–29.

Yates, J. (1997) 'Racial incarceration disparity among states', *Social Science Quarterly* 78: 1001–10.

Zimring, F. and Hawkins, G. (1991) *The scale of imprisonment*. Chicago, IL: University of Chicago Press.

Zimring, F. and Hawkins, G. (1995) *Incapacitation: penal confinement and the restraint of crime*. New York: Oxford University Press.

5 The *macho* penal economy

Mass incarceration in the United States – a European perspective

DAVID DOWNES

INTRODUCTION

American exceptionalism in deviance and control, for most of the 20th century, consisted of exceptionally high rates of serious crime, notably homicide, robbery, hard drug dealing and gang violence in both its juvenile and organized crime forms. Theorizing about crime, especially in the *anomie* tradition, has been massively influenced by this major contrast with the general run of European experience. So there has been a certain experience of cognitive dissonance as, over the past two decades, crime rates in the USA have levelled off and recently fallen, whilst those in some European countries have risen, in the case of serious property crimes, to surpass the US rates. Moreover, these trends have occurred despite a sharpening of the contrasts between the USA and Europe[1] in the alleged root causes of crime: the extent of inequalities of wealth and income, poverty and the apotheosis of the winner/loser culture (James, 1993). An aetiological crisis (see Young, 1986), due to crime trends spinning out of alignment with predictions drawn from the major social theories, was avoided only by the phenomenal growth of the US prison population. Even powerful causes can be over-ridden by so devastating a penal response, though there are the awkward facts that state by state increases in imprisonment correlate only weakly with crime rate fluctuations, especially crimes of violence (Currie, 1998).

The aetiological crisis may, however, simply have been displaced to another site. Social theorists have long maintained that the criminal justice and penal systems are poor guarantors of crime prevention and reduction. Structural and cultural variables are seen as far more potent in explaining and predicting trends in crime and their variations. But the US penal explosion, which has now persisted for over two decades, eluded both prediction and convincing explanation. Why, in short, did nobody see this coming? An earlier generation of sociologists had been taken to task by Everett Hughes for failing to foresee the scale of racial conflict in the late 1950s and early 1960s, due to their attachment to Parsonian systems theory. It may well be that the 1970s' equivalent was the assumption that governments would respect the view, shared by most criminologists, that deterrence and incapacitation would not, except at an unacceptably high human and financial cost, serve significantly to reduce crime. The argument that the price was worth paying (Wilson, 1975, is the *fons et origo* of this case) was a paradigmatic break. Sufficiently pursued, the penal route, it was claimed, *does* pay off. A decade or two later, the American example's appeal to governments elsewhere, especially those of a New Right persuasion, is that prison does indeed 'work'. And it works not just by keeping vast numbers of offenders off the streets. It also works by showing how a deregulated capitalism can have its cake and eat it: a market economy can produce a market society without a rocketing crime rate.

No comparable democratic society has embraced what Leon Radzinowicz (1991) termed 'penal regression' with remotely equivalent fervour. Of the other high imprisonment societies, China remains pre-democratic, and Russia, the former Soviet bloc countries and South Africa, are – for very different reasons – in transition from massively oppressive regimes. In the 1980s, by contrast, a New Right Britain did the opposite, to everyone's surprise. It was only in the 1990s, clearly influenced by the American example, that the appeal of a 'prison works' strategy was seen as ideologically more palatable, politically advantageous and also cheaper than crime reduction bought by substantial increases in employment and welfare services. And in The Netherlands, a high-cost welfare society, imprisonment also came to be seen as the only resort where welfare and lesser punishments had failed. The Netherlands too has quintupled its prison population over the past two decades, albeit from a far lower base and, as yet, to no more than the European average.

There are, however, several examples of resistance to this trend (Stern, 1998). The Scandinavian countries have maintained very high welfare spending with relatively low and, in the case of Finland, striking falls in imprisonment levels. France and Germany have maintained a steady state despite rising crime rates. Closest to home, Canada has preserved roughly stable crime and imprisonment levels for two decades,[2] an achievement that is rarely mentioned in Anglo-American debate on penal policy. And, of course, there are some states within the USA which have bucked the trend in significant respects (Kuhn, 1999; Tonry, 1999).

A great deal rides on whether or not, and the extent to which, the USA is an exceptionalist outlier in the penal sphere or both a prefiguration and a driver of things to come. If the era of global capitalism is both highly criminogenic *and* punitive, as Nils Christie (1993) has so forcefully argued; and if, as his colleague Thomas Mathiesen (1990) has proposed, the more developed societies resort heavily to penal innovations in periods of rapid changes in their political economy – as in the late 16th, late 18th and now late or post-20th centuries – then we can expect the latter course to be followed. Global capitalism is not necessarily 'late' capitalism. 'We are still in the early stages of capitalism. Our lives are still shaped on all sides by pre-capitalist residues, though they are under assault as never before' (Collini, 2000).[3] It may be better seen as its belated onset, in the sense that capitalism until now has been much constrained by its context. Nineteenth-century capitalism was still subject to pre-capitalist encirclement. Second, it was constantly pressured by diverse socialist movements from within and, after 1917, State socialism from without. It consequently adapted Bismarckian welfare defences to ward off revolution and civil strife. It is only now that it is off the leash. Third, imperialism may have exported capitalism on a global scale, but it was not global capitalism. It was mainly British, French, or Dutch, and these countries tended to fetter capitalist development for nationalistic or paternalistic reasons. It is only now, in the post-communist, post-colonial era that a more purely global capitalism holds sway, albeit largely of an American model.

There is a fourth and arguably more fundamental characteristic of this new, purer form of capitalism. Until now, capitalism has been not only constrained but also facilitated by traditional, massively taken for granted social values and forms of conduct. Emile Durkheim may, as David Greenberg (1999) has argued, have proved a poor predictor of penal trends. But his dictum that contract rests on 'non-contractual elements' of trust and co-operation, born of social solidarity, summarizes acutely how capitalist successes so far have rested implicitly on forms of social relations which it is now in the process of dissolving. To John Gray (1998) and Richard Sennett (1998), global capitalism is corrosive of both social cohesion and the bases of character. Karl Marx would not have been surprised by this analysis. Ironically, far from being eclipsed by the fall of communism, Marxism has never looked so good, though it is Marx the diagnostician of capitalism rather than the prognosticator of communism who appears to be back on track (Hobsbawm, 1998). None of which explains why, well in advance of the fall of communism and with a far from negligible public sector, the USA switched to so immense an investment in imprisonment.

AMERICAN EXCEPTIONALISM: CAUSE OR CONSEQUENCE?

In his review of possible explanations for the trends towards mass incarceration in the USA, Michael Tonry (1999) classifies current theories into five types: empirical (crime-led); psephological (public opinion-led); journalistic (media manipulation of crime as a 'wedge' issue, political (what Jonathan Simon has termed 'governing through crime' in the context of issue fragmentation); and historical (a cycle of tolerance and intolerance towards key forms of deviance). Tonry concludes that no factor taken alone can account for so gross a development as the quintupling of the US prison population over 25 years, but that the historical approach may provide a basis for the other factors to weigh in. He rejects most of the theories on comparative grounds: other countries, with far lower prison numbers than the USA have also experienced the empirical, psephological, journalistic and political shifts concerned and, it might be added, also have their own versions of swings between periods of tolerance and intolerance. American history is indeed unique, but less for its cyclical patterns than for the culture that shapes them.

In short, American exceptionalism in the penal sphere must be related to American exceptionalism itself, as a broad, unifying mythology that stretches back, with remarkable cultural continuity, to the Puritan settlement. As Melossi and Lettiere note, quoting Thomas Dumm

> 'the emergence of the penitentiary in the United States was a project *constitutive* of liberal democracy. That is, the penitentiary system formed the epistemological project of liberal democracy, creating conditions of knowledge of self and other that were to shape the political subject required for liberal and democratic values to be realised in practice . . .' . . . We could in a sense say that the American penitentiary was erected by the Founding Fathers of the Nation as an imposing and monumental Gateway to the Republic. (1998: 24–5)

Though the origins of the penitentiary lay in 17th-century Holland, it was only in

Jacksonian America that 'it became the task of the prison to do nothing less than ensure the future safety of the Republic' (Rothman, 1995: 115).

In similar vein, Deborah Madsen (1998) traces the extraordinary extent to which the founding notions of the 'federal covenant', the 'saving remnant' and the 'elect' or 'redeemer nation' continue to animate, and set the terms for, current political and cultural discourse. America as the 'city on a hill' was charged with a divine mission to build a model society on earth – the New World – which would, by force of example, serve to purify the Old World they had left behind, but not abandoned. Especially relevant for deviance and control are the concepts of 'declension' – the falling away from the high ideals of the original 'errand' – and the 'federal covenant', whereby any moral backsliding by a community would threaten the salvation of the whole. Drawing on the work of Perry Miller and others, Madsen traces American exceptionalism as the animating force in Benjamin Franklin's self-exemplification of American virtues; in the 'American Renaissance' of Emerson, Hawthorne, Melville, Thoreau and Whitman; in the mythology of the western genre in cinema; in the abolitionist case against slavery, most notably by prominent slaves themselves; in the legitimation of the annexation of former Mexican and Caribbean territories; and in the case for promulgating war in Vietnam. The notion of the American Dream, so beloved of anomie theorists, captures only limited aspects of American exceptionalism – the stress on individualism and the right to happiness through virtue – and neglects its other components – the dangers of and penalties for declension, and the injunction for America to be 'not only a model nation, but also the world's guardian, regulating the conduct of other nations, and representing the world's last and best chance of salvation' (Madsen, 1998: 38).

Suitably secularized and modernized, American exceptionalism furnishes a vocabulary of motives for mass incarceration to be viewed as an inescapably utopian mission. It may have been pragmatically punitive in its origins. In *Thinking about crime* (1975), for example, James Q. Wilson argued 'for a sober view of man and his institutions that would permit reasonable things to be accomplished, foolish things abandoned, and utopian things forgotten' (quoted in Rutherford, 1996: 25–6). But in its rapid politicization and development beyond all comparable limits, it has become a utopian experiment: a social cleansing by penal means. That appeal, along with its popular accreditation for crime reduction, helps account for its widespread acceptance and lack of effective opposition, especially by the judiciary, whose discretionary powers have been greatly weakened by mandatory sentencing. It also provides an *imprimatur* for its export on a global scale. And, like many utopias, it has become dystopia, a cataclysm for those most adversely affected by its realization.

Against this view, it can be said that American exceptionalism may account for the Salem witch-hunts of the late 17th century but hardly for the sudden shift to mass incarceration in the late 20th century. As a constant, if evolving, foundation of American culture, it ran for over 300 years without producing this effect. Yet it has only been in the late 20th century that American exceptionalism ran out of, or rather ruled out, alternative options with regard to deviance and control. Two such options have, until the recent past, been the rehabilitative ideology and radical social reform. A third, the prospect of new frontiers, has – Madsen argues – been self-cancelling, as the exceptionalist drive of the pioneers ceded to settlement. New frontiers are now – following the fall of communism – new markets and technological means of penetrating them.

Rehabilitative movements have flourished both long and extensively, both within prisons and outside them, in the USA; and greater claims arguably have been made for their success than elsewhere (Rothman, 1971, 1980; Melossi and Lettiere, 1998). The use of the indeterminate sentence in California was a particularly florid example of its penal expression. It was perhaps only to be expected, therefore, that in the post-Martinson, 'Nothing Works' era after 1974, the movement to overthrow the rehabilitative agenda would have its greatest impact in the USA. This movement reached much further than psycho-analytically or psychiatrically based approaches. It seemed to wipe out the political will to experiment adequately with social and economic approaches to crime prevention and reduction. Hence, the major argument of Elliott Currie, Jerome Miller and other critics of penal expansionism – that the alternative to prison is not doing nothing, it is spending equivalent amounts on well-resourced community alternatives – met with the same 'nothing works' response.

Second, what David Garland (1996) has termed the 'solidarity project', the post-Enlightenment ideal of extending full and active citizenship to all subjects, was effectively dispensed with by the Reagan Presidency. Before then, the New Deal, and the Great Society and War on Poverty programmes had held open the possibility that the United States would move towards a 'welfare state' along European lines. Even in the 1970s and under Richard Nixon, affirmative action and the extension of Head Start projects perpetuated that hope. But the advent of 'Reaganomics', and the Bush and Clinton years, have effectively removed all but a vestigial welfare safety net for most and, for some (e.g. unwed mothers in certain states) not even that. Between 1981 and 1993, there was no increase in the proportion of GDP (21 percent) spent on welfare in the USA (Hills, 1997: 10). This was not due, in the richest nation on earth, to the 'limits of welfare' being reached, but to the perception of the economic leadership that welfare undercut market disciplines (Parenti, 1999).

A related aspect is supplied from academe – the repudiation, notably by James Q. Wilson and Charles Murray, of the search for 'root causes' of and the affirmation of penal incapacitation as the sole sure remedy for crime on the streets. If individuals are entirely responsible for crime, structural and cultural theorizing is inadmissible. Prisons are not in themselves a utopian device, as in earlier eras, such as Jacksonian America (Rothman, 1971). Rather, utopia consists in the removal of criminals from American society by penal means.[4] It rests on exclusion and banishment rather than inclusion and hopes of reform (Young, 1999). Human warehousing (Cohen, 1985) rather than normalization (King and Morgan, 1980) or minimal 'just deserts' (Von Hirsch, 1976) is all that is required. Roy King's study of 'Supermax' prisons in the USA (King, 1999) confirms that they, in particular, are an over-used facility antithetical to both humane containment and rehabilitation. Nor is there evidence to suggest that their expansion has 'freed up' the rest of the system for more humanitarian and constructive regimes.

A COMPARATIVE PERSPECTIVE ON PENAL FUTURES

In their comparative analyses of incarceration trends, both Tonry and Kuhn rightly stress the unique scale of US incarceration and the extent to which it 'dwarfs' that in comparable European societies. As noted above, Tonry goes on to reject certain much-touted 'causes' of the American phenomenon due to their co-existence with the far lower prison populations of Europe, Australasia and Canada. But that logic holds only as things currently stand. If these 'causes' are weighed in terms of their future potential rather than their current impact, then it may be only a matter of time before they begin to exert more influence in these countries too. The cliché that what happened in California yesterday is happening in the rest of America today, and will happen in Europe tomorrow, cannot be lightly dismissed. The challenge is to assess how far the recipe for the US mass incarceration is in embryo in European and other societies. In addition, having gone this route alone, the US is actively exporting it, and key groups in comparable societies are eager to adopt it. It may be more, not less, difficult for other societies to resist its appeal when the USA is both its role model and its advocate, both in the 'law and order' and in other political and economic respects.

Crime is not the problem?

Zimring and Hawkins (1997) have convincingly shown the extent to which crime rates in the USA, with the single exception of lethal violence, are now relatively normal compared with several European societies. It is a peculiar irony of American exceptionalist mythologizing that the right to bear arms, which harbour the potential for instant lethal violence, is regarded as sacrosanct, while the right to bear drugs, whose potential is rarely so, is regarded as taboo. Hence 'crime is not the problem' as a cause of US mass incarceration, as only a quarter of admissions to prisons are for violence (Tonry, 1999: 8).[5] But the fact that European crime rates have reached US proportions, while it may be reassuring from an American perspective, is disquieting from a European vantage-point. Signs of relative normalcy to the one may portend the advent of pathology to the other. Burglary and car theft may be non-lethal offences but they are still profoundly unsettling, especially when experienced as repeat victimizations. It may well be, as Katharine Beckett (1997) has shown, that public anxieties about crime register most strongly after media and political campaigns rather than rises in crime rates or drug use. As Chambliss (1999) argues, politicians and criminal justice agencies typically quote the worst trends for the most serious crimes, even if they are plea bargained away! But rising crime rates still set the context within which such campaigns resonate. And, once in train, penal expansionism gains the credit when crime rates fall, even when other explanations, such as falling unemployment and rising prosperity, may be more plausible reasons.

The most damaging crime phenomena are those periods in which a quantum leap in crime rates coincides with allied sequences of events yielding a virulent symbolism of social breakdown. Thus, the mid-1960s to the mid-1970s in the USA combined steep rises in crime with a doubling of the homicide rate; the assassinations of John and Robert Kennedy, Martin Luther King and Malcolm X; major urban riots, both racial and anti-war; and extremist political violence. There were elements of 'la grande peur' of revolutionary France in the atmosphere of the times. In Britain, the 1980s saw a doubling of the crime rate and, especially in 1989–92, when the crime rate rose by 50 percent, in a context of rioting and high unemployment following deindustrialization, the sense of a breakdown of social order was very strong. The murder of a 2-year-old boy, James Bulger, by two older boys, provided the climax to a decade of growing fear of crime that symbolized a sense of social changes spinning out of control. In The Netherlands, the rising crime rate during 1979–84 resembled a cliff face compared with earlier trends. Combined with fears about hard drug use and drug-related crime, it provided conditions ripe for a toughening of criminal justice and penal policy. In all three countries, but to very different degrees, the scene was set for prison populations rising to unprecedented heights.

The definition of the problem, heavily influenced by political and media agendas, seems crucial in explaining whether structural or punitive measures are deployed in response. In the USA and to a lesser extent in Britain, the most influential explanation imputed rising crime and riots to a newly jobless marauding underclass (Taylor, 1999). In The Netherlands, 'depillarization', the erosion of the institutionalized bases of informal social control in the family, denominational groupings, the school and the community, was seen as the principal cause in the influential *Society and crime* report (Ministry of Justice, 1985). This explanation probably did more to arouse anxieties than to allay them, and the publication of the first International Victim Survey in 1987, showing The Netherlands to be apparently the most crime-prone nation surveyed, compounded such fears. Other Western European countries to have experienced such trends have avoided or resisted so penal a response, though several – e.g. Italy, Spain, Portugal – have raised their prison populations markedly (Ruggiero et al., 1995). In others, – e.g. Austria, France – politically fascistic parties have gained ground.

Crime thus holds the potential to symbolize social breakdown in ways which mobilize popular and elite support for punitive formal controls to be stepped up to previously impermissible heights and lengths. Seismic shifts can occur in the regulatory character not only of the criminal justice field (Feeley and Simon, 1992) but across the entire culture of control (see Garland, 2001). As a result, even when crime has ceased to be *the* problem, changes have been set in motion which are immensely difficult to modify and may be impossible to reverse. In this welter of disturbing change, imprisonment offers one touchstone of secure social order. Prisons are the guarantee that *ultimately* law and order will be enforced or restored. Modes of punishment are profoundly expressive (Garland, 1990), and the symbolic potency of imprisonment in particular offers politicians endless dramaturgical possibilities, conveying multiple messages to different audiences (Sparks, forthcoming). It is *the* sign that governments are prepared to do whatever it takes to wage war on crime. In some penal climates it attains a kind of fiscal benefit of clergy, as an experiment that cannot fail – if crime goes down, prisons gain the credit; but if it goes up, we clearly need more of the same medicine whatever the cost.

The politics of law and order

With some allowance for time-lags, Tonry rightly sees much common experience between the USA and European societies on this front. In Britain, crime control emerged as a partisan issue only in the 1970 General Election, then even more resoundingly in 1979 (Downes and Morgan, 1997). In the USA, it first surfaced with Goldwater in 1964, in The Netherlands 20 years later. In France, Germany and the Scandinavian countries, it remains much less prominent, despite highly visible episodes of youthful disorder and growing drug use. Though variation persists, two trajectories are discernible. The first is that, once embarked on a course of 'governing through crime', with the heightened emotionalism and bidding-up of punitive measures that this entails, no society has managed to find a way of extricating itself from that upwards spiral. Part of that pattern is at least *some* convergence between the USA and Europe at the ideological level. It may well be that Americans have given less weight than Europeans to social and economic factors in offending behaviour (Kuhn, 1999: 19), but rehabilitation also connotes self-improvement aided by counselling and treatment, a long-established if now marginalized American practice. At the European end:

> analogous to the conversion of the welfare state since the 1980s into . . . a 'market economy', diminishing the responsibility of the state to its citizens and heavily emphasising individual responsibility, causes of criminal behaviour are no longer seen as lying in the criminal's social background, life situation and the circumstances of the offence, but in the moral fault of the actor resulting in acts of free will for which he is fully responsible. (Junger-Tas, 1998: 19)

The second is that economic growth in the richest countries has in part depended on inflows of migrant workers, has fostered immigration from former colonies and prompted refugees to seek haven on a scale not easily accommodated without conflict. The problems involved in integrating diverse culturally distinctive groups into highly unequal societies can all too readily be translated into crime control terms.

In Britain, only since 1992 have both major parties engaged in 'populist punitiveness' (Bottoms, 1995). The Tories had long contrived to cast Labour as a party neglectful of the police, 'soft' on crime and tolerant of public disorder born of industrial militancy. Labour had pursued the alternative case that rising crime was largely due to social and economic inequalities (Downes and Morgan, 1994). As Shadow Home Secretary during 1979–92, Roy Hattersley also pressed a Rawlsian case, the need to combine social justice with civil liberties (Bowling, 2000). Between 1989–92, Britain experienced a major recession, with male unemployment rising to 15 percent; a prison population falling from 50,000 to 42,000; and a crime rate that rose by almost 50 percent. For the first time in over 30 years, the Conservative lead over Labour as the party best able to guarantee law and order vanished. Labour pressed home their advantage, not by emphasizing the links between economic factors and rising crime but by stressing the leniency of sentencing. Tony Blair's celebrated sound-bite on the need to be 'tough on crime, tough on the causes of crime' nicely allowed for both, but the sub-text, being 'tough on criminals', was what emerged in policy terms (Pease, 1998; see also Ryan, 1999). This strategy owed much to the American Democratic Party's approach to avoiding a repetition of the Dukakis debacle of 1988. Clinton was 'smart' as well as 'tough' on crime (Rutherford, 1999). To neutralize Michael Howard's 'Prison Works' policy, Jack Straw, both in Opposition and in government, formulated policies (some enacted in the 1998 Crime and Disorder Act, some either still forthcoming or meeting resistance) which Labour would hardly have countenanced before 1992. These include

- activating minimum mandatory penalties for burglary, drug-dealing and violence (authorized by a statute passed by the outgoing Conservative government);
- the creation of Anti-Social Behaviour Orders which, inter alia, blur the distinction between criminal and civil law burdens of proof (see Ashworth et al., 1998);
- local authority powers to impose curfews for juveniles;
- renaming the Probation and After-Care Service the 'Community Punishment and Rehabilitation Service' (a measure to which 85 percent of Chief Probation Officers are opposed);
- reducing the threshold for returning probationers to court from three breaches to two

(a breach being such conduct as failing to attend a meeting with the officer at the agreed time); and automatic withdrawal of social security benefits for up to six months for a second breach;

- the extension of privatized prison management from three prisons to 14;
- the ending of *doli incapax* (the presumption of lack of offending awareness) for offenders under the age of 14;
- the replacement of Social Security payments by subsistence vouchers for asylum seekers;
- the prosecution of 'squeegee merchants' and beggars;
- drug testing of arrestees at police stations;
- extending disclosure to employers of previous convictions to all offences.

Much of this catalogue is inspired by the American example of 'zero tolerance' policing and prosecution. The effect is that both major parties have engaged in raising the punitive stakes, and the prison population in England and Wales rose from 42,000 to 65,000 in six years.

There are, it must be said, compensating liberal components to offset the generally punitive drift of these measures. For example

- Labour have embarked on a generously funded programme of 'restorative justice' and community crime reduction projects for disaffected youth, stressing reparation, mediation and mentoring for young offenders and those at risk of crime;
- Jack Straw took the brave decision to mount a public enquiry into the Stephen Lawrence case, in which the hugely bungled investigation by the Metropolitan Police of the murder of a black teenager by local white youths was defined as 'institutional racism' by the resulting Report;
- the UK, a long-term but reluctant signatory to the European Convention on Human Rights, has now incorporated its provisions into domestic law;
- the age of consent for homosexual relations should be reduced to 16, to match that for heterosexual relations.

The net result of all these measures remains, however, markedly punitive and penally expansionist, though some expert commentary (e.g. Morgan, 1998) sees Straw as acting '*sotto voce*' to 'manage' the prison population at roughly its current level. And the community measures are heavily dependent on marked improvements in the major public sector services of health, education and housing, which remain significantly under-funded by comparison with most European countries (Hills, 1997; Downes, 1998). Should crime rates recommence their annual rise, and the evaluation of community measures prove negative or equivocal, a further ratcheting up of prison populations seems inevitable.

The second common trajectory crucial to the politics of law and order is that

the concern with crime and fear of victimization has grown out of all proportion to the actual increases in criminality; fear which typically is most focused on traditional 'street crimes' and crimes allegedly committed by powerless minority groups . . . Across Europe and in the US, increasing proportions of the prison population consist of 'minorities' and foreigners. (Marshall, 1996: 31)

In Europe, contradictory impulses are at work. On the one hand, the shared political aspiration is for a Europe *sans frontières*, with freedom of trade and movement, upheld by the European Court, the Convention on Human Rights, etc. On the other hand, the inflows of refugees, migrant workers and immigrants from both former communist and colonial societies provokes resentments that have, as Loïc Wacquant (1999) has stressed, fed into the politics of far Right ethnocentrism. One attempt at resolution is to legislate for equal opportunities but also to step up penalties for the offences in which the most discriminated against ethnic minorities are disproportionately involved (Tonry, 1995). The over-representation of Afro-Caribbean compared to white prisoners in Britain is much the same as in the USA. In The Netherlands, the proportion of non-Dutch prisoners rose from 12 percent in 1981 to 26 percent in 1992; and a growing proportion are from second-generation ethnic minorities (Van Swaaningen and De Jonge, 1995; Downes, 1998: 150). While much controversy surrounds the view that such minorities are disproportionately involved in crime, the perception has grown that they are unusually disaffected, resistant to welfare measures and recalcitrant. In this situation, even liberal elites are prone to disillusioned acceptance of exclusionary measures: in England, black children are permanently excluded from school at three times the rate of white children; and the scale of expulsions overall rose greatly during the 1990s to 12,668 in 1996/7 (10,400 in 1998/9) (Department for Education and Employment, 10 May 2000). These trends all hold potential for penal expansion.

Risk and security

More common ground between Europe and the USA can be found in the combination of a heightened awareness of victimization by crime and greater expectations of personal security and public safety. Expectations about safety and security have increased hugely in the post-war period. The Social Democratic ideal of cradle-to-grave work and welfare; immense improvements in medical care and surgery; the post-war settlement that, despite the nuclear threat, held out the prospect of peaceful international relations; and the makings of a system of world governance promised future stability. In the lives of most people in the democracies of the West, and with the single exception of the Vietnam war, victimization by crime was the principal source of risk that could not be personally controlled or ameliorated. Oral histories tend to confirm this sense of crime as an increasingly unwarranted scourge (Hood and Joyce, 1999). It has fuelled the growth of such movements as victim rights and victim support (Rock, 1987, 1990, 1998) and the vast and growing investment in situational crime prevention: mass electronic surveillance, target hardening, security checks and gated communities are now so pervasive that the crime rate might well be termed the displacement rate. Cars left unalarmed, property left unguarded and houses only minimally secured are now bad insurance risks, with the worst-hit communities becoming uninsurable. The more repressive the controls, the more regressive becomes the crime, with poorer areas – notoriously the deindustrialized wastelands – plagued by multiple victimization (Davies, 1998). The promise of situational control (Clarke, 1980) was that the contested terrain of 'root causes' could be ignored. But while such controls may have helped contain crime rates, they have hardly been reduced at all substantially. Insofar as crime rates persist at a high level or even increase despite such measures – which has immense implications for the exclusion and control of deviant groups and individuals – the potential for yet further resort to imprisonment is ever-present.

Among the more potent images of risk and insecurity are the mentally ill, decanted from dwindling institutions to insubstantial community care. What gets noticed in the community are the visibly distressed and deviant, whose often-unkempt appearance, verbal aggression and odd behaviour disturb harassed commuters and busy shoppers. Though it is no comfort to victims, their contribution to lethal violence is minute, but what there is has fuelled demands for 'something to be done' about the most dangerous, severely disordered personalities. The current British Home Office proposal (1999) is that indefinite detention should be the provision, even in the absence of offending behaviour. Given the difficulties of diagnosis, this is a recipe for expanding incarceration to a fresh target group of uncertain dimensions.

THE *MACHO* ECONOMY

The USA in the 1980s seemed to many observers (e.g. Paul Kennedy, 1993) to be losing its pre-eminence as *the* world power economically if not militarily. The 1990s saw its position not only restored but subject to a certain triumphalism. There remains, however, one contender against the US model of political economy: the social democratic 'welfare state', mixed economies, primarily of Europe, but also Canada, Australia and New Zealand. In this model, fundamentally capitalist societies intervene in the market for social, welfare and civic ends, especially in the fields of education, health, housing, income maintenance and personal social services. It has been a remarkable attempt, particularly in Scandinavia, to retain what Lionel Jospin termed 'a market economy but not a market society', and to protect the more vulnerable from pitiless economic forces on a more systematic basis than the vagaries of private charity.

International commentary often takes the USA to be some kind of ultracapitalist lost cause in terms of welfare spending. But this is a travesty. In 1993, even after a decade of Reaganomic tax cuts for the rich and welfare cuts for the poor, US spending on public welfare services still amounted to some 21 percent of GDP, compared to 26 percent in the UK and 29 percent in Germany (Hills, 1997). The UK and Germany are, on this measure, closer to the USA than to Scandinavian countries, where over 40 percent of GDP is devoted to public sector welfare. On health, the USA spent a slightly *higher* proportion of GDP on its public health sector than the British spent on the National Health Service, and over twice as much if private health spending is included. On education and social security they are roughly the same, though the US system favours the better off much more than in Britain; really big differences only obtain in housing. What this implies is the underlying strength of constituencies within the USA for a substantial mixed economy of welfare, rather than an absolute difference between the USA and Europe.

For the past two decades, however, the pressures towards privatization and a reduction of public spending have gathered pace. The impact of different interpretations of the 'Third Way' (Giddens, 1999) will be crucial in determining how far this tendency will be pushed. The debate is increasingly couched in terms of the greater success of deregulated market economies, most notably the USA, by comparison with the more 'corporatist' economies of Europe, with the UK occupying an intermediate position following the partial continuation of New Right privatizations by New Labour. At stake is the continuing commitment to far more substantial public sector investment in the lead countries of Scandinavia, The Netherlands, Belgium, France, Germany and Italy.

The sheer size of the US prison population has now become an important factor in this macroeconomic matrix as never before. As Beckett and Western (1997) have clearly spelt out, the US prison population now amounts to some 2 percent of the male labour force. As a result of prisoners being excluded from the labour force count, a convention which merits re-examination, this factor alone has reduced the official figure for male unemployment by some 30–40 percent since the early 1990s. And it is this unemployment figure that is endlessly cited, on both sides of the Atlantic, as a major sign of the superiority of the deregulated economy of the USA compared with the more corporatist economies of Western Europe. Few financial commentators seem aware of the significance of the penal factor – only Larry Elliott (*Guardian*, 13 December 1999) has, to my knowledge, referred to it all, and then only in passing. Making some allowance for the huge job creation aspect of imprisonment for custodial and allied staff, especially in areas of high unemployment, would enhance its significance even further. It is a tragic irony that a major flaw in the political economy of the USA – its grotesquely high prison population – unduly inflates what is taken to signify a major success – its unusually low unemployment rate. Moreover, it is by now well established, thanks to the work of Michael Tonry (1995), Jerome Miller (1996) and Mark Mauer (1997), that these effects are most pronounced and devastating in the case of young black males, with one in three either in prison or under the penal disciplines of probation or parole. The penal factor has denuded some black inner-city neighbourhoods of young men: the female-headed household can now, but for children and the elderly, be writ large as communities virtually composed of women. And in the ghetto areas documented by William Julius Wilson, more or less devoid of economic activity, very high unemployment rates persist which would be even starker but for the high rate of imprisonment, fuelled by involvement in the drug trade. Yet informed commentators can still write: 'The economy is booming, and American blacks are today less likely to be out of work than Europeans. (Black unemployment is down to under 8 per cent.)' (Thernstrom, 1999). Taking those in prison into account, that figure would be at least 16 percent.

It may be, therefore, that mass imprisonment in the USA will make its impact on Europe less by the direct export of its components, such as privatization, and mandatory and tougher sentencing, and more by its masked impact on macroeconomic policy, encouraging a retreat from substantial welfare services, from the involvement of trade unions in economic regulation and from employment safeguards. 'If Europe continues to follow the lead of the US by continuing the gradual dismantlement of the welfare state, excluding growing segments of the population from full participation in society, Europe too may become a polarized society of winner versus losers' (Marshall, 1996: 32) with all that that implies by way of crime and its penal control.

In this retreat from welfarism, Britain leads the way: New Labour is

on course to keep public spending at a lower level (as a proportion of the whole economy) than any government since Harold Macmillan's 35 years ago . . . Even if the extra money voted in the comprehensive spending review results in health, education and transport rising as a proportion of GDP in 1999–2000 and beyond, the changes are unlikely to make a radical difference to the average during the whole life of the present government. (Travers, 1999)[6]

The National Health Service has run for 20 years or more on at least 1 percent below average expenditure for the European OECD countries. That is currently £8 billion a year, which amounts over the 20-year period to a total of £160 billion of denied investment. Despite its efficiency, no system could flourish on such austere resourcing. As the health budget covers mental health, it is no surprise that 'care in the community' is at a low ebb. As, unlike mental hospitals, prisons are an ever-open door for whomever they are sent by the courts, transcarceration is more of a reality now than in the past, with prisoners suffering disturbingly high rates of some of the most serious mental illnesses.

There are at least four other respects in which the US penal phenomenon feeds into important debates in a distorting fashion. First, it is associated with both a successive stabilization and actual reductions in the US crime rate *and* with an unprecedentedly long period of economic growth. Both factors combine to lend mass incarceration an aura of hard-won success, of benefits outweighing costs, which may prove influential in other countries. It hallows the export of private prison systems by Wackenhut and Correctional Corporation of America. The fact that the economic growth is despite, not because of, the prison explosion may be swamped in the rush to buy into its apparent success.

Second, as Beckett and Western argue, imprisonment damages employment prospects after release and heightens risks of recidivism. The criminogenic effects of custody are met in circular fashion by yet more incarceration. This helps explain why the US prison population has risen so incessantly beyond all seeming limits, and suggests that the USA is now locked into a penal economy which is both self-replicating and subject to a multiplier effect due to progressively steepening mandatory sentences.

Third, and paradoxically, the tight labour market created in part by mass imprisonment *may* be one reason for the falls in crimes against property, as a consequence of rising prosperity and even low wage employment (W. Wilson, 1997). It is, however, the imprisonment and not the employment that gains popular credit.

Fourth, there is a *macho* quality to the long US boom that may be heightened by mass incarceration. High prison populations hold inflationary implications, due to the tight labour markets on which they exert a concealed effect, and due also to the huge, largely unproductive nature of the investment involved. These are currently masked by the low inflation achieved in the USA partly by productivity gains from information technology, but partly from high levels of foreign investment (Atkinson, 2000). A certain *machismo* inheres, however, in the steep disparity between Stock Market valuations and company profits; the size of the current account deficit; and high levels of consumer debt. When the downturn comes, it could be that mass incarceration will exert a Keynesian, stabilizing effect, to be sustained for economic reasons. But a recession will fall most damagingly on those ex-offenders and ex-prisoners who have been employed, if at all, in the most precarious and least protected jobs, and whose employability has been most eroded by custody. These pressures predictably heighten their risk of recidivism and reimprisonment (Beckett and Western, 1997). The interaction between these two trends could spell the even greater expansion of the prison population to well above the 2 million mark.

It is also the case that a *macho* economy produces a *macho* society. When economic strength and cut-throat profitability are the drivers of conduct; when job stability and decent wages are a folk memory; when skilled professionals can be told to clear their desks within the hour; when you are only as good as your last deal; and when secrecy in takeovers, asset stripping and head-hunting are conducted with sublime disregard for ethics, then the basis for some sort of Kantian respect for persons in social relationships can hardly be said to exist. The *machismo* of the street, in drug dealing, hustling and physical intimidation, with its lack of eye contact, demand for 'respect' (Bourgois, 1995) and contempt for weakness, is – as William Julius Wilson has said – a poor basis for primary labour market employment. It is, however, a good preparation for street crime and survival in prison. The *machismo* of the powerless is a symmetrical parody of that of the powerful in a winner/loser culture.

CONCLUSIONS

'Europe has to withstand the American 'example'! . . . It is improbable that it will become like the US in the future. The latter has given them too bad an example of what a failure can look like' (Kuhn, 1996: 39). One can only hope that this is indeed to be the case. But the burden of this analysis is that the components of a steep rise in imprisonment in Europe, especially in Britain, have been assembled. At the macroeconomic level, the case against more regulated economies is strengthened by fallacies about low unemployment fostered by mass incarceration itself. And Europe does not have to *match* the US rate of imprisonment for Europe to experience the makings of a social and political disaster: even to reach half the US level, or 330 per 100,000, would mean tripling current rates of imprisonment in Europe. The off-the-scale character of US imprisonment may even induce complacency elsewhere that their prison populations are so much lower that even steep rises in their terms would be comparatively negligible.

It is certainly the case that Europe and other societies should resist the US example on the penal front. But what are the prospects for resistance within the USA itself? Here there is much common ground with Europe. 'We think of the US as a nation dedicated to private enterprise. Yet [unlike in Britain] its water supply remains in public hands, as do some important rail lines; and there are no plans to privatise the federal mails' (Blackburn, 2000: 25). And, as noted above, education, health and social security remain major public services, despite the huge inroads of the grossly enlarged criminal justice and penal systems. In other words, there is a basis for interpretations of American exceptionalism to be reclaimed from the New Right by the constituencies which created the New Deal and the Great Society programmes. It may be that those constituencies have been fragmented by deindustrialization and suburbanization, but the potential for their reassembly surely lies in the need for security against the hazards of the 'risk society' that can only be collectively provided.

The crime form most unique to American society, lethal violence, presents awesome problems of regulation, but Zimring and Hawkins have documented the links with lack of gun control to provide a case which can be tirelessly put for far greater restrictions, even if they are dubious about its prospects. On racial discrimination and drug law enforcement, we should heed William Julius Wilson's prescription on joblessness and inequality: that although they affect young black men most adversely, they are transracial problems that are best dealt with as needing common solutions.

Taken together, these three strands provide a front on which to contest the case for mass incarceration. Otherwise, the country which invented the juvenile court but is now executing juveniles, and in which no presidential candidate opposes capital punishment, will carry on, and seek to carry others with it, as if it had no alternative.

Acknowledgements

My thanks to David Piachaud, Paul Rock and Andrew Wilson for timely help and stimulating criticism. It was David Piachaud who coined the term 'the *macho* economy' to parody those economists who dismiss what goes on at the micro-level as of no account. I am also grateful to Kate Malleson, Maurice Punch, Mick Ryan and Jo Sparkes for ready answers on what, for me, were difficult points.

Notes

1 Except Britain, where poverty levels came to surpass those in the USA.
2 One sign of active resistance to the American trend is the Canadian Solicitor General's web-site Home Page *Myths and realities: dispelling myths about Canada's criminal justice system* (4 February 2000), which explicitly challenges the morality and efficacy of US penal policy.
3 David Greenberg's Commentary (this volume) criticizes this approach by linking the long-term decline in violence in England since the 13th century with the rise of the spirit of capitalism. I prefer to see the two as mutually dependent on the establishment of the rule of law, a settled state with authorities strong enough to uphold it, and the long haul to democratic citizenship. Moreover, the immense decline in rates of homicide had already been substantially accomplished by the advent of capitalism in the late 18th century.
4 Thus, for example, the 1995 Republican political agenda *Restoring the Dream* contained 'the toughest crime package approved by the House of Representatives in decades', stepping up already huge budgets for additional prison construction from 8 to 10.5 billion dollars, converting elements of Democrat social spending into law enforcement programmes, limiting the scope for death penalty appeals, allowing 'good faith' exemptions to exclusionary rules on evidence, making victim restitution mandatory for federal crimes and easing the deportation of criminal aliens (see Windlesham, 1998: 129–30; and throughout for an impressively documented analysis of the past two decades of law and order politics in the USA).
5 Against this view, Matthews (1999) argues, citing Lynch (1988) and the work of Farrington and Langan (1992) and Farrington et al. (1994), that the USA is not especially punitive once the more serious character of crime in America is taken into account: 'The differences between the USA and England and Wales are largely a product of different rates of crime rather than major differences in sentencing practice . . . However, the USA tends to impose longer prison sentences for those convicted' (Matthews, 1999: 99). This conclusion seriously understates substantial differences between the two societies, and between the USA and other Western European countries, in sentences for non-violent crimes and drug offences, the fastest growing component of US incarceration rates. Even Lynch (1995), who is also keen to challenge the image of the USA as relatively punitive, summarizes Farrington and Langan's (1992) data as follows:

The probability of incarceration following conviction was not radically different across nations for violent crimes, but it was substantially different for property crimes . . . A person found guilty of burglary in the United States had a .74 probability of a custodial sentence but only a .40 chance in England and Wales . . . The large differences in time served between the United States and the other countries occurs for property crimes – burglary and larceny. (Lynch, 1995: 33–4)

For burglary, the same source gives the US average of time served as 10.6 months compared with 6.8 months in England and 5.3 in Canada. For larceny, the mean time served is 7 months in the USA compared with 4.65 in England and 2 months in Canada. For drug offences, the differences are even more substantial. And, as Currie notes, these figures are mostly based on mid-1980s data, so that 'after nearly a decade and a half of relentlessly stiffening sentences [in the US] . . . our comparative severity has increased substantially' (Currie, 1998: 19). Moreover, while within offence differences, such as carrying weaponry, may account for steeper sentences for robbery, this factor is far less likely to apply to burglary and larceny (see Zimring and Hawkins, 1997: 44–6). Matthews' argument is, however, a timely reminder that we lack up-to-date, close-grained analyses of comparative sentencing practice. The urge to normalize American punitiveness also encourages playing down, or ignoring, what is happening at the extremes of the sentencing spectrum, as distinct from its middle range. Thus 'it is curious that those who argue that the US is not especially punitive generally fail to mention that we are the only industrial democracy that still makes significant use of the death penalty for homicide (Currie, 1998: 17). And for the least serious offences, the USA has pioneered, or reactivated, an array of 'quality of life' crimes, for whose violation the risks of arrest, detention and subsequent imprisonment are now greatly increased (Parenti, 1999: Ch. 4).

6 The March 2000 Budget changes the picture for health spending, adopting annual increases far higher than those previously enacted, and aiming to raise government resourcing of the National Health Service to European average levels by 2007. With this exception, New Labour policies on welfare are tending towards a liberal-democratic rather than the social-democratic tradition of previous Labour and most Western European governments.

References

Ashworth, A. et al. (1998) 'Neighbouring on the oppressive: the government's "Anti-Social Behaviour Order" proposals', *Criminal Justice* 16(1): 7–14.

Atkinson, M. (2000) 'Dollar beware', *Guardian* 18 January.

Beckett, K. (1997) *Making crime pay: law and order in contemporary American politics.* New York: Oxford University Press.

Beckett, K. and Western, B. (1997) 'The penal system as labor market institution: jobs and jails, 1980–95', *Overcrowded Times* 8(6).

Blackburn, R. (2000) 'How to bring back collectivism', *New Statesman* 17 January 2000.

Bottoms, A. (1995) 'The philosophy and politics of punishment and sentencing', in C. Clarkson and R. Morgan (eds) *The politics of sentencing reform.* Oxford: Clarendon Press.

Bourgois, P. (1995) *In search of respect.* Cambridge: Cambridge University Press.

Bowling, B. (1999) 'The rise and fall of New York murder: zero tolerance or crack's decline?', *British Journal of Criminology* 39(4).

Bowling, B. (2000) 'New Labour, racism, crime and justice', paper presented to the British Society of Criminology, 19 January.

Chambliss, W. (1999) *Power, politics, and crime.* Boulder, CO: Westview.

Christie, N. (1993) *Crime control as industry: towards gulags, western style?* London: Routledge.

Clarke, R. (1980) 'Situational crime prevention', *British Journal of Criminology* 20(2): 136–47.

Cohen, S. (1985) *Visions of social control.* Cambridge: Polity.

Collini, S. (2000) 'The end of the world as we know it', *Guardian* 1 January.

Currie, E. (1998) *Crime and punishment in America.* New York: Holt.

Davies, N. (1998) *Dark heart.* London: Chatro & Windus.

Department for Education and Employment (2000) *Permanent exclusions from schools and exclusion appeals, England 1998/9 (provisional).* London: Government Statistical Service.

Downes, D. (1998) 'The buckling of the shields: Dutch penal policy 1985–95', in R. Weiss and N. South (eds) *Comparing prison systems.* Amsterdam: Gordon & Breach.

Downes, D. (1998) 'Toughing it out: from Labour opposition to Labour government', *Policy Studies* 19(3/4): 191–8.

Downes, D. and Morgan, R. (1997) 'Dumping the hostages to fortune: the politics of law and order', in M. Maguire, R. Morgan and R. Reiner (eds) *The Oxford handbook of criminology, 2nd edn.* Oxford: Clarendon Press.

Farrington, D. and Langan, P. (1992) 'Changes in crime and punishment in England and America in the 1980s', *Justice Quarterly* 9: 5–46.

Farrington, D., Langan, P. and Wikstrom, P. (1994) 'Changes in crime and punishment in England, America and Sweden in the 1980s and 1990s', *Studies in Crime and Crime Prevention*, 104–31.

Feeley, M. and Simon, J. (1992) 'The new penology: notes on the emerging strategy on corrections and its implications', *Criminology* 30(4): 449–74.

Garland, D. (1990) *Punishment and modern society.* Oxford: Clarendon Press.

Garland, D. (1996) 'The limits of the sovereign state: strategies of crime control in contemporary society', *British Journal of Criminology* 36(4): 445–71.

Garland, D. (2001) *The culture of control: crime and social order in contemporary society.* Oxford: Clarendon Press.

Giddens, A. (1999) *The third way.* Cambridge: Polity.

Gray, J. (1998) *False dawn: the delusions of global capitalism.* Cambridge: Granta.

Greenberg, D. (1999) 'Punishment, division of labor, and social solidarity', in W. Laufer and F. Adler (eds) *The criminology of criminal law: advances in criminological theory, vol. 3.*

Hills, J. (1997) *The future of welfare: a guide to the debate.* York: Rowntree Foundation.

Home Office (1999) *Managing dangerous people with severe personality disorder: proposals for policy development.* London: Home Office, July.

Hood, R. and Joyce, K. (1999) 'Three generations: oral testimonies on crime and social change in London's East End', *British Journal of Criminology* 39(1).

James, O. (1993) *Juvenile violence in a winner/loser culture*. London: Free Association Books.

Junger-Tas, J. (1998) 'Dutch Penal Policies Changing Direction' *Overcrowded Times*, 9(5).

Kennedy, P. (1993) *Preparing for the twenty-first century*. New York: Random House.

King, R. (1999) 'The rise and rise of supermax: an American solution in search of a problem?', *Punishment & Society* 1(2): 163–86.

King, R. and Morgan, R. (1980) *The future of the prison system*. Farnborough: Gower.

Kuhn, A. (1996) 'Incarceration rates: Europe versus USA', *European Journal on Criminal Policy and Research (Developments in the Use of Prisons)* 4(3): 46–73.

Kuhn, A. (1999) 'Incarceration rates around the world', *Overcrowded Times* 10(2).

Lynch, J. (1988) 'A comparison of prison use in England, Canada, West Germany and the United States', *Journal of Criminal Law and Criminology* 79: 108–217.

Lynch, J. (1995) 'Crime in international perspective', in J. Wilson and J. Petersilia (eds) *Crime*. San Francisco, CA: ICS Press.

Madsen, D. (1998) *American exceptionalism*. Edinburgh University Press.

Marshall, I. (1996) 'How exceptional is the United States? crime trends in Europe and the US', *European Journal on Criminal Policy and Research (Europe Meets US in Crime and Policy)* 4(2): 7–35.

Mathiesen, T. (1990) *Prison on trial: a critical assessment*. London: Sage.

Matthews, R. (1999) *Doing time: an introduction to the sociology of imprisonment*. London: Macmillan.

Mauer, M. (1997) *Intended and unintended consequences: state racial disparities in imprisonment*. Washington, DC: The Sentencing Project.

Melossi, D. and Lettiere, M. (1998) 'Punishment in the American democracy: the paradoxes of good intentions', in R. Weiss and N. South (eds) *Comparing prison systems*. Amsterdam: Gordon & Breach.

Miller, J. (1996) *Search and destroy: African-American males in the criminal justice system*. Cambridge University Press.

Ministry of Justice (1985) *Society and crime: a policy plan for the future*. The Hague: Ministry of Justice.

Morgan, R. (1998) 'Imprisonment in England and Wales: flood tide, but on the turn?', *Overcrowded Times* 9(5).

Parenti, C. (1999) *Lockdown America: police and prisons in the age of crisis*. London: Verso.

Pease, K. (1998) 'Crime, Labour and the wisdom of Solomon', *Policy Studies* 19(3/4): 255–66.

Radzinowicz, L. (1991) 'Penal regressions', *Cambridge Law Journal* 50: 422–44.

Rock, P. (1986) *The view from the shadows*. Oxford: Clarendon Press.

Rock, P. (1990) *Helping victims of crime*. Oxford: Clarendon Press.

Rock, P. (1998) *After homicide: practical and political responses to bereavement*. Oxford: Clarendon Press.

Rothman, D. (1971) *The discovery of the asylum: social order and disorder in the new republic*. Boston, MA: Little, Brown.

Rothman, D. (1980) *Conscience and convenience: the asylum and its alternatives in progressive America*. Boston, MA: Little, Brown.

Rothman, D. (1995) 'Perfecting the prison: United States, 1789–1865', in N. Morris and D. Rothman (eds) *The Oxford history of the prison: the practice of punishment in western society.* New York: Oxford University Press.

Ruggiero, V., Ryan, M. and Sim, J. (eds) (1995) *Western European penal systems: a critical anatomy.* London: Sage.

Rutherford, A. (1996) *Transforming criminal policy.* Winchester: Waterside.

Rutherford, A. (1999) 'New Labour, new Democrats, new criminality', paper given at Mannheim Centre, London School of Economics, 21 January.

Ryan, M. (1999) 'Penal policy making towards the millennium: elites and populists; New Labour and the new criminology', *International Journal of the Sociology of Law* 27: 1–22.

Sennett, R. (1998) *The corrosion of character: the personal consequences of work in the new capitalism.* New York: Norton.

Simon, J. (1993) *Poor discipline: parole and the social control of the underclass.* Chicago University Press.

Sparks, R. (forthcoming) 'State punishment in advanced capitalist societies.' University of Keele: Dept. of Criminology.

Stern, V. (1998) *A sin against the future: imprisonment in the world.* London: Penguin.

Taylor, I. (1999) *Crime in context: a critical criminology of market societies.* Cambridge: Polity.

Thernstrom, A. (1999) 'The kids are all right: why fears that America has lost its moral compass are misplaced', *Times Literary Supplement* 30 July.

Tonry, M. (1995) *Malign neglect: race, crime and punishment.* New York: Oxford University Press.

Tonry, M. (1996) 'The effects of American drug policy on black Americans, 1980–1996', *European Journal of Criminal Policy and Research (Europe Meets US in Crime and Policy)* 4(2) 36–62.

Tonry, M. (1999) 'Why are US incarceration rates so high?', *Overcrowded Times* 10(3).

Travers, T. (1999) 'Squaring the circle', *Guardian* 22 September.

Van Swaaningen, R. and De Jonge, G. (1995) 'The Dutch prison system and penal policy in the 1990s: from humanitarian paternalism to penal business management', in V. Ruggiero, M. Ryan and J. Sim (eds) *Western European penal systems: a critical anatomy.* London: Sage.

Von Hirsch, A. (1976) *Doing justice.* New York: Hill & Wang.

Wacquant, L. (1999) ' "Suitable enemies": foreigners and immigrants in the prisons of Europe', *Punishment and Society* 1(2): 215–22.

Walmsley, R. (1999) *World prison population list.* London: Home Office.

Wilson, J. (1975) *Thinking about crime.* New York: Basic Books.

Wilson, W. (1997) *When work disappears: the world of the new urban poor.* New York: Knopf.

Windlesham, Lord (1998) *Politics, punishment, and populism.* Oxford University Press.

Young, J. (1986) 'The failure of criminology: the need for a radical realism', in R. Matthews and J. Young (eds) *Confronting Crime* London: Sage.

Young, J. (1999) *The exclusive society: social exclusion, crime and difference in late modernity.* London: Sage.

Zimring, F. and Hawkins, G. (1997) *Crime is not the problem: lethal violence in America.* New York: Oxford University Press.

6 *Novus ordo saeclorum*?

A commentary on Downes, and on Beckett and Western

DAVID F. GREENBERG

The sociological study of state punishment policies and practices – long a minor criminological specialty – is currently undergoing a renaissance. Stimulated at least in part by the historically unprecedented growth of American prison populations over the past 30 years, the study of prison populations and the reasons they change has attracted new researchers and has stimulated new lines of rich theorizing, as exemplified by the articles in this collection.

Several features distinguish this new work from its antecedents. It no longer looks at punishment in isolation from other social institutions; it considers historical change, and some of it is cross-national. In contrast with the economic reductionism of some earlier work, the new studies, without abandoning economic considerations, pay attention to politics.

The relationships Beckett and Western find between penal and welfare policies, and between imprisonment rates and race, have now been found in several studies of American imprisonment rates (Wallace, 1981; Michalowski and Pearson, 1987; Greenberg and West, 1998) and in cross-national research (Greenberg, 1999), and must be considered firmly established. As they suggest, locking people up or giving them money might be considered alternative ways of handling marginal, poor populations – repressive in one case, generous in the other.

It may be that this linkage between different responses to marginal populations can be extended further. Several years ago, Michael Lynch and his collaborators suggested that five social institutions – prison, psychiatric hospital, school, welfare, and the armed services – serve as major control institutions, and might substitute for one another (Lynch et al., 1996). This suggestion might be fruitfully pursued. Some American data on trends suggest that these alternatives do, to a degree, serve as substitutes for one another: as prison populations have been rising over the past few decades, psychiatric hospital populations have been shrinking (Scull, 1984; Mechanic and Rochefort, 1990; Caplow and Simon, 1999), but the evidence for substitution effects is conflicting (Young, 1986).

Some features of Beckett and Weston's statistical analysis merit discussion. Their estimation procedures assume that imprisonment rates are influenced by crime rates, but do not influence them. However, if imprisonment reduces crime rates (e.g. through incapacitation or deterrence) to an appreciable degree, these procedures will underestimate the tendency of crime rates to increase imprisonment rates (Greenberg, 1978: 36–49).

Recent research bears on the extent to which imprisonment prevents crime. Some investigators conclude that each additional imprisonment reduces the number of index crimes by about 15 (Marvell and Moody, 1994; Levitt, 1996). If this figure is accurate, Beckett and Western's treatment of crime rates as exogenous would be invalid. However, a back-of-the-envelope calculation suggests that this figure is too large. In 1997, 13.2 million index crimes were reported, and there were 1.2 million people in prison (Maguire and Pastore, 1999: 260, 462). If all the index crimes were committed by people in prison (and none committed by people on probation or parole, or not under correctional supervision), that would come to 11 per person. However, even if the true figure is smaller than the estimates by a factor of 10, the crime prevention effect of imprisonment would be nontrivial. On the other hand, Useem et al. (1999), in what is the most careful and rigorous study of deterrence to date, find no clear evidence of it. If they are correct, the unidirectionality of influence in Beckett and Western's model may be appropriate.

Beckett and Western's conclusion, based on models involving interaction terms of AFDC payments and year, that imprisonment rates are not strongly related to crime rates, is surprising not only because it is contrary to what one might commonsensically expect, but also because others have found the relationships to be substantial in single year cross-sectional analyses, time-series analyses, and panel designs (Michalowski and Pearson, 1987; Jacobs and Helms, 1996; Greenberg and West, 1998). The cross-sectional correlation between the violent crime rate in 1995 and the imprisonment rate in 1996 is about 0.7, just as strong as in the previous decade. Controlling for level of AFDC payments slightly increases the correlation. It would be remarkable for such a strong effect to be rendered small and insignificant through the introduction into the pooled model of period effects and welfare-year interactions. Because multicollinearity in Beckett and Western's models is sky-high, especially in these models, it is difficult to place much faith in this result.

The question of exogeneity of the predictors also arises with regard to unemployment. Western and Beckett (1999) have argued, as has Freeman (1996), that the imprisonment of large numbers of individuals lowers official unemployment rates by removing them from the paid labor market. If Beckett and Western are right in their analysis of imprisonment and unemployment, statistical methods are needed that will allow for the mutual influence of imprisonment and unemployment on one another, rather than assuming that causal influences flow only from unemployment to imprisonment.

Here, too, some quick-and-dirty estimates suggest that in this earlier work, Western and Beckett overstate the extent to which imprisonment reduces unemployment rates. Most American prison inmates are not unemployed at the time of their arrest. In 1974, 62 percent of sentenced inmates were employed full time during the month before their arrest, and another 7 percent were employed part time. Just 12 percent were looking for work, and another 5 percent said they wanted work, although they were not looking for it (National Criminal Justice Reference Service, 1979: 13–14). Thus, at most, 17 percent of the inmates would be counted as unemployed under Department of Labor criteria.

Similar figures are found in more recent studies. In 1986, 69 percent of state prison inmates were employed in the month before they were arrested; almost all of them full time. The percentages in 1991 were quite similar (Beck et al., 1993: 3). In 1996, 64 percent of jail inmates were employed during the month before their arrest, only moderately lower than the 75 percent of the general population that was employed in the previous year (Harlow, 1998). An independent source of information – the National Longitudinal Study of Youth – indicates that 74.4 percent of young males involved in crime also worked at lawful jobs (Freeman, 1996).

Another line of reasoning also suggests that imprisonment does not play a large role in artificially reducing unemployment figures. If unemployment is dropping because imprisonment removes unemployed people from the ranks of those counted, then a drop in unemployment statistics will not be accompanied by a corresponding rise in employment. This prediction is easily tested. Between 1992 (when unemployment rates peaked) and 1998, male unemployment in the United States dropped by 3.4 million and female unemployment by 1.15 million. In these same years, male employment rose by 6.25 million, and female employment by 6.72 million (Council of Economic Advisors, 1999: 370). The main reason unemployment dropped was not that the number of males in prison rose during these years rose by 417,816, and the number of females by 37,926; it was because the economy was expanding. Unemployed workers were finding jobs, men and women, black and white, were being drawn into the labor force.[1] This line of reasoning suggests that Beckett and Western's assumption of unemployment's exogeneity may be valid, notwithstanding their earlier work.

Beckett and Western's analysis suggests that state prison populations can be predicted quite well, but their model will not be nearly as successful in explaining change. The dummy variables for year represent trends not explained by the variables in the model. Some of the variables in their analysis (e.g. *percentage black*), contribute to the cross-sectional variation; yet, as they changed little between 1975 and 1995, they will not explain change in prison populations. Though imprisonment rates are higher in states that have more blacks, it is not because the percentage of the US population that is black rose greatly between 1975 and 1995 that imprisonment rates rose so dramatically in those years.

One can see the limitations of analyses that predict levels of imprisonment for understanding change by considering the hypothetical case in which differences in state imprisonment rates are established at some time in the distant past, and in subsequent years increase uniformly. Provided the predictors also change in a uniform manner, a regression on data from later years will show the same results as a regression estimated in earlier years, but will disclose nothing whatsoever about patterns of change. Looking at actual patterns, the correlation between per capita state prison populations in 1976 and 1986 is 0.92; between 1986 and 1996, 0.91. With correlations this high, 82–4 percent of the variance in 1986 and 1996 imprisonment rates is explained by the imprisonment rates a decade earlier, leaving only a modest amount of variance to be explained by other state characteristics. The lesson is clear: to find out about change, one needs to analyze change explicitly (Kessler and Greenberg, 1981).

Beckett and Western conclude that the relationship between imprisonment and welfare policy has become stronger over time, so that welfare and penal policies increasingly cluster into coherent 'policy regimes.' A partial regression coefficient, controlling for a number of other variables, is not the best way to assess the degree to which welfare and penal policies go together. The zero-order correlation between the imprisonment rate and the the average monthly AFDC payment is a better indicator of this coherence. In 1976 this correlation was –.58, rising to –.42 in 1986, and then dropping to –.46 in 1996. Though the correlation was consistently negative, high imprisonment rates were less likely to go with low welfare rates in 1996, after a long period of cutbacks on welfare and an enormous growth in prison populations, than two decades earlier. Moreover, the correlation between the *change* in imprisonment rate and the *change* in the AFDC payment between 1976 and 1986 is just –.051. Between 1986 and 1996, it was .026. There was, essentially, no relationship between change in one variable and change in the other. Individual cases illustrate the lack of relationship. Between 1981 and 1997, the imprisonment rate in California rose by a factor of 4.17; adjusted for inflation, the level of AFDC payments rose by a modest 17 percent. By the argument of Beckett and Western's article, it should have fallen.

Nationally, there has been a shift away from welfare (adjusted for inflation, AFDC payments fell before the program was abolished), and toward greater use of imprisonment. To the extent that these shifts reflect a change in the thinking that lies behind both policies, using one variable to predict the other may be a little misleading. It is a little like using the length of people's left leg to predict the length of their right leg. Both are indicators of someone's height. If imprisonment and welfare are both products of the same mind-set, the critical issue is to understand the sources of this mind-set, and why it changed between the 1960s and subsequent decades, with consequences for both imprisonment and welfare.

Implicit in the statistical procedures used by Beckett and Western and all previous analysts of state imprisonment rates is the assumption that each state formulates its penal policies independently of every other state. This seems unlikely. Governors meet periodically to discuss state policy. It would be surprising if they did not at times attend to policy innovations and their outcomes in other states. Politicians and mass media deliver crime-related messages to a national audience. Just after the period covered in the Beckett and Western study, federal legislation was enacted providing subsidies to states for prison construction.[2] Developments like these can produce national trends without contributing to cross-sectional variation among the states, or variation among the states in growth rates.

Equally common to this body of research is the limitation inherent in a statistical analysis linking a policy outcome to its putative causes. Statistical research can establish connections between a state's demographic, socio-economic and political characteristics and policy outcomes, but we cannot be confident about the processes at work unless we study the actual policy-making process. Transcending the limitations of current research will require supplementing statistical analysis of policies with qualitative analyses of how those policies were adopted.

* * *

David Downes' article is both thoughtful and troubling. For years, criminologists have criticized expansionist prison policies, arguing that they were at best ineffective, and at worst counter-productive. Yet expansion has continued unchecked. Downes notes that where this sort of self-reproducing growth becomes established, it may be very difficult to reverse. If he is correct, we are now seeing the dawning of a *novus ordo saeclorum* – a 'new order of the age' – not the age of Aquarius, but the age of social control, not just in the United States, but in Europe as well.

Jonathan Simon (1997) has used the phrase 'governing through crime' to character-ize this new order. It is one in which normative regulation is carried out largely through the crime control apparatus. As a statement of how behavior is currently regulated, the phrase exaggerates. Family and school still play a large role in socialization; so do churches, peers and the mass media. In addition, states do much more than enforce norms: they also perform many other functions related to the smooth operation of a complex society. Nevertheless Simon does point to a pronounced trend toward greater use of the crime control apparatus to bring about behavioral conformity.

There are good institutional reasons for Downes' pessimism. In many states, local rural economies have become heavily dependent on prisons for employment. Their resi-dents can be expected to oppose prison closings. Unions representing correctional officers are now major contributors to political campaigns; their political clout will have to be overcome if their members' jobs are threatened by decarceration.

Against the argument of irreversibility, one may recall that there have been massive reductions in prison populations in the past. French and English prison populations fell dramatically beginning in the late 19th century (McConville, 1995; O'Brien, 1995). Perhaps the political context has changed in such a way that reductions of this magni-tude could no longer take place, but then again, perhaps not. To my knowledge, no one has studied the earlier reductions closely enough to ascertain just how they were accom-plished. It seems plausible, though, that decades of large reductions in levels of serious crime made people of the late 19th century feel more secure, reducing the demand for prisons[3] (Tobias, 1967: 37–44; Jones, 1982: 117–29).

Downes further suggests that the nightmare of an out-of-control penal policy may be spreading from America to Europe. In recent years, nations like The Netherlands, which have historically had extremely low prison populations, have seen remarkable increases; indeed, Dutch prison populations, though still low by American standards, are no longer low by European standards, and have experienced more rapid growth than those in the United States – halted only by a political decision to stop the increase (Koomer, n.d., Kuhn, 1996; Tak and Van Kalmthout, 1998).

The percentage of foreigners in European prisons ranges from about 9 percent (Austria) to 40 percent (Switzerland) – rates that are several times as large as for the rest of the population. Many are immigrants and asylum seekers (Albrecht, 1991; Wacquant, 1999a, 1999b). If immigrants are the European equivalent of African-Americans, then the parallel to the American pattern is quite close. In the past, Europeans could criticize Americans for their uniquely punitive response to crime. With the gap narrowing, Americans may soon be in a position to respond with Horace,[4] '*Quid rides? Mutato nomine de te fabula narratur*' – 'What are you laughing at? Change the name and the joke is on you.'

Running through Downes' article is the concern that 'global capitalism may be both highly criminogenic and punitive.' Criminological theory gives us many reasons for thinking that this characterization of capitalism is apt. As Downes observes, capitalism is generally understood to weaken precapitalist forms of social solidarity. Marxists contend that it increases economic inequality and poverty, while at the same time encouraging consumption. It promotes geographical mobility, inhibiting the formation of bonds that social disorganization theory tells us should discourage crime. In this century, it has drawn women out of the household into the paid labor force away from home, increasing their vulnerability to stranger violence, and leaving the home unguarded during the day. Routine activities theorists argue that these developments increase crime. The rise and fall of prison populations in response to unemployment independently of crime rates in several different countries (Chiricos and Delone, 1992; Jacobs and Helms, 1996) suggests that anxieties associated with the business cycle in market economies contribute to punitiveness.

Seemingly, the sharp drop in American crime rates that has taken place in the United States since 1994, suggests that something is wrong with this logic. During much of this time span, employment levels and economic inequality were both rising. Downes argues that unemployment and crime would have soared had it not been for prison expansion. At a time when global competition threatens social-democratic welfare measures in Europe (Avi-Yonah, 2000), many Europeans might find it tempting to follow the American example. Indeed, it seems that some European nations are already moving decisively in this direction (Wacquant, 1998, 1999a, 1999b). This temptation might well extend not only to prison expansion, but also to the adoption of government surveillance measures and aggressive policing strategies. This is a policy regime that would substantially diminish freedom in order to fight crime and contain troublesome populations.

There is clearly much to warrant Downes' concerns. In a number of countries during the past several decades, deregulation has increased economic inequality. Reductions in corporate taxes undertaken to forestall capital flight have shifted the tax burden to individuals, presenting governments with the unhappy choice of curtailing welfare benefits or raising taxes on individuals even further. Both options carry significant political costs (Avi-Yonah, 2000), and might tend to increase crime.

At the same time, Downes' remarks may also reflect an overly sentimental attachment to the welfare state and regulation. Like other writers who have expressed similar concerns (Taylor, 1997, 1999), Downes conveys the impression that free markets always increase inequality and unemployment and generate higher crime rates, while state regulation reduces inequality and unemployment, thereby keeping crime rates within bounds. However, state interventions can redistribute wealth to the wealthy as well as to the poor, increasing inequality. The subordination of black Americans and the creation of the black urban ghetto was in substantial measure a product of state regulation, not its absence (Sowell, 1981; Massey and Denton, 1993; Duster, 1996).

I would like to complicate Downes' analysis of the relationship between crime, prisons, and markets in several ways. First, the long-term relationship between crime and the development of capitalism suggests something very different from what Downes suggests. The best estimates that can be made for homicide rates in egalitarian simple societies, where markets are limited or non-existent, are quite high by comparison with those in contemporary United States (Knauft, 1987, 1991). English homicide rates exhibit a long-term secular decline from the 13th century until just a few decades ago. Over a period of seven centuries, the rates fell by a factor of 10 to 20. Assault rates cannot be reconstructed before the beginning of the 19th century, but from then until the middle of the 20th century, they too seem to have dropped (Hair, 1971; Zehr, 1976; Gurr, 1981; Stone, 1983, 1985; Sharpe, 1985; Cockburn, 1991). If it can be agreed that market institutions grew in importance in England in this period, it would seem that markets do more than cause crime. In much of the last millennium they evidently reduced violence.

Most of the decline took place before the temperance movement reduced the consumption of alcohol, before the establishment of a full-time salaried police force carried law enforcement into the community, before penitentiaries took law violators out of circulation, and before medical progress reduced the rate at which injuries led to death. Gurr (1981) suggests that the gradual bourgeoisification of society led to the gradual disarmament of the male population, and the acceptance of nonviolent methods for resolving interpersonal disputes. Once the factory was introduced, it may have inculcated a more orderly, sober way of life that was not conducive to illegal interpersonal violence. It was simply no longer acceptable in circumstances where it once had been (Soman, 1980). It was the sensibilities associated with the greatly reduced elimination of violence in everyday life that gave rise to the establishment of societies for the prevention of cruelty to animals, opposition to judicial torture, campaigns to abolish corporal and capital punishment, and pacifism.

More recent rises in violence may represent a reversal of these trends. Perhaps we really are in a new era. But it is also possible that these trends are ephemeral, little blips in a long-run trend away from violence. That homicide and robbery rates in the United States for the past 50 years are, essentially, a random walk, in which annual increases and decreases occur on a completely random basis (Greenberg, forthcoming), suggests that not too much should be made of short-run increases. Over the short-term, random change can look a lot like a trend.

Figures for trends in property crime are harder to obtain for earlier centuries, though there is some indication that they, too, were dropping in early modern England (Sharpe, 1985). Possibly the mass production of cheap consumer goods that can be stolen easily brought about increases in property crime rates much earlier than homicide rates. This might be seen as an indirect consequence of one of the triumphs of market economies – they have raised the standard of living of the masses.

Recent discussions of increases in the imprisonment rates of various European countries trace them, in part, to public demand generated by rising crime rates, sometimes enhanced by anxiety over social change, unrest or disorder. Between 1960 and 1985, recorded crime rates in England and Wales, the Federal Republic of Germany, France, The Netherlands and Sweden all rose by factors of three to six (van Dijk, 1991). Under these circumstances it does not seem surprising that prison populations in these nations rose; what surprises is that they did not rise faster and farther. That they did not demonstrates, I think, how entrenched an ideological commitment to the incorporation, rather than the exclusion, of marginal populations has been in much of Europe.[5]

Assuming for the sake of argument that prison population growth in the United States and in some European countries has been a response to popular demand occasioned by crime rates that were persistently high, the decline in crime rates now underway ought to reduce that demand. Surveys suggest that this is already happening. Between 1989 and 1998, the percentage of Americans who say that there was more crime than a year ago dropped from 84 percent to 52 percent. The percentage who believe too little is being spent on halting the rising crime rate dropped from 73 percent to 61 percent. The percentage who think that the courts are not harsh enough dropped from 84 percent to

74 percent. Support for the death penalty fell from 74 percent to 68 percent (Maguire and Pastore, 1999: 116, 123, 129, 135, 137). These shifts are not large, but if crime rates continue to drop, or if they level off, they may become large. It would be of some interest to know whether the drop in crime rates that began in the UK around 1993 (Maguire, 1997) has produced a similar drop in alarm about crime, and in punitiveness.

The cross-sectional relationship many researchers have found between neighborhood poverty and unemployment on the one hand, and crime on the other, has usually been understood as due to the criminogenic effect of unemployment.[6] However, high levels of crime in a neighborhood can increase unemployment by driving out businesses, and discouraging new investment (Schumach, 1977). With crime dropping, neighborhoods like Harlem, which have suffered from high rates of crime and unemployment, are attracting business investment. If opportunities for gainful, lawful employment discourage theft, violence and narcotics trafficking, then crime rates may diminish further as a result.[7]

In the past year, mass-circulation magazines and nationally-read newspapers like the *New York Times* have published articles attacking harsh sentencing practices, and have called for a rethinking of the war on drugs. Illinois has instituted a moratorium on capital punishment. Intolerance of police violence is growing. The timing of these developments suggests that falling crime rates may be creating a new willingness to rethink crime control strategies.

As Downes notes, economists generally attribute the high levels of unemployment in Britain and continental Europe to the high burdens and costs of regulation, and to an overly generous welfare state, which discourage businesses from hiring. The fact that economic growth rates are higher in the common law countries, which have historically been more sympathetic to markets (Mahoney, 2000) is consistent with this understanding. In the conventional criminological understanding, the disappearance of work should increase crime. If this common-sense view of why unemployment rates in Europe have been so high is valid, the long-term consequences of deregulation may be salutary. Reducing obstacles to investment may stimulate European economies, increasing employment and raising wages, thereby making abstention from crime more appealing. In the short run, of course, the dislocations created by deregulation and welfare cutbacks can be wrenching, and may have significant consequences for crime (Taylor, 1997, 1999). But these adjustments, however painful, should not be confused with long-term trends, which may be quite different.

A distinction between long and short-term effects is also relevant in considering the penological status of immigrants in European countries. Xenophobia has, no doubt, multiple sources, but one of them is obviously competition for scarce jobs. In the short run, increased labor mobility across national lines may intensify prejudices against foreigners. Barriers to lawful employment may direct immigrants and their descendants to illegal forms of entrepreneurial activity. Prejudice on the part of the host population may subject immigrants to heavy-handed, discriminatory law enforcement, swelling prison populations (Chapin, 1997; Wacquant, 1998, 1999a, 1999b). All these phenomena are familiar from American history. Nineteenth-century American writings on crime repeatedly linked crime with one immigrant group after another (Brace, 1872; Platt, 1969).

Yet the long-term effects of globalization may be quite different. The establishment of the European Union may strengthen European economies, and lead to so much labor mobility that foreigners will no longer seem so strange. Interaction between host and foreigners in the work place may reduce prejudice (Estlund, 1999), and undermine punitive sentiments toward law violators of foreign origin. Americans no longer worry about the high crime rates of the Irish, Italians, and Jews. Perhaps America and Europe have a future that does not include a carceral archipelago.

Notes

1 Suggestions have been made that this expansion in employment, which cut the unemployment rate for black workers from 14.1 percent in January of 1993 to 7.2 percent in April of 2000, may be a better explanation for the drop in crime rates than the expansion of the prison population.

2 The legislation referred to here is the Violent Criminal Incarceration Act of 1995 (HR 667).

3 In France, the continued use of transportation of lesser offenders to penal colonies in Africa and South America long after England had given it up (O'Brien, 1982: 258–96) may also have helped make the drop in prison populations possible.

4 *Satirae* I.1.69. Marx (1867) quoted this passage without attribution in the preface to the first edition of *Kapital* as he explained to his German readers why he was giving so much attention to the development of industrial capitalism in England. England, he implied, was not an exception, only a forerunner.

5 Elsewhere I have shown that differences among the European countries in prison populations can be substantially explained as a consequence of the degree to which the country embraces an incorporative stance toward its less well-off citizens (Greenberg, 1999). See Downes (1988) for a comparative analysis of how The Netherlands and England and Wales responded to increased rates of crime between 1950 and 1975.

6 There is ample evidence for this from data on individuals. Aggregate relationships are less clear, possibly because aggregate unemployment, in addition to increasing motivation for crime, can reduce opportunities to commit it (Cantor and Land, 1985; Greenberg, forthcoming).

7 Increases in crime rates also increase out-migration, particularly of higher-income residents. The resulting erosion of the tax base can leave a city without the financial resources to deal with crime and other problems, and may also reduce informal social control. Businesses may leave the city to accommodate their white-collar employees (Grubb, 1982; Cullen and Levitt, 1999; Dugan, 1999), further increasing unemployment.

References

Albrecht, H.-J. (1991) 'Ethnic minorities: crime and criminal justice in Europe', in F. Heidensohn and M. Farrell (eds) *Crime in Europe*. New York: Routledge.

Avi-Yonah, R.S. (2000) 'Globalization, tax competition and the fiscal crisis of the welfare state', *Harvard Law Review* 113(May).

Beck, A., Gilliard, D., Greenfeld, L., Harlow, C., Hester, T., Jankowski, L., Snell, T., Stephan, J. and Morton, D. (1993) *Survey of state prison inmates, 1991*. Office of Justice Programs, Bureau of Justice Statistics NCJ-136949. Washington, DC: US Department of Justice.

Brace, C.L. (1872) *The dangerous classes of New York and twenty years' work among them.* New York: Wynkoop & Hallenbeck.

Cantor, D. and Land, K.C. (1985) 'Unemployment and crime rates in the post-World War II United States: a theoretical and empirical analysis', *American Sociological Review* 50: 317–32.

Caplow, T. and Simon, J. (1999) 'Understanding prison population and population trends', in M. Tonry and J. Petersilia (eds) *Prisons, crime and justice: a review of research.* Chicago, IL: University of Chicago Press.

Chapin, W.D. (1997) 'Ausländer raus? The empirical relationship between immigration and crime in Germany', *Social Science Quarterly* 78: 543–58.

Chiricos, T.G. and Delone, M. (1992) 'Labor surplus and punishment: a review and assessment of theory and evidence', *Social Problems* 39(4): 421–46.

Cockburn, J.S. (1991) 'Patterns of violence in English society: homicide in Kent, 1560–1985', *Past and Present* 131: 70–106.

Council of Economic Advisors (1999) *Annual report.* Washington, DC: US Government Printing Office.

Cullen, J.B. (1999) 'Crime, urban flight, and the consequences for cities', *Review of Economics and Statistics* 81: 159–69.

Downes, D. (1988) *Contrasts in tolerance.* Oxford: Clarendon Press.

Dugan, L. (1999) 'The effect of criminal victimization on a household's moving decision', *Criminology: An Interdisciplinary Journal* 37: 903–30.

Duster, T. (1996) 'Individual fairness, group preferences, and the California strategy', *Representations* 55: 41–58.

Estlund, C.L. (1999) 'Working together: the workplace in civil society', Columbia Law School Public Law and Legal Theory Working Paper No. 3.

Freeman, R.B. (1996) 'Why do so many young American men commit crimes and what might we do about it?', *Journal of Economic Perspectives* 10: 25–42.

Greenberg, D.F. (1978) *Mathematical criminology.* New Brunswick, NJ: Rutgers University Press.

Greenberg, D.F. (1999) 'Punishment, division of labor, and social solidarity', in W.S. Laufer and F. Adler (eds) *The criminology of criminal law: advances in criminological theory.*

Greenberg, D.F. (forthcoming) 'The time series analysis of crime rates', *Journal of Quantitative Criminology.*

Greenberg, D.F. and West, V. (1998) 'Growth in state prison populations, 1971–1991', paper presented to the Law and Society meeting.

Grubb, W.N. (1982) 'The flight to the suburbs of population and employment, 1960–1970', *Journal of Urban Economics* 11: 348–67.

Gurr, T.R. (1981) 'Historical trends in violent crime: a critical review of the evidence', in M. Tonry and N. Morris (eds) *Crime and justice: an annual review of research.* Chicago, IL: University of Chicago Press.

Hair, P.E.H. (1971) 'Deaths from violence in Britain: a tentative secular survey', *Population Studies* 25: 5–24.

Harlow, C.W. (1998) *Profile of jail inmates, 1996.* Bureau of Justice Statistics Special Report. Washington, DC: US Department of Justice.

Jacobs, D. and Helms, R.E. (1996) 'Towards a political model of incarceration: a time-series examination of multiple explanations for prison admissions rates', *American Journal of Sociology* 102: 323–57.

Jones, D. (1982) *Crime, protest, community and police in nineteenth-century Britain.* Boston, MA: Routledge & Kegan Paul.

Kessler, R.C. and Greenberg, D.F. (1981) *Linear panel analysis: models of quantitative change.* New York: Academic Press.

Knauft, B.M. (1987) 'Reconsidering violence in simple human societies: homicide among the Gebusi of New Guinea', *Current Anthropology* 28: 457–500.

Knauft, B.M. (1991) 'Violence and sociality in human evolution', *Current Anthropology* 32: 391–428.

Koomer, M.M. (n.d.) 'Reaching the European level: the case of the Dutch prison system', unpublished paper.

Kuhn, A. (1996) 'Imprisonment trends in Western Europe', *Overcrowded Times* 7 (February): 1, 4–9.

Levitt, S.D. (1996) 'The effect of prison population size on crime rates: evidence from prison overcrowding litigation', *Quarterly Journal of Economics* 111: 319–52.

Lynch, M., Nalla, M., Stretetsky, P. and Hogan, M. (1996) 'Expanding the expansion of the social control perspective', paper presented to the American Society of Criminology.

McConville, S. (1995) *English local prisons, 1860–1900: next only to death.* New York: Routledge.

Maguire, K. and Pastore, A.L. (eds) (1999) *Sourcebook of criminal justice statistics 1998.* US Department of Justice, Bureau of Justice Statistics. Washington, DC: United States Government Printing Office.

Maguire, M. (1997) 'Crime statistics, patterns, and trends: changing perceptions and their implications', in M. Maguire, R. Morgan and R. Reiner (eds) *The Oxford handbook of criminology, 2nd edn.* Oxford: Clarendon Press.

Mahoney, P.G. (2000) 'The common law and economic growth: Hayek might be right', University of Virginia School of Law Legal Studies Working Paper 00-8.

Marvell, T.B. and Moody, C.E. (1994) 'Prison population and crime reduction', *Journal of Quantitative Criminology* 10: 109–39.

Marx, K. (1867) *Das kapital: kritik der politischen oekonomie. Buch I: der produktionsprocess des kapitals.* Hamburg: Otto Meissner.

Massey, D.S. and Denton, N.A. (1993) *American apartheid: segregation and the making of the underclass.* Cambridge, MA: Harvard University Press.

Mechanic, D. and Rochefort, D.A. (1990) 'Deinstitutionalization: an appraisal of reform', *Annual Review of Sociology* 16: 301–27.

Michalowski, R.J. and Pearson, M.A. (1987) 'Punishment and social structure at the state level: a cross-sectional comparison of 1970 and 1980', *Journal of Research in Crime and Delinquency* 27: 52–78.

National Criminal Justice Reference Service (1979) *Profile of state prison inmates: sociodemographic findings from the 1974 survey of inmates of state correctional facilities.* National Prisoner Statistics Special Report SD-NPS-SR-4. Washington, DC: US Government Printing Office.

O'Brien, P. (1982) *The promise of punishment: prisons in nineteenth-century France.* Princeton, NJ: Princeton University Press.

O'Brien, P. (1995) 'The prison on the Continent: 1865–1965', in N. Morris and D.J. Rothman (eds) *The Oxford history of the prison: the practice of punishment in Western society.* New York: Oxford University Press.

Platt, A.M. (1969) *The child savers: the invention of delinquency.* Chicago, IL: University of Chicago Press.

Schumach, M. (1977) 'Thefts by youths in Queens lead dozen plants to say they'll move', *New York Times* 13 April: A1, D7.

Scull, A.T. (1984) *Decarceration: community treatment and the deviant – a radical view.* New Brunswick, NJ: Rutgers University Press.

Sharpe, J.A. (1985) 'The history of violence in England: some observations', *Past and Present* 108: 206–24.

Simon, J. (1997) 'Governing through crime', in L.M. Friedman and G. Fisher (eds) *The crime conundrum: essays on criminal justice.* Boulder, CO: Westview.

Soman, A. (1980) 'Deviance and criminal justice in Western Europe, 1300–1800: an essay in structure', *Criminal Justice History: An International Annual* 1: 1–28.

Sowell, T. (1981) *Markets and minorities.* New York: Basic Books.

Stone, L. (1983) 'Interpersonal violence in English society, 1300–1980', *Past and Present* 101: 22–33.

Stone, L. (1985) 'A rejoinder', *Past and Present* 108: 216–24.

Tak, P.J.P. and Van Kalmthouht, A.M. (1998) 'Prison population growing faster in the Netherlands than in US', *Overcrowded Times* 9(3): 1, 12–16.

Taylor, I. (1997) 'The political economy of crime', in M. Maguire, R. Morgan and R. Reiner (eds) *The Oxford handbook of criminology, 2nd edn.* Oxford: Clarendon Press.

Taylor, I. (1999) *Crime in context: a critical criminology of market societies.* Boulder, CO: Westview Press.

Useem, B., Piehl, A.M. and Liedka, R.V. (1999) *The crime-control effect of incarceration: reconsidering the evidence.* Final Report to the National Institute of Justice (98-IJ-CX-0085).

Van Dijk, J. (1991) 'More than a matter of security: trends in crime prevention in Europe', in F. Heidensohn and M. Farrell (eds) *Crime in Europe.* New York: Routledge.

Wacquant, L. (1998) 'La tentation pénale en Europe', *Actes de la Recherche en Sciences Sociales* 124 (Sept.): 3–6.

Wacquant, L. (1999) 'Suitable enemies: foreigners and immigrants in the prisons of Europe', *Punishment and Society* 1: 215–22.

Wacquant, L. (1999b) *Les prisons de la misère* Paris: Raison d'Agir.

Wallace, D. (1981) 'The political economy of incarceration trends in late US capitalism: 1971–1977', *Insurgent Sociologist* 10: 59–66.

Western, B. and Beckett, K. (1999) 'The U.S. penal system as a labour market institution', *American Journal of Sociology* 104: 1030–1061.

Zehr, H. (1976) *Crime and the development of modern society: patterns of criminality in nineteenth century Germany and France.* Totowa, NJ: Rowman & Littlefield.

7 Deadly symbiosis

When ghetto and prison meet and mesh

LOÏC WACQUANT

You know they got me trapped in this prison of seclusion
Happiness, living on tha street is a delusion
Even a smooth criminal one day must get caught
Shot up or shot down with tha bullet that he bought
Nine millimeter kicking, thinkin' about what tha street do to me
'Cause they never talk peace in tha black community
All we know is violence, do that job in silence
Walk tha city streets like a rat pack of tyrants
Too many brothers daily headin' for tha big penn
Niggas comin' out worse off than when they went in.

    Tupac Shakur, 'Trapped' (Reprinted by permission of
    Universal Music Publishing Group)

*Dedicated to the loving memory of DeeDee Armour
who is now coaching in that great big gym in the heavens*

REFRAMING BLACK HYPER-INCARCERATION

Three brute facts stare the sociologist of racial inequality and imprisonment in America in the face as the new millenium dawns. First, since 1989 and for the first time in national history, African Americans make up a majority of those walking through prison gates every year. Indeed, in four short decades, the ethnic composition of the US inmate population has *reversed*, turning over from 70 percent white at the mid-century point to nearly 70 percent black and Latino today, although ethnic patterns of criminal activity have not been fundamentally altered during that period (LaFree et al., 1992; Sampson and Lauritzen, 1997).

Second, the rate of incarceration for African Americans has soared to astronomical levels unknown in any other society, not even the Soviet Union at the zenith of the Gulag or South Africa during the acme of the violent struggles over apartheid. As of mid-1999, close to 800,000 black men were in custody in federal penitentiaries, state prisons and county jails, a figure corresponding to *one male out of every twenty-one* (4·6 percent) and one out of every nine ages 20 to 34 (11·3 percent). An additional 68,000 black women were locked up, a number higher than the *total* carceral population of any one major western European country (Beck, 2000).[1] Several studies, starting with a series of well-publicized reports by the Sentencing Project, have documented that, on any given day, upwards of one-third of African-American men in their twenties find themselves behind bars, on probation or on parole (Donziger, 1996: 104–5). And, at the core of the formerly industrial cities of the North, this proportion often exceeds two-thirds.

A third trend interpellates the social analyst of race, state, and punishment in the United States: the past two decades have witnessed a swift and steady *deepening of the gap* between the imprisonment rates of blacks and whites (from about one for 5 to one for 8·5), and this rising 'racial disproportionality' can be traced directly to a single federal policy, namely, the War on Drugs launched by Ronald Reagan and expanded by the administrations of George Bush and William Jefferson Clinton. In 10 of the 38 states in which this black-white disparity has grown, African Americans are imprisoned at more than ten times the rate of their compatriots of European origin.[2] The political elite of the country is well placed to take note the phenomenon since the jurisdiction that sports the highest racial gap in the land is none other than the District of Columbia, where blacks were 35 times more likely than whites to be put behind bars in 1994 (Mauer, 1997).

These grim statistics are well-known and agreed upon among students of crime and justice – though they have been steadfastly ignored or minimized by analysts of urban poverty and policy, who have yet to register the enormously disruptive impact that imprisonment has on low-income black communities, as shown by Miller (1997). What remains in dispute are the causes and mechanisms driving this sudden 'blackening' which has turned the carceral system into one of a few national institutions dominated by African Americans, alongside professional sports and selected sectors of the entertainment industry. Most analysts have focused on trends in crime and endeavored to decompose the source of black over-representation in prison by sorting and sifting through patterns of criminality, bias in arrest, prosecution, and sentencing, and prior criminal records (see Blumstein, 1993, for a model study, and Tonry, 1995: 56–79, for a vigorous and rigorous review). A few have expanded their compass to measure the influence of such non-judicial variables as the size of the black population, the poverty rate, unemployment, inflation, income, value of welfare payments, region, support for religious fundamentalism, and political party in office (e.g., Lessan, 1991; Yates, 1997; Greenberg and West, 1999). But none of these factors, taken separately or jointly, accounts for the sheer magnitude, rapidity, and timing of the recent racialization of US imprisonment, especially as crime rates have been flat and later declining over that period. For this, it is necessary, first, to take a longer historical view and, second, to break out of the narrow 'crime-and-punishment' paradigm to reckon the extra-penological role of the penal system as instrument for the management of dispossessed and dishonored groups.[3]

In this article, I put forth two interconnected theses, the first *historical*, replacing the carceral institution in the full arc of ethnoracial division and domination in the United States, the second *institutional*, explaining the astounding upsurge in black incarceration in the past three decades as a result of the obsolescence of the ghetto as a device for caste control and the correlative need for a substitute apparatus for keeping (unskilled) African Americans 'in their place', i.e. in a subordinate and confined position in physical, social, and symbolic space. I further argue that, in the post-Civil Rights era, the remnants of the dark ghetto and the fast-expanding carceral system of the United States have become tightly linked by a triple relationship of functional equivalency, structural homology, and cultural fusion. This relationship has spawned a *carceral continuum* that ensnares a supernumerary population of younger black men, who either reject or are rejected by the deregulated low-wage labor market, in a never-ending circulus between the two institutions. This carceral mesh has been solidified by two sets of concurrent and interrelated changes: on the one end, sweeping economic and political forces have reshaped the structure and function of the urban 'Black Belt' of mid-century to *make the ghetto more like a prison*. On the other end, the 'inmate society' that inhabited the penitentiary system of the US during the postwar decades has broken down in ways that *make the prison more like a ghetto*. The resulting symbiosis between ghetto and prison not only enforces and perpetuates the socioeconomic marginality and symbolic taint of the urban black subproletariat, feeding the runaway growth of the penal system that has become a major component of the post-Keynesian state. It also plays a pivotal role in the remaking of 'race' and the redefinition of the citizenry via the production of a racialized public culture of vilification of criminals.

A fuller analysis, extending beyond the black ghetto, would reveal that the increasing use of imprisonment to shore up caste division in American society partakes of a broader 'upsizing' of the penal sector of the state which, together with the drastic 'downsizing' of its social welfare sector, aims at imposing desocialized wage labor as a norm of citizenship for the deskilled fractions of the postindustrial working class (Wacquant, 1999a). This emerging *government of poverty* wedding the 'invisible hand' of the deregulated labor market to the 'iron fist' of an intrusive and omnipresent punitive apparatus is anchored, not by a 'prison industrial complex', as political opponents of the policy of mass incarceration maintain (e.g. Davis, 1998), but by a *carceral-assistential complex* which carries out its mission to surveil, train and neutralize the populations recalcitrant or superfluous to the new economic and racial regime according to a gendered division of labor, the men being handled by its penal wing while (their) women and children are managed by a revamped welfare-workfare system designed to buttress casual employment. It is this shift from the social to the penal treatment of poverty and its correlates at the bottom of the class and caste structure, subsequent to the denunciation of the Fordist-Keynesian social contract, that has brought the prison back to the societal center, counter to the optimistic forecasts of its impending demise by analysts of the criminal justice scene in the early 1970s.

To recognize that the hypertrophic growth of the penal institution is one component of a more comprehensive restructuring of the American state to suit the requirements of neoliberalism is not to negate or even minimize the special office of race in its advent. If the prison offered itself as a viable vehicle of resolving the 'black question' after the crisis of the ghetto – that is, for reformulating it in a way that both *invisibilizes it and reactives it* under new disguises: crime, 'welfare dependency', and the 'underclass' – it is surely because America is the one society that has pushed the market logic of commodification of social relations and state devolution the furthest (Esping-Andersen, 1987; Handler, 1997). But, conversely, if the US far outstrips all advanced nations in the international trend towards the penalization of social insecurity, it is because, just as the dismantling of welfare programs was accelerated by the conflation of blackness and undeservingness in national culture and politics (Gilens, 1999), the 'great confinement' of the rejects of market society, the poor, the mentally ill, the homeless, the jobless and the useless, can be painted as a welcome 'crackdown' on *them*, those dark-skinned criminals issued from a pariah group still considered alien to the national body. Thus, just as the color line inherited from the era of Southern slavery directly determined the mishappen figure of America's 'semi-welfare state' in the formative period of the New Deal (Lieberman, 1998), the handling of the 'underclass' question by the prison system at the close of the 20th century is key to fashioning the visage of the post-Keynesian state in the 21st.

FOUR PECULIAR INSTITUTIONS

To ascertain the pivotal position that the penal apparatus has come to assume within the system of instruments of (re)production of ethnoracial hierarchy in the post-Civil Rights era, it is indispensable to adopt an historical perspective of the *longue durée* so as to situate the prison in the full lineage of institutions which, at each epoch, have carried out the work of race making by drawing and enforcing the peculiar 'color line' that cleaves American society asunder.[4] Put succinctly, the task of *defining, confining, and controling* African Americans in the United States has been successively shouldered by four 'peculiar institutions': slavery, the Jim Crow system, the urban ghetto, and the novel organizational compound formed by the vestiges of the ghetto and the expanding carceral system, as set out in Table 1.

The first three of these institutions, chattel slavery until the Civil War, the Jim Crow regime of racial exclusion operative in the agrarian South from Emancipation to the Civil Rights revolution, and the ghetto in the 20th century Northern industrial city, have, each in its own manner, served two joined yet discordant purposes: to recruit, organize, and extract labor out of African Americans, on the one hand; and to demarcate and ultimately seclude them so that they would not 'contaminate' the surrounding white society that viewed them as as irrevocably inferior and vile because devoid of ethnic honor. These two goals of *labor extraction and social ostracization* of a stigmatized category are in tension with one another inasmuch as to utilize the labor power of a group inevitably entails bringing it into regular intercourse with oneself and thereby invites the blurring or transgression of the boundary separating 'us' from 'them'. Conversely, to immure a group in a separate physical and sociosymbolic space can make it more difficult to draw out and deploy its labor in the most efficient way. When the tension between these two purposes, exploitation and ostracization, mounts to the point where it threatens to undermine either of them, its excess is drained, so to speak, and the institution re-stabilized, by resort to *physical violence*: the customary use of the lash and ferocious

TABLE 1 The four 'peculiar institutions' and their basis

PECULIAR INSTITUTION	FORM OF LABOR	CORE OF ECONOMY	DOMINANT SOCIAL TYPE
Slavery (1619–1865)	unfree fixed labor	plantation	slave
Jim Crow (South, 1865–1965)	free fixed labor	agrarian and extractive	sharecropper
Ghetto (North, 1915–1968)	free mobile labor	segmented industrial manufacturing	menial worker
Hyperghetto + Prison (1968–)	fixed surplus labor	polarized postindustrial services	welfare recipient & criminal

suppression of slave insurrections on the plantation, terroristic vigilantism and mob lynchings in the post-bellum South, and periodic bombings of Negro homes and pogroms against ghetto residents (such as the six-day riot that shook up Chicago in 1919) ensured that blacks kept to their appointed place at each epoch.[5]

But the built-in instabilities of unfree labor and the inherent anomaly of caste partition in a formally democratic and highly individualistic society guaranteed that each 'peculiar institution' would in time be undermined by the weight of its internal contradictions as well as by mounting black resistance and external opposition,[6] to be replaced by its successor regime. At each new stage, however, the apparatus of ethnoracial domination would become less total and less capable of encompassing all segments and all dimensions of the social life of the pariah group. As African Americans differentiated along class lines and acceded to full formal citizenship, the institutional complex charged with keeping them 'separate and unequal' grew more differentiated and diffuse, allowing a burgeoning middle and upper class of professionals and salary earners to *partially* compensate for the negative symbolic capital of blackness by their high-status cultural capital and proximity to centers of political power, while lower-class blacks remained burdened by the triple stigma of 'race', poverty, and putative immorality.[7]

1. Slavery (1619–1865)

From the first years of the colony to the Civil War, slavery was the institution that determined the collective identity and individual life chances of Americans of African parentage. Orlando Patterson (1982: 334 and passim) has rightly insisted that slavery is essentially 'a relation of domination and not a category of legal thought', and, moreover, a relation unusual for the inordinate amounts of material and symbolic violence it entails. In the Americas (as opposed to, say, in the Islamic world, where it served no productive purpose), this violence was channeled to fulfil a definite economic end: to appease the nearly insatiable appetite of the plantation for labor. The forcible importation of Africans and West Indians, and the rearing of their descendants under bondage (the US enslaved population tripled to reach 4 million in the half-century after the slave trade was cut off in 1808), supplied the unfree and fixed workforce needed to produce the great staples that were the backbone of North America's preindustrial economy, tobacco, rice, sugar, and cotton.

In the early colonial period indentured servitude was economically more advantageous than slavery but, by the second half of the 17th century, the increase in life expectancy, the growth of the tobacco trade, the need to encourage further voluntary immigration and the relative powerlessness of African captives compared to European migrants and native Americans combined to make slaves the preferred source of labor (Morgan, 1975). After the Revolution, human bondage was abolished along the Eastern seaboard and prohibited north and west of the Ohio River, but it spread and solidified throughout the South, as the economic value of slaves rose in concert with the increase in the demand for cotton and the scarcity of labor in the new territories of the Southwest. Once it generalized, slavery transformed all of society, culture, and politics in its image, fostering the concentration of economic and state power in the hands of a small slaveholder class tied to lower-class whites by patronage relations and to their slaves by a paternalistic code and elaborate rituals of submission that reinforced the latter's lack of cultural autonomy and sense of inferiority (Williamson, 1986: 15–27).

Whereas in the early decades of the colony the status of slave and servant were virtually indistinguished – the terms were even used interchangeably – by the 19th century the dichotomous opposition between bondsmen and freemen had been racialized: the militant defense of slavery generated an elaborate ideology justifying the subhuman condition imposed upon blacks by their inferior biological makeup, exemplified by the animalistic traits, in turn childish and bestial, attributed to the archetypal figure of Sambo. In the decades leading to the Civil War, the specter of insurrection and of the abolition of bondage resulted in increased hostility toward manumission, miscegenation, and 'passing' by Negroes, as well as in the generalization of a rigid twofold racial schema, based on the mythology that God had created blacks to be slaves and that one drop of 'Negro blood' made one a Negro – persons of mixed descent were believed to be against nature and fated to physical extinction (Davis, 1992: 41–2). Slavery as a system of unfree labor thus spawned a suffusive racial culture which, in turn, remade bondage into something it was not at its outset: a color-coded institution of ethnoracial division.[8]

2. Jim Crow (South, 1865–1965)

Emancipation posed a double and deadly threat to Southern society: the overthrow of bondage made slaves formally free laborers, which potentially eliminated the cheap and abundant workforce required to run the plantation economy; black access to civil and political rights promised to erode the color line initially drawn to bulwark slavery but since entrenched in both the South and the North of the country. In a first phase, during Reconstruction, the Dixie ruling class promulgated the Black Codes to resolve the first problem by establishing 'forced labor and police laws to get the freedman back to the fields under control' (Woodward, 1971: 250–1). In a second phase, through the 1880s, the white lower classes, pressed by the dislocations wrought by declining farm prices, demographic pressure and capitalist industrialization, joined with the plantation elite to demand the political disenfranchisement and systematic exclusion of former slaves from all major institutions (Wilson, 1980: 57–61): the Jim Crow regime of racial segregation was born which would hold African Americans in its brutal grip for nearly a century in the Southern states and beyond.[9]

Under this regime, backed by custom and elaborate legal statutes, superexploitative sharecropping arrangements and debt peonage fixed black labor on the land, perpetuating the hegemony of the region's agrarian upper class – and the work discipline of the antebellum plantation: the lash remained in use in Mississipi into the interwar years. The economic opportunities of African Americans were severely restricted not only in the cotton fields but also in the emerging mining and industrial towns of the uplands by limiting their employment to the most dirty and dangerous 'nigger work'. Former slaves and their descendants were prohibited from attending churches and schools with whites (in some states, biracial education was even made unconstitutional). And they were methodically banished from the ballot box thanks to an assortment of residency requirements, poll taxes, literacy tests, 'grandfather clauses' and disqualifying criminal offenses.[10]

Most crucially, the second 'peculiar institution' sharply curtailed social contacts between whites and blacks by relegating the latter to separate residential districts and to the reserved 'colored' section of commercial establishments and public facilities, saloons and movie houses, parks and beaches, trolleys and buses, waiting rooms and bathrooms.

Any and all forms of intercourse that might imply social equality between the 'races' and, worse yet, provide an occasion for sexual contact across the color line were rigorously forbidden and zealously surveiled, and any infringement, real or imagined, savagely repressed. The hysterical dread of 'racial degeneracy' believed to ensue from mixing, and justified by the self-evident query 'Would you want your sister to marry a nigger?' (Dollard, 1937: 62), climaxed in periodic explosions of mob violence, beatings, whippings, and rioting against blacks who failed to 'stay in their place' and display proper caste deference. In the last two decades of the 19th century, some 2,060 African Americans were lynched, one third of them after being accused of sexual assault or mere improprieties towards white women (Williamson, 1982: 292). These veritable carnivals of caste rage, during which the bodies of 'bad niggah' were ritually desecrated by burning, mutilation, and public exhibition, were fanned by the press, tacitly supported by the churches, and encouraged by the complicity of the forces of order and immunity from the authorities. African Americans could hardly turn to the courts for protection since the latter openly put the law of caste above the rule of law: lynchings were perpetrated by lower-class 'rednecks' but with the consent and approval of white 'quality', for, as a Mississippi gentleman put it, 'race is greater than law now and then, and protection of women transcends all law, human and divine' (cited by McMillen, 1990: 240).

3. The ghetto (North, 1914–1968)

The very ferocity of Jim Crow on both the labor and the ostracization fronts sowed the seeds of its eventual ruin, for blacks fled the South by the millions as soon as the opportunity came. Three forces combined to rouse them to desert Dixie and rally to the surging metropolitan centers of the Midwest and Northeast in the half-century following the outbreak of World War I. The first was the economic crisis of cotton agriculture caused by the boll weevil and later by mechanization, as well as arrested urbanization in the South due to the industrial underdevelopment of the region (Fligstein, 1981). The second was the booming demand for unskilled and semiskilled labor in the steel mills, packinghouses, factories and railroads of the North, as the war cut off immigration from Europe and employers sent their recruiting agents scurrying through the South to entice African Americans to come work for them (Marks, 1989). But economic push and pull factors merely set conditions of possibility: the trigger of the Great Migration that transformed the black community from a landless peasantry to an industrial proletariat, and with it the visage of American society *in toto*, was the irrepressible will to escape the indignities of caste and its attendant material degradation, truncated life horizon, and rampant violence – the outmigration of blacks was heaviest in those counties of the Deep South where lynchings were most frequent (Tolnay and Beck, 1992). These indignities were made all the more intolerable by the ongoing incorporation of 'white ethnics' into national institutions and by the paradoxical role that the US played on the world stage as champion of those very freedoms which it denied Negros at home. The trek up to Chicago, Detroit, New York and Philadelphia was thus undertaken by Southern blacks not only to 'better their condition' but also to board the 'train of freedom' (to recall the title of a well-known poem by Langston Hughes) on a journey filled with biblical imagery and political import (Grossman, 1989: esp. 16–37): it was a race-conscious gesture of collective defiance and self-affirmation.[11]

Yankee life did offer salutory relief from the harsh grip of Southern caste domination and significantly expand the life chances of the former sharecroppers, but it did not turn out to be the 'promised land' of racial equality, economic security, and full citizenship for which migrants yearned. For, in the Northern metropolis, African Americans came upon yet another device designed to allow white society to exploit their labor power while keeping them confined to a separate *Lebensraum*: the ghetto. As the Negro population rose, so did the animosity of whites towards a group they viewed as 'physically and mentally unfit', 'unsanitary', 'entirely irresponsible', and therefore 'undesirable as neighbors', in the terms reported to the 1920 Chicago Commission on Race Relations (cited in Spear, 1967: 22). Patterns of ethnoracial discrimination and segregation that had hitherto been inconsistent and informal hardened in housing, schools, and public accomodations such as parks, playgrounds and beaches. They were extended to the polity, where the promotion of a small cadre of black politicians handpicked by party leaders served to rein in the community's votes to the benefit of the white-controlled city machine (Katznelson, 1976: 83–5). They were systematized in the economy, where a 'job ceiling' set conjointly by white employers and unions kept African Americans trapped in the lower reaches of the occupational structure, disproportionately concentrated in semi-skilled, manual, and servant work that made them especially vulnerable to business downturns (Drake and Cayton, 1945: 223–35; Wilson, 1980: 71–6). And, when they tried to breach the color bar, for instance by attempting to settle outside of their reserved perimeter in violation of restrictive covenants, blacks were assaulted on the streets by white 'athletic clubs' and their houses bombed by so-called 'neighborhood improvement societies'. They had no choice but to take refuge in the secluded territory of the Black Belt and to try to build in it a self-sustaining nexus of institutions that would both shield them from white rule and procure the needs of the castaway community: a 'Black Metropolis' lodged 'in the womb of the white', yet hermetically sealed from it (Drake and Cayton, 1945: 80).[12]

This 'black city within the white', as black scholars from DuBois and Frazier to Oliver Cox and Kenneth Clark have consistently characterized the ghetto (Wacquant, 1998a), discharged the same two basic functions that slavery and the Jim Crow system had performed earlier, namely, to harness the labor of African Americans while cloistering their tainted bodies, so as to avert both the specter of 'social equality' and the odium of 'miscegenation' that would inevitably result in loss of ethnic honor for whites. But it differed from the preceding 'peculiar institutions' in that, by granting them a measure of organizational autonomy, the urban Black Belt enabled African Americans to fully develop their own social and symbolic forms and thereby accumulate the group capacities needed to escalate the fight against continued caste subordination.[13] For the ghetto in full-fledged form is, by its very makeup, a *double-edged sociospatial formation*: it operates as an instrument of *exclusion* from the standpoint of the dominant group; yet it also offers the subordinate group partial *protection* and a platform for succor and solidarity in the very movement whereby it sequesters it.

Specifying the workings of the ghetto as mechanism of ethnoracial closure and control makes readily visible its *structural and functional kinship with the prison*: the ghetto is a manner of 'ethnoracial prison' in that it encloses a stigmatized population which evolves within it its distinctive organizations and culture, while the prison functions as a 'judicial ghetto' relegating individuals disgraced by criminal conviction to a secluded space harboring the parallel social relations and cultural norms that make up the 'society of captives'.[14] This kinship explains why, when the ghetto was rendered inoperative in the sixties by economic restructuring that made African-American labor expendable and mass protest that finally won blacks the vote, the carceral institution offered itself as a substitute apparatus for enforcing the shifting color line and containing the segments of the African-American community devoid of economic utility and political pull. The coupling of the transformed core of the urban Black Belt, or hyperghetto, and the fast-expanding carceral system that together compose America's fourth 'peculiar institution' was fortified by two concurrent series of changes that have tended to 'prisonize' the ghetto and to 'ghettoize' the prison. The next two sections examine each of these trends in turn.

FROM COMMUNAL GHETTO TO HYPERGHETTO: HOW THE GHETTO BECAME MORE LIKE A PRISON

The *fin-de-siècle* hyperghetto presents four main characteristics that differentiate it sharply from the communal ghetto of the Fordist-Keynesian era and converge to render its social structure and cultural climate more akin to those of the prison. I consider each in turn by drawing a schematic contrast between the mid-century 'Bronzeville' depicted by St. Clair Drake and Horace Cayton (1945) in *Black Metropolis* and the South Side of Chicago as I observed it some forty years later through fieldwork, official statistics, and survey data.

1. Class segregation overlays racial segregation

The dark ghetto of mid-century held within itself a full complement of classes, for the simple reason that even the black bourgeoisie was barred from escaping its cramped and compact perimeter while a majority of adults were gainfully employed in a gamut of occupations. True, from the 1920s onward, Chicago's South Side featured clearly demarcated subdivisions stratified by class, with the small elite of doctors, lawyers, teachers, and businessmen residing in the stabler and more desirable neighborhoods adjacent to white districts at the southern end, while the families of laborers and domestic workers massed themselves in areas of blight, crime and dissolution towards the northern end (Frazier, 1932). But the social distance between the classes was limited by physical propinquity and extensive family ties; the black bourgeoisie's economic power rested on supplying goods and services to its lower-class brethens; and all 'brown' residents of the city were united in their common rejection of caste subordination and abiding concern to 'advance the race', despite its internecine divisions and the mutual panning of 'big Negroes' and 'riff-raff' (Drake and Cayton, 1945: 716–28). As a result, the postwar ghetto was *integrated both socially and structurally* – even the 'shadies' who earned their living from such illicit trades as the 'numbers game', liquor sale, prostitution and other *risqué* recreation, were entwined with the different classes.

Today's black bourgeoisie still lives under strict segregation and its life chances continue to be curtailed by its geographic and symbolic contiguity with the African-American (sub)proletariat (Patillo-McCoy, 1999). Nonetheless, it has gained considerable physical distance from the heart of the ghetto by establishing satellite black neighborhoods at its periphery inside the city and in the suburbs.[15] Its economic basis has shifted from the direct servicing of the black community to the state, with employment in public bureaucracies accounting for most of the growth of professional, managerial and technical positions held by African Americans over the past thirty years. The genealogical ties of the black bourgeoisie to the black poor have also grown more remote and less dense. What is more, the historic center of the Black Belt has experienced massive depopulation and deproletarianization, such that a large majority of its residents are no longer employed: two-thirds of the adults in Bronzeville did not hold a job in 1980, compared to fewer than half thirty years earlier (cf. Table 2); and three out of every four households were headed by women, while the official poverty rate hovered near the 50 percent mark.

This marked lowering and homogenization of the social composition of the ghetto makes it akin to the monotonous class recruitment of the carceral institution, dominated as the latter is by the most precarious fractions of the urban proletariat of the unemployed, the casually employed, and the uneducated. Fully 36 percent of the half-million detainees housed by US jails in 1991 were jobless at the time of their arrest and another 15 percent worked only part-time or irregularly. One-half had not finished high school and two-thirds earned less than a thousand dollars a month that year; in addition, every other inmate had been raised in a home receiving welfare and a paltry 16 percent were married (Harlow, 1998). Residents of the hyperghetto and clients of the carceral institution thus present germane profiles in economic marginality and social dis-integration.

2. Loss of a positive economic function
The transformed class structure of the hyperghetto is a direct product of its evolving position in the new urban political economy ushered by post-Fordism. We have seen that, from the Great Migration of the interwar years to the 1960s, the dark ghetto served a positive economic function as reservoir of cheap and pliable labor for the city's factories. During that period, it was 'directly exploited by outside economic interests, and it provide[d] a dumping ground for the human residuals created by economic change. These economic conditions [we]re stabilized by transfer payments that preserve[d] the

TABLE 2 The changing class structure of Chicago's South Side, 1950–1980 *

	1950		1980	
	TOTAL	%	TOTAL	%
Proprietors, managers, professional & technical	5,270	3.3	2,225	3.2
Clerical, sales	10,271	6.4	5,169	7.5
Operative, laborers, craftsmen	42,372	26.7	6,301	9.3
Private household and service workers	25,182	15.8	5,203	7.5
Total employed adults	83,095	52.2	18,898	27.5
Adults not employed	75,982	47.8	50,148	72.5
Total adult population	159,077	100	69,046	100

* Comprising the three community areas of Grand Boulevard, Oakland, and Washington Park; adults are persons 15 and over for 1950, 18 and over for 1980.

Source: Chicago Fact Book Consortium, *Local Community Fact Book*, Chicago, Center for the Study of Family and Community, 1955, and Chicago Review Press, 1985.

ghetto in a poverty that recreate[d] itself from generation to generation', ensuring the ready availability of a low-cost workforce (Fusfeld and Bates, 1982: 236). By the 1970s, this was no longer true as the engine of the metropolitan economy passed from manufacturing to business and knowledge-based services, and factories relocated from the central city to the mushrooming industrial parks of the suburbs and exurbs, as well as to anti-union states in the South and to foreign countries.

Between 1954 and 1982, the number of manufacturing establishments in Chicago plunged from 10,288 to 5,203, while the number of production workers sank from nearly half a million to a mere 172,000. The demand for black labor plummeted accordingly, rocking the entire black class structure (Wacquant, 1989: 510–11), given that half of all employed African Americans in Chicago were blue-collar wage earners at the close of World War II. Just as mechanization had enabled Southern agriculture to dispense with black labor a generation earlier, 'automation and suburban relocation created a crisis of tragic dimension for unskilled black workers' in the North, as 'for the first time in American history, the African American was no longer needed in the economic system' of the metropolis (Rifkin, 1995: 79; also Sugrue, 1995: 125–52). The effects of technological upgrading and postindustrialization were intensified by (1) unflinching residential segregation, (2) the breakdown of public schools, and (3) the renewal of working-class immigration from Latin America and Asia to consign the vast majority of uneducated blacks to economic redundancy. At best, the hyperghetto now serves the *negative economic function of storage of a surplus population* devoid of market utility, in which respect it also increasingly resembles the prison system.

3. State institutions of social control replace communal institutions

The organizations that formed the framework of everyday life and anchored the strategies of reproduction of urban blacks in the 1950s were group-based and group-specific establishments created and run by African Americans. The black press, churches, lodges and fraternal orders, social clubs and political (sub)machine knit together a dense array of resources and sociability that supported their quest for ethnic pride and group uplift. To its 200,000 members, the five hundred religious congregations that dotted the South Side were not only places of worship and entertainment but also a potent vehicle for individual and collective mobility within the specific order of the ghetto that cut across class lines and strengthened ingrown social control, even as black proletarians chaffed in endless 'protest against the alleged cupidity and hypocrisy of church functionaries and devotees' (Drake and Cayton, 1945: 710–11, 650).

In the economic realm also, African Americans could seek or sustain the illusion of autonomy and advancement. Now, Negro entreprise was small scale and commercially weak, the three most numerous types of black-owned firms being beauty parlors, grocery stores and barber shops. But the popular 'doctrine of the 'Double-Duty Dollar', according to which buying from black concerns would 'advance the race' (Drake and Cayton, 1945: 430–1, 438–9), promised a path to economic independence from whites, and the 'numbers game' seemed to prove that one could indeed erect a self-sustaining economy within Black Metropolis. With some 500 stations employing 5,000 and paying yearly wages in excess of a million dollars for three daily drawings, the 'policy racket' was at once big business, a fixture of group fellowship, and a popular cult. Protected by criss-crossing ties and kickbacks to court officials, the police, and politicians, the 'policy kings' were regarded as 'Race Leaders, patrons of charity, and pioneers in the establishment of legitimate business' (Drake and Cayton, 1945: 486; also Light, 1977).

By the 1980s, the organizational ecology of the ghetto had been radically altered by the generalized devolution of public institutions and commercial establishments in the urban core as well as by the cumulative demise of black associations caused by the confluence of market withdrawal and state retrenchment (Wacquant, 1998a). The physical infrastructure and business base of the South Side had been decimated, with thousands of boarded-up stores and abandoned buildings rotting away along deserted boulevards strewn with debris and garbage. Arguably the most potent component of the communal ghetto, the church lost its capacity to energize and organize social life on the South Side. Storefront operations closed in the hundreds and the congregations that have endured either battle for sheer survival or battle local residents: in the early 1990s, on 63rd Street near Stony Island Avenue, the Apostolic Church of God, lavishly financed and patronized by an expatriate black bourgeoisie, was engaged in a trench war with the surrounding poor population which viewed it as an invader, so that the church had to fence itself up and hire a phalanx of security guards to enable its members to come into the neighborhood and attend its three services on Sunday.[16] Similarly, the black press has grown outside of the ghetto but virtually disappeared within it as a vector of public opinion: there were five black weeklies in Bronzeville when World War II broke out; forty years later, the *Chicago Defender* alone remains in existence and then, only as a pale shadow of its former glorious self – it is sparsely distributed even at the heart of the South Side whereas an estimated 100,000 read it and everyone discussed it fervently in the 1940s.[17]

The vacuum created by the crumbling of the ghetto's indigenous organizations has been filled by *state bureaucracies of social control*, themselves largely staffed by the new black middle class whose expansion hinges, not on its capacity to service its community, but on its willingness to assume the vexing role of *custodian* of the black urban subproletariat on behalf of white society. By the 1980s, the institutions that set the tone of daily life and determined the fate of most residents on Chicago's South Side were (1) astringent and humiliating welfare programs, bolstered and replaced by 'workfare' after 1996, designed to restrict access to the public aid rolls and push recipients into the low-wage labor market; (2) decrepit public housing that subjected its tenants and the surrounding population to extraordinary levels of criminal insecurity, infrastructural blight and official scorn (its management was so derelict that the Chicago Housing Authority had to put under federal receivership); (3) permanently failing public health and public schools operating with resources, standards, and results worthy of Third World countries; and (4), not least, the police, the courts, and on-the-ground extensions of the penal system such as probation officers, parole agents, and 'snitches', recruited by the thousands by law enforcement agencies, often under threat of criminal prosecution, to extend the mesh of state surveillance and capture deep into the hyperghetto (Miller, 1997: 102–3).[18]

4. Loss of 'buffering function' and the depacification of everyday life

Along with its economic function of labor pool and the extensive organizational nexus it supported, the ghetto lost its capacity to buffer its residents from external forces. It is no longer Janus-faced, offering a sheltered space for collective sustenance and self-affirmation in the face of hostility and exclusion, as in the heyday of the Fordist-Keynesian era. Rather, it has devolved into a one-dimensional machinery for naked relegation, a human warehouse wherein are discarded those segments of urban society deemed disreputable, derelict, and dangerous. And, with the conjoint contraction of the wage-labor market and the welfare state in the context of unflinching segregation, it has become saturated with economic, social, and physical insecurity (Massey and Denton, 1993; Krivo and Peterson, 1996). Pandemic levels of crime – gunfire and assaults have become habitual, with homicide rates topping 100 for 100,000 at the core of the South Side in 1990 – have further depressed the local economy and ruptured the social fabric. The depacification of everyday life, shrinking of networks, and informalization of survival strategies have combined to give social relations in the hyperghetto a distinct carceral cast (Kotlowitz, 1991; Jones and Newman, 1997; Wacquant, 1998b): fear and danger pervade public space; interpersonal relations are riven with suspicion and distrust, feeding mutual avoidance and retraction into one's private defended space; resort to violence is the prevalent means for upholding respect, regulating encounters, and controling territory; and relations with official authorities are suffused with animosity and diffidence – patterns familiar to students of social order in the contemporary US prison (e.g., Carroll, 1974; Jacobs, 1977; Irwin, 1980).

Two examples illustrate well this increasing conformance of the hyperghetto to the carceral model. The first is the *'prisonization' of public housing*, as well as retirement homes, single-room occupancy hostels, homeless shelters, and other establishments for collective living, which have come to look and feel just like houses of detention.[19] 'Projects' have been fenced up, their perimeter placed under beefed-up security patrols and authoritarian controls, including identification-card checks, signing in, electronic monitoring, police infiltration, 'random searches, segregation, curfews, and resident counts – all familiar procedures of efficient prison management' (Miller, 1997: 101). Over the past decade, the Chicago Housing Authority has deployed its own police force and even sought to institute its own 'misdemeanor court' to try misbehaving tenants on the premises. Residents of the Robert Taylor Homes, at the epicenter of the South Side, have been subjected to video surveillance and required to bear special ID cards as well as pass through metal detectors, undergo patdown searches, and report all visitors to a housing officer in the lobby (Venkatesh, 2000: 123–30). In 1994, the CHA launched massive paramilitary sweeps under the code name 'Operation Clean Sweep,' involving pred-dawn surprise searches of buildings leading to mass arrests in violation of basic constitutional rights quite similar to the periodic 'shakedowns' intended to rid prison wards of shanks and other contraband. As one elderly resident of a District of Columbia project being put under such quasi-penal supervision observed: 'It's as though the children in here are being prepared for incarceration, so when they put them in a real lock-down situation, they'll be used to being hemmed in' (cited by Miller, 1997: 101).

Public schools in the hyperghetto have similarly deteriorated to the point where they operate in the manner of *institutions of confinement* whose primary mission is not to educate but to ensure 'custody and control' – to borrow the motto of many departments of corrections. Like the prison system, their recruitment is severely skewed along class and ethnoracial lines: 75 percent of the pupils of Chicago's establishments come from families living under the official poverty line and nine of every ten are black or Latino. Like inmates, these children are herded into decaying and overcrowded facilities built like bunkers, where undertrained and underpaid teachers, hampered by a shocking penury of equipment and supplies – many schools have no photocopying machines, library, science laboratory, or even functioning bathrooms, and use textbooks that are thirty-year-old rejects from suburban schools – strive to regulate conduct so as to maintain order and minimize violent incidents. The physical plant of most establishments resembles fortresses, complete with concertina wire on outside fences, bricked up windows, heavy locks on iron doors, metal detectors at the gates and hallways patroled by armed guards who conduct spot checks and body searches between buildings. Over the years, essential educational programs have been cut to divert funds for more weapons scanners, cameras, emergency telephones, sign-in desks, and security personnel, whose duty is to repel unwanted intruders from the outside and hem students inside the school's walls.[20] Indeed, it appears that the main purpose of these school is simply to 'neutralize' youth considered unworthy and unruly by holding them under lock for the day so that, at minimum, they do not engage in street crime. Certainly, it is hard to maintain that educating them is a priority when half of the city's high schools place in the bottom 1 percent of establishments nationwide on the American College Test and two thirds of ghetto students fail to complete their cursus while those who do graduate read on average at the 8th grade level (*Chicago Tribune*, 1992: 12–3). At any rate, the carceral atmosphere of schools and the constant presence of armed guards in uniform in the lobbies, corridors, cafeteria, and playground of their establishment habituates the children of the hyperghetto to the demeanor, tactics, and interactive style of the correctional officers many of them are bound to encounter shortly after their school days are over.

FROM 'BIG HOUSE' TO WAREHOUSE:
HOW THE PRISON BECAME MORE LIKE A GHETTO

The two decades following the climax of the Civil Rights movement not only witnessed a sea change in the function, structure and texture of the dark ghetto in the postindustrial metropolis. The racial and class backlash that reconfigured the city also ushered a sweeping transformation in the purpose and social organization of the carceral institution. Summarily put, the 'Big House' that embodied the correctional ideal of melioristic treatment and community reintegration of inmates[21] gave way to a race-divided and violence-ridden 'warehouse' geared solely to neutralizing social rejects by sequestering them physically from society – in the way that a classical ghetto wards off the threat of defilement posed by the presence of a dishonored group by encaging it within its walls, but in an ambience resonant with the fragmentation, dread, and despair of the post-Fordist hyperghetto. With the explosive growth of the incarcerated population leading to rampant overcrowding, the rise in the proportion of inmates serving long sentences, the spread of ethnically-based gangs, the flood of drug offenders and especially of young offenders deeply rooted in the informal economy and oppositional culture of the street, the 'inmate society' depicted in the classic prison research of the postwar decades foundered, as John Irwin (1990: vi) observes in his 1990 preface to *The Felon*:

There is no longer a single, overarching convict culture or social organization, as there tended to be twenty years ago when *The Felon* was written. Most prisoners restrict their association to a few other prisoners and withdraw from prison public life. A minority associates with gangs, gamble, buy and sell contraband commodities, and engage in prison homosexual behavior. If they do so, however, they must act 'tough' and be willing to live by the new code, that is, be ready to meet threats of violence with violence.

It is not easy to characterize the changes which have remade the American prison in the image of the ghetto over the past three decades, not only because of the 'astonishing diversity' of establishments and regimes across levels of the carceral system and the different states (Morris, 1995: 228), but also because we have remarkably little on-the-ground data on social and cultural life inside the contemporary penitentiary. Sociologists have deserted the institution – with a firm push from corrections administrations that have grown increasingly closed and secretive – just as it was ascending to the front line of the instruments for the regulation of poverty and race. With the partial exception of women's facilities, field studies based on direct observation have virtually disappeared, as research on imprisonment shifted from close-up accounts of the internal order of the prison, its hierarchies, values, and mores, to distant analyses of incarceration rates, the dynamics and cost-effectiveness of penal management, sentencing, and fear of crime based primarily on official statistics, administrative reports, litigation findings, and large-scale surveys (DiIulio, 1991; Simon, 2000).[22] Nonetheless, one can provisionally single out five tendencies that fortify the structural and functional meshing of ghetto and prison in the large (post)industrial states that have put the United States on the path to mass imprisonment.

1. The racial division of everything

The relatively stable set of positions and expectations defined primarily in terms of criminal statuses and prison conduct that used to organize the inmate world has been replaced by a chaotic and conflictual setting wherein 'racial division has primacy over all particular identities and influences all aspects of life' (Irwin, 1990: v; also Carroll, 1982; Johnson, 1996; Hassine, 1999: 71–8). The ward, tier, cell and bed-bunk to which one is assigned; access to food, telephone, television, visitation and in-house programs; one's associations and protections, which in turn determine the probability of being the victim or perpetrator of violence: all are set by one's ethnic community of provenance. Elective loyalty to inmates as a generic class, with the possibility of remaining non-aligned, has been superseded by forced and exclusive loyalty to one's 'race' defined in rigid, caste-like manner, with no in-between and no position of neutrality – just as within the urban ghetto. And the central axis of stratification inside the 'pen' has shifted from the vertical cleavage *between prisoners and guards*, marked by the proscription to 'rat on a con', exploit other inmates, and 'talk to a screw', to horizontal cleavages *among prisoners* between blacks, Latinos, and whites (with Asians most often assimilated to whites and Middle Easterners given a choice of voluntary affiliation).

In Sykes's (1958) classic account, the 'argot roles' that compose the social structure and cultural fabric of the prison are all *specific to the carceral cosmos*: 'rats' and 'center men' are defined as such because they betray the core value of solidarity among inmates by violating the ban on communication with custodians; 'merchants' peddle goods in the illicit economy of the establishment while 'gorillas' prey on weak inmates to acquire cigarettes, food, clothing, and deference; similarly, 'wolfs', 'punks' and 'fags' are descriptors of sexual scripts adopted behind bars. Finally 'ball busters' and 'real men' are categories defined by the type of intercourse they maintain with guards: defiant and hopeless, the former give 'screws' a hard time while the latter 'pull their own time' without displaying either subservience or aggression. In John Irwin's (1990) portrait of the social organization of convicts in California prisons in the 1960s, the inmate subculture is not a response to prison deprivation but an import from the street. Yet it is the criminal identities of 'thief', 'convict' and 'square' that nonetheless predominate behind bars. In today's warehouse prison, by contrast, racial affiliation has become the 'master status trait' (Hughes, 1945) that submerges all other markers and governs all relations and spaces, from the cells and the hallways to the dining hall, the commissary and the yard.[23]

To be sure, American prisons, both North and South, have always been strictly segregated along ethnoracial lines. But these lines used to *crosscut and stabilize* penitentiary demarcations as the social worlds of black and white inmates ran parallel to each other in 'separate but equal' fashion, so to speak (Jacobs, 1983: 75–6). In the aftermath of the black mobilization of the 1960s and the rapid 'darkening' of the imprisoned population, racial cleavages have grown to *undercut and supplant* carceral ones. And the perennial pattern of separation and avoidance that characterized race relations in the postwar years has been amplified by open hostility and aggression, particularly through the agency of gangs.

2. The 'code of the street' overwhelms the 'convict code'

Along with racial division, the predatory culture of the street, centered on hypermasculinist notions of honor, toughness, and coolness has entered into and transfigured the social structure and culture of jails and prisons. The 'convict code', rooted in solidarity among inmates and antagonism towards guards (Sykes and Messinger, 1960), has in effect been swamped by the 'code of the street' (Anderson, 1998), with its ardent imperative of individual 'respect' secured through the militant display and actualization of readiness to mete out physical violence. Accordingly, 'the old 'hero' of the prison world – the 'right guy' – has been replaced by outlaws and gang members. These two types have raised toughness and mercilessness to the top of prisoners' value systems' (Irwin, 1990: vii). Ethnically-based street gangs and 'supergangs', such as the Disciplines, El Rukn, Vice Lords, and Latin Kings in Illinois, the Mexican Mafia, Black Guerrilla Family, and Aryan Brotherhood in California, and the Netas in New York City, have taken over the illicit economy of the prison and destabilized the entire social system of inmates, forcing the latter to shift from 'doing your own time' to 'doing gang time'. They have even precipitated a thorough restructuring of the administration of large-scale prison systems, from Illinois to California to Texas (Jacobs, 1977: 137–74; Irwin, 1980: 186–92; Martin and Ekland-Olson, 1987).

Together with the compositional changes of the prison's clientele, the rising tide of drugs circulating *sub rosa*, and the consolidation of racially-based gangs, the eclipse of the old inmate structure of power has resulted in increased levels of interpersonal and group brutality.[24] So that 'what was once a repressive but comparatively safe 'Big House' is now often an unstable and violent social jungle' (Johnson, 1996: 133) in which social intercourse is infected with the same disruption, aggression, and unpredictability as in the hyperghetto. Today's prisoners 'complain about the increased fragmentation and disorganization that they now experience. Life in prison is no longer organized but instead is viewed as capricious and dangerous' (Hunt et al., 1993: 407). Those who return behind bars after spending extended periods outside invariably find that they do not recognize 'the joint' and that they can no longer get along with their fellow inmates due to the prevailing anomie.[25] When my best friend and informant from Chicago's South Side, Ashante, was sent to serve a six-year sentence in a low-security facility in downstate Illinois after having 'stayed clean' on the outside for a decade following a stint of eight years at Stateville penitentiary, he promptly requested a transfer to a maximum-security prison: he was dismayed by the arrogance and unruliness of 'young punks' from the streets of Chicago who ignored the old convict code, disrespected inmates with extensive prison seniority, and sought confrontation at every turn. Ashante knew well that, by moving to Stateville or Pontiac, he would endure a much more restrictive regimen in a more dreary physical setting with access to fewer programs, but he believed that a more predictible environment ruled by the norms of the 'inmate society' of old made for a less risky sojourn.[26] The increased entropy and commotion that characterizes prison life today explains that 'it is not uncommon to find ten percent of the population of large prison in protective custody' (Morris, 1995: 248). It accounts also for the proliferation of 'supermax' penitentiaries across the country as authorities strive to restore order by relegating 'the worst of the worst', inmates in special facilities where they are kept in near-total lockdown under detention regimes so austere that they are indistinguishable from torture in the light of international human rights covenants (King, 1999).

3. Purging the undesirables

The 'Big House' of the postwar decades was animated by a consequentialist theory of punishment that sought to resocialize inmates so as to lower the probability of re-offense once they returned society, of which they were expected to become law-abiding if not productive members. Following the official repudiation of the philosophy of rehabilitation in the 1970s (Allen, 1981), today's prison has for sole purpose to *neutralize* offenders – and individuals thought to be likely to violate the law, such as parolees – both *materially*, by removing them physically into an institutional enclave, and *symbolically*, by drawing a hard and fast line between criminals and law-abiding citizens. The 'law-and-order' paradigm that has achieved undivided hegemony in crime and justice policy over the past two decades jettisons any notion of prevention and proportionality in favor of direct appeals to popular resentment through measures that dramatize the fear and loathing of crime viewed as the abhorrent conduct of defective individuals.[27] 'Such appeals to resentment', writes Hirsch (1999: 676), 'reflect an ideology of purging "undesirables" from the body politic' in which incarceration is essentially a means for social and moral excommunication. That makes the mission of today's prison identical to that of the classical ghetto, whose *raison d'être* was precisely to quarantine a polluting group from the urban body.

When the prison is used as an implement for social and cultural purging, like the ghetto, it no longer points beyond itself; it turns into a self-contained contraption which fulfils its function, and thus justifies itself, by its mere existence. And its inhabitants learn to live in the here-and-now, bathed in the concentrate of violence and hopelessness brewing within the walls. In his autobiographical description of the changing social structure and culture of a maximum-security facility in Pennsylvania over the past sixteen years, inmate Victor Hassine (1999: 41) captures well the devolution of the Big House, pointing to eventual reentry into society, into a Warehouse leading nowhere but to a wall of despair:

> Through this gradual process of deterioration, Graterford the prison became Graterford the ghetto, a place where men forgot about courts of law or the difference between right and wrong because they were too busy thinking about living, dying, or worse. Reform, rehabilitation, and redemption do not exist in a ghetto. There is only survival of the fittest. Crime, punishment, and accountability are of little significance when men are living in a lawless society where their actions are restrained only by the presence of concrete and steel walls. Where a prison in any real or abstract sense might promote the greater good, once it becomes a ghetto it can do nothing but promise violent upheaval.

4. The proto-racialization of judicial stigma

The contemporary prison can be further likened to the ghetto in that, in the revanchist penal climate of the past two decades, the stigma of penal conviction has been prolonged, diffused, and reframed in ways that assimilate it to an ethnoracial stigma attached *ad aeternitum* to the body of its bearer. In other liberal-democratic societies, the status dishonor and civic disabilities of being a prisoner are temporary and limited: they affect offenders while they are being processed by the criminal justice system and typically wear off upon coming out of prison or shortly thereafter; to ensure this, laws and administrative rules set strict conditions and limits to the use and diffusion of criminal justice information. Not so in the United States, where, on the contrary, (1) convicts are subjected to ever-longer and broader post-detention forms of social control and symbolic branding that durably set them apart from the rest of the population; (2) the criminal files of individual inmates are readily accessible and actively disseminated by the authorities; (3) a naturalizing discourse suffused with genetic phraseology and animalistic imagery has swamped public representations of crime in the media, politics, and significant segments of scholarship.

All but two states require *postprison supervision* of offenders and 80 percent of all persons released from state penitentiaries are freed under conditional or community release; the average term spent on parole has also increased steadily over the past two decades to surpass 23 months in 1996 – nearly equal to the average prison term served of 25 months (Petersilia, 1999). At the same time, parole services have become entirely focused on the administrative enforcement of safety and security, to the near-total neglect of job training, housing assistance, and substance abuse treatment, even though official records indicate that over three- fourths of inmates suffer from psychotropic dependency. With fully 54 percent of offenders failing to complete their term of parole in 1997 (compared to 27 percent in 1984), and parole violators making up a third of all persons admitted in state penitentiaries every year (two-thirds in California), parole has become an appendage of the prison which operates mainly to extend the social and symbolic incapacities of incarceration beyond its walls. With the advent of the Internet, corrections administrations in many states, among them

Illinois, Florida, and Texas, have put their entire inmate data bases on line, further stretching the perimeter of penal infamy by making it possible for anyone to delve into the 'rap sheet' of prisoners via the World Wide Web, and for employers and land-lords to discriminate more broadly against ex-convicts in complete legality (Wacquant, 1999a: 76–7).[28]

This general movement towards longer and more encompassing post-detention measures of criminal justice supervision finds an extreme instantiation in the manage-ment of sex offenders under the regime of 'Megan's Laws' voted in 1996 by federal and state governments in a mad rush to appease displaced popular ire over child abuse. These laws mandate that authorities not only keep a registry of all (ex-)sex offenders in their jurisdiction, for periods extending up to life, but also notify the public of their whereabouts via mailings, posters, media announcements and CD-Roms containing the files of ex-offenders coded by geographic area (Martin, 1996), thus making per-manent and highly visible the blemish attached to their conviction. In Louisiana, for instance, the (ex-)sex offender himself must notify in writing his landlord, neighbors, and the director of the local school and municipal parks of his penal status; he must also post warnings of his presence in a community newspaper within thirty days of his arrival. The law further authorizes 'all forms of public notification', including posters, handbills, and bumper stickers – a judge can even request that the offender wear 'a dis-tinctive garb' that will readily identify him as a sex offender (Cooper, 1998), in the manner of the yellow star or hat donned by Jews in the principalities of Medieval Europe and Hitler's Germany. Upon release of this information, former sex offenders have been routinely insulted, publicly humiliated, harassed and attacked; many have lost their jobs and been forced to relocate to escape the open hostility of their neigh-bors; a few have reacted by committing suicide. Reinforced by the systematic media (mis)representation of sex offenders as congenital perverts whose behavior cannot be prevented or corrected, Megan's Laws send the unmistakable message, 'once an offender, always an offender',[29] turning judicial stigma into negative symbolic capital that cannot be shed and will therefore weigh on its bearer for life, like the stain of 'race' construed as a dishonoring form of denegated ethnicity.

The resurgence and popularity of genetic pseudo-explanations of crime is another indicator of the bent towards the compulsive *racialization of criminals*, whose counter-part is the elective *ethnicization of crime victims*, who have recently been fabricated into a quasi-ethnic group (Best, 1997), complete with its distinctive idiom, insignia, pageantry, and official organizations that mobilize to demand 'affirmative action' from the state on behalf of their members. One illustration from among a myriad: the com-pendium on crime edited by James Q. Wilson and Joan Petersilia, in which 'twenty-eight leading experts look at the most pressing problem of our time' (according to the book's front cover blurb), opens with two long chapters that review 'Criminogenic Traits' and 'Biomedical Factors in Crime' (Herrnstein, 1995; Brennan et al., 1995). For Richard Herrnstein (1995: 40, 41, 62, 56–7, 58), a renowned Harvard psychologist and co-author, with ultraright-wing ideologue Charles Murray, of the infamous treatise in schol-arly racism, *The Bell Curve*, serious crimes are not culturally or historically defined but *male in se*, 'crimes that are wrong in themselves'. Now, 'it would be an overstatement to say "once a criminal always a criminal", but it would be closer to the truth [sic] than to deny the evidence of a unifying and long-enduring pattern of encounters with the law for most serious offenders'. This pattern cannot be explained by 'accidents, situations, and social forces', as these only 'modulate the criminogenic factors' of low intelligence, antisocial personality and male chromosomes.[30] The genetic roots of crime are further confirmed by the fact that offenders are 'disproportionately nonectomorphic meso-morphs' (chunky and muscular with large bones) and sport 'lower heart rates', 'lower nervous system responsiveness to sudden stimuli', and 'atypical patterns [of] brain waves'. Herrnstein regrets that research has turned up 'only weak association between male hormones and criminal behavior or antisociality' but he promptly consoles himself by asserting that the Y chromosome elevates criminal behavior in 'supermales' and 'increases the risk of criminal incarceration by a factor of about ten' – based on the fact that the proportion of XYY male prisoners is ten times that in the general population.[31] Interestingly enough, Herrnstein does not discuss ethnoracial differences in criminality and, in his conclusion, he even disingenuously disavows – on feigned epistemological grounds – any effort to 'frame questions about behavior in terms of causes' (although he has repeatedly turned correlation into causation in this very chapter). But it requires little effort to infer from his argumentation that, 'just as night follows day', the hyper-incarceration of blacks must be caused in part by their innate criminal propensity, given what he calls 'a scientific consensus that criminal and antisocial behavior can have genetic roots' (Herrnstein, 1995: 62, 58).[32]

5. Bifurcated socioracial patterning of carceral recruitment and authority

Today's prison further resembles the ghetto for the simple reason that an overwhelm-ing majority of its occupants originate from the racialized core of the country's major cities, and returns there upon release, only to be soon caught again in the police dragnet to be sent away for another, longer sojourn behind bars in a self-perpetuating cycle of escalating socioeconomic marginality and legal incapacitation. To take but one example, in the late 1980s, three of every four inmates serving a sentence in the prisons of the entire state of New York came from only *seven* black and Latino neighborhoods of New York City, which also happen to be the poorest areas of the metropolis, chief among them Harlem, the South Bronx, East New York, and Brownsville (Ellis, 1993). Every year these segregated and dispossessed districts furnished a fresh contingent of 25,000-odd inmates while 23,000 ex-convicts were discharged, most of them on parole, right back in these devastated areas. A conservative estimate, given a statewide felony recidivism rate of 47 percent, is that within a year, some 15,000 of them found their way back 'upstate' and under lock.[33] The fact that 46 percent of the inmates of New York state prisons issue from neighborhoods served by the 16 worst public schools of the city (Davidson, 1997: 38) ensures that their clientele will be duly replenished for years to come.

The contemporary prison system and the ghetto not only display a similarly skewed recruitment and composition in terms of class and caste. The former also duplicates the authority structure characteristic of the latter in that it places a population of poor blacks under the direct supervision of whites – albeit, in this case, lower-class whites. In the communal ghetto of the postwar, black residents chaffed under the rule of white land-lords, white employers, white unions, white social workers and white policemen (Clark, 1965). Likewise, at century's end, the convicts of New York City, Philadelphia, Balti-more, Cleveland, Detroit and Chicago, who are overwhelming African-American, serve their sentence in establishments staffed by officers who are overwhelmingly white (see Figure 1). In Illinois, for instance, two-thirds of the state's 41,000 inmates are blacks who live under the watch of a 8,400 uniformed force that is 84 percent white. With the proliferation of detention facilities in rural areas, perversely, the economic stability and social welfare of lower-class whites from the declining hinterland has come to hinge on the continued socioeconomic marginality and penal restraint of ever-larger numbers of subproletarian blacks from the urban core.

The convergent changes that have 'prisonized' the ghetto and 'ghettoized' the prison in the aftermath of the Civil Rights revolution suggest that the inordinate and mounting over-representation of blacks behind bars does not stem simply from the discriminatory targeting of specific penal policies such as the War on Drugs, as proposed by Tonry (1995), or from the sheer destabilizing effects of the increased penetration of ghetto neighborhoods by the penal state, as Miller argues (1997). Not that these two factors are not at work, for clearly they are deeply involved in the hyper-incarceration of African Americans. But they fail to capture the precise nature and the full magnitude of the transformations that have interlocked the prison and the (hyper)ghetto via a relation of *functional equivalency* (they serve one and the same purpose, the coercive confinement of a stigmatized population) and *structural homology* (they comprise and comfort the same type of social relations and authority pattern) to form a *single institutional mesh* suited to fulfil anew the mission historically imparted to America's 'peculiar institutions'.

The thesis of the structural-functional coupling of the remnants of the ghetto with the carceral system is supported by *the timing of racial transition*: with a lag of about a dozen years, the 'blackening' of the carceral population has followed closely on the heels of the demise of the Black Belt as a viable instrument of caste containment in the

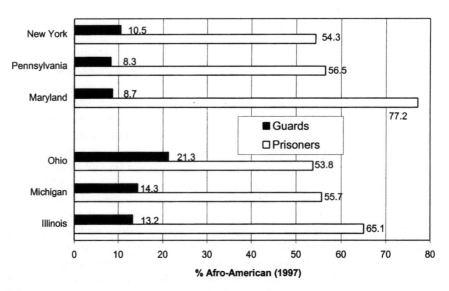

•Figure 1 Black prisoners guarded by white correctional officers
Source: Camp and Camp (1998: pp. 13 and 130)

urban-industrial settting, just as, a century earlier, the sudden penal repression of African Americans had helped to shore up 'the walls of white supremacy as the South moved from an era of racial bondage to one of racial caste' (Oshinsky, 1996: 57). It is also verified by the *geographic patterning* of racial disproportionality and its evolution: outside of the South – which for obvious historical reasons requires a separate analysis – the black-white gap in incarceration is more pronounced and has increased faster in those states of the Midwest and Northeast that are the historic cradle of the Northern ghetto (Mauer, 1997).

The intertwining of the urban Black Belt and the carceral system is further evidenced, and in turn powerfully abetted, by the *fusion of ghetto and prison culture*, as vividly expressed in the lyrics of 'gangsta rap' singers and hip hop artists (Cross, 1993), in graffitti and tattooing (Phillips, 1999: 152–67), and in the dissemination, to the urban core and beyond, of language, dress, and interaction patterns innovated inside of jails and penitentiaries. The advent of hyper-incarceration for lower-class blacks and Latinos has in effect rendered moot the classic dispute, among scholars of imprisonment, between the 'deprivation thesis,' canonized by Gresham Sykes, and the 'importation thesis,' proposed in response by John Irwin and Donald Cressey. This alternative has been transcended by the melting of street and carceral symbolism, with the resulting mix being *re-exported* to the ghetto and diffused throughout society via the commercial circuits catering to the teenage consumer market, professional sports, and even the mainstream media.[34] Witness the widespread adolescent fashion of baggy pants worn with the crotch down to mid-thigh and the resurgent popularity of body art featuring prison themes and icons – more often than not unbeknownst to those who wear them.

HOW PRISON IS REMAKING 'RACE' AND RESHAPING THE CITIZENRY

I indicated earlier that slavery, the Jim Crow system and the ghetto are 'race making' institutions, which is to say that they do not simply *process* an ethnoracial division that would somehow exist outside of and independently from them. Rather, each *produces* (or co-produces) this division (anew) out of inherited demarcations and disparities of group power and inscribes it at every epoch in a distinctive constellation of material and symbolic forms.[35] And all have consistently *racialized* the arbitrary boundary setting African Americans apart from all others in the United States by actively denying its cultural origin in history, ascribing it instead to the fictitious necessity of biology.

The highly particular conception of 'race' that America has invented, virtually unique in the world for its rigidity and consequentiality, is a direct outcome of the momentous collision between slavery and democracy as modes of organization of social life *after* bondage had been established as the major form of labor conscription and control in a underpopulated colony home to a precapitalist system of production (Fields, 1982). The Jim Crow regime reworked the racialized boundary between slave and free into a rigid caste separation between 'whites' and 'Negros' – comprising all persons of known African ancestry, no matter how minimal – that infected every crevice of the postbellum social system in the South (Powdermaker, 1939). The ghetto, in turn, imprinted this dichotomy onto the spatial makeup and institutional schemas of the industrial metropolis. So much so that, in the wake of the 'urban riots' of the 1960s, which in truth were uprisings against intersecting caste and class subordination, 'urban' and black became near-synonymous in policy making as well as everyday parlance. And the 'crisis' of the city came to stand for the enduring contradiction between the individualistic and competitive tenor of American life, on the one hand, and the continued seclusion of African Americans from it, on the other.[36]

As a new century dawns, it is up to the fourth 'peculiar institution' born of the adjoining of the hyperghetto with the carceral system to remould the social meaning and significance of 'race' in accordance with the dictates of the deregulated economy and the post-Keynesian state. Now, the penal apparatus has long served as an accessory to ethnoracial domination by helping to stabilize a regime under attack or bridge the hiatus between successive regimes: thus the 'Black Codes' of Reconstruction served to keep African-American labor in place following the demise of slavery while the criminalization of civil rights protests in the South in the 1950s aimed to retard the agony of Jim Crow. But the role of the carceral institution today is different in that, for the first time in US history, it has been elevated to the rank of main machine for 'race making'.

Among the manifold effects of the wedding of ghetto and prison into an extended carceral mesh, perhaps the most consequential is the practical revivification and *official solidification of the centuries-old association of blackness with criminality* and devious violence. Along with the return of Lombroso-style mythologies about criminal atavism and the wide diffusion of bestial metaphors in the journalistic and political field (where mentions of 'superpredators', 'wolf-packs', 'animals' and the like are commonplace), the massive over-incarceration of blacks has supplied a powerful common-sense warrant for 'using color as a proxy for dangerousness' (Kennedy, 1997: 136). In recent years, the courts have consistently authorized the police to employ race as 'a negative signal of increased risk of criminality' and legal scholars have rushed to endorse it as 'a rational adaptation to the demographics of crime', made salient and verified, as it were, by the blackening of the prison population, even though such practice entails major inconsistencies from the standpoint of constitutional law (Kennedy, 1997: 143, 146). Throughout the urban criminal justice system, the formula 'Young + Black + Male' is now openly equated with 'probable cause' justifying the arrest, questioning, bodily search and detention of millions of African-American males every year (Gaynes, 1993).

In the era of racially targetted 'law-and-order' policies and their socio-logical pendant, racially skewed mass imprisonment, the reigning public image of the criminal is not just that of 'a *monstruum* – a being whose features are inherently different from ours' (Melossi 2000: 311), but that of a *black* monster, as young African-American men from the 'inner city' have come to personify the explosive mix of moral degeneracy and mayhem.[37] The conflation of blackness and crime in collective representation and government policy (the other side of this equation being the conflation of blackness and welfare) thus reactivates 'race' by giving a legitimate outlet to the expression of anti-black animus in the form of the public vituperation of criminals and prisoners. As writer John Edgar Wideman (1995: 504) points out,

It's respectable to tar and feather criminals, to advocate locking them up and throwing away the key. It's not racist to be against crime, even though the archetypal criminal in the media and the public imagination almost always wears 'Willie' Horton's face. Gradually, 'urban' and 'ghetto' have become code words for terrible places where only blacks reside. Prison is rapidly being re-lexified in the same segregated fashion.

Indeed, when 'to be a man of color of a certain economic class and milieu is equivalent in the public eye to being a criminal', being processed by the penal system is tantamount to being made black, and 'doing time' behind bars is at the same time 'marking race' (Wideman, 1995: 505).[38]

A second major effect of the penalization of the 'race question' via the hypertrophic expansion of the prison system has been to thoroughly *depoliticize* it. For reframing the problems posed by the maintenance of ethnoracial division in the wake of the ghetto's demise as issues of law enforcement automatically delegitimates any attempt at collective resistance and redress. Established organizations of civic voice for African Americans cannot confront head on the crisis of hyperincarceration in their community for fear that this would seem to validate the very conflation of blackness and crime in public perception that fuels this crisis. Thus the courteous silence of the NAACP, the Urban League, the Black Congressional Caucus, and black churches on the topic, even as the penal tutelage of African Americans has escalated to heights experienced by no other group in history, even under the most repressive authoritarian regimes and in Soviet-style societies. This reticence is further reinforced by the fact, noted long ago by W.E.B. DuBois, that the tenuous position of the black bourgeoisie in the socioracial hierarchy rests critically on its ability to distance itself from its unruly lower-class brethen: to offset the symbolic disability of blackness, middle-class African Americans must forcefully communicate to whites that they have 'absolutely no sympathy and no known connections with any black man who has committed a crime' (DuBois cited in Christianson, 1998: 228).

Even riots, the last weapon of protest left to an urban subproletariat spurned by a political system thoroughly dominated by the white suburban electorate and corporations, have been rendered purposeless by mass penal confinement. It is commonly believed that 'race riots' in the United States crested in the 1960s and then vanished, save for anomalous outbursts such as in Miami in 1980 and Los Angeles in 1992. In reality, the ghetto uprisings of 1963–1968 have been succeeded by a rolling *wave of upheavals inside of prisons*, from Attica and Soledad to facilities throughout Michigan, Tennessee, Oklahoma, Illinois, West Virginia, and Pennsylvania, among others (Morris, 1995: 248–9; Useem and Kimball, 1989). But, by moving from the open stage of the streets to the closed perimeter of penitentiaries, these outbursts differed from their predecessors of the 1960s in three important ways. First, ghetto riots were highly visible and, through the media, interpellated the highest authorities in the land. Carceral riots, on the contrary, were never conspicuous to start with (unless they caused major destruction), and they have rapidly grown less and less perceptible to the point of virtually *disappearing* from the public scene.[39] Next, they have received *administrative* responses from within the correctional bureaucracy in lieu of political responses from without, and these responses have only compounded the problem: the approach of the state to inmate belligerence in the 1950s was to 'intensify the therapeutic thrust in prisons' (Rotman, 1995: 189); thirty years later, it is to intensify the drive to 'classify, separate, and isolate' (Irwin, 1980: 228), to toughen discipline, routinize the use of 'lockdown', and to multiply 'special housing units' and 'supermax' facilities. A third difference between the uproarious ghetto riots of decades past and the diffuse, muffled, carceral riots that have replaced them is that they typically pit, not blacks against whites, but *one subordinate ethnic group against another*, such as blacks versus Mexicans, thereby further diminishing the likelihood that they will receive a broad sociopolitical interpretation connecting them to the transformed ethnoracial order on the outside.[40] By entombing poor blacks in the concrete walls of the prison, then, the penal state has effectively smothered and silenced subproletarian revolt.

By assuming a central role in the post-Keynesian government of race and poverty, at the crossroads of the deregulated low-wage labor market, a revamped 'welfare-workfare' apparatus designed to support casual employment, and the vestiges of the ghetto, the overgrown carceral system of the United States has become a major engine of symbolic production in its own right.[41] It is not only the preeminent institution for signifying and enforcing blackness, much as slavery was during the first three centuries of US history. Just as bondage effected the 'social death' of imported African captives and their descendants on American soil (Patterson, 1982), *mass incarceration also induces the civic death* of those it ensnares by extruding them from the social compact. Today's inmates are thus the target of a threefold movement of exclusionary closure:

1. Prisoners are denied access to valued *cultural capital*: just as university credentials are becoming a prerequisite for employment in the (semi-)protected sector of the labor market, inmates have been expelled from higher education by being made ineligible for Pell Grants, starting with drug offenders in 1988, continuing with convicts sentenced to death or lifelong imprisonment without the possibility of parole in 1992, and ending with all remaining state and federal prisoners in 1994. This expulsion was voted by Congress for the sole purpose of accentuating the symbolic divide between criminals and 'law-abiding citizens' in spite of overwhelming evidence that prison educational programs drastically cut recidivism as well as help to maintain carceral order (Page, 2000).

2. Prisoners are systematically excluded from *social redistribution* and public aid in an age when work insecurity makes access to such programs more vital than ever for those dwelling in the lower regions of social space. Laws deny welfare payments, veterans benefits and food stamps to anyone in detention for more than 60 days. The Work Opportunity and Personal Responsibility Act of 1996 further banishes most ex-convicts from Medicaid, public housing, Section 8 vouchers, and related forms of assistance. In spring of 1998, President Clinton denounced as intolerable 'fraud and abuse' perpetrated against 'working families' who 'play by the rules' the fact that some prisoners (or their households) continued to get public payments due to lax bureaucratic enforcement of these prohibitions. And he proudly launched 'unprecedented federal, state, and local co-operation as well as new, innovative incentive programs' using the latest 'high-tech tools to weed out any inmate' who still received benefits (Clinton, 1998), including the disbursement of bounties to counties who promptly turn in identifying information on their jail detainees to the Social Security administration.

3. Convicts are banned from *political participation* via 'criminal disenfranchisement' practiced on a scale and with a vigor unimagined in any other country. All but four members of the Union deny the vote to mentally competent adults held in detention facilities; 39 states forbid convicts placed on probation from exercising their political

rights and 32 states also interdict parolees. In 14 states, ex-felons are barred from voting even when they are no longer under criminal justice supervision – *for life* in ten of these states. The result is that nearly 4 million Americans have temporarily or permanently lost the ability to cast a ballot, including 1.47 million who are not behind bars and another 1.39 million who served their sentence in full (Fellner and Mauer, 1998). A mere quarter of a century after acceding to full voting rights, one black man in seven nationwide is banned from the electoral booth through penal disenfranchisement and seven states permanently deny the vote to more than one fourth of their black male residents.

Through this *triple exclusion*, the prison, and the criminal justice system more broadly, contribute to the ongoing *reconstruction of the 'imagined community' of Americans* around the polar opposition between praiseworthy 'working families'- implicitly white, suburban, and deserving – and the despicable 'underclass' of criminals, loafers, and leeches, a two-headed antisocial hydra personified by the dissolute teenage 'welfare mother' on the female side and the dangerous street 'gang banger' on the male side – by definition dark-skinned, urban, and undeserving. The former are exalted as the living incarnation of genuine American values, self-control, deferred gratification, subservience of life to labor;[42] the latter is vituperated as the loathsome embodiment of their abject desecration, the 'dark side' of the 'American dream' of affluence and opportunity for all believed to flow from morality anchored in conjugality and work. And the line that divides them is increasingly being drawn, materially and symbolically, by the prison.

On the other side of that line lies an institutional setting unlike any other. Building on his celebrated analyses of Ancient Greece, classical historian Moses Finley (1968) has introduced a fruitful distinction between 'societies with slaves' and 'genuine slave societies'. In the former, slavery is but one of several modes of labor control and the division between slave and free is neither impermeable nor axial to the entire social order. In the latter, enslaved labor is epicentral to both economic production and class structure, and the slave-master relation provides the pattern after which all other social relations are built or distorted, such that no corner of culture, society and self is left untouched by it. The astronomical overrepresentation of blacks in houses of penal confinement and the increasingly tight meshing of the hyperghetto with the carceral system suggests that, owing to America's adoption of mass incarceration as a queer social policy designed to discipline the poor and contain the dishonored, lower-class African Americans now dwell, not in a society with prisons as their white compatriots do, but in *the first genuine prison society* of history.

Acknowledgements

A shorter version of this paper was presented at the Conference on Mass Imprisonment in the United States: Social Causes and Consequences, New York University Law School, 26 February 2000. It benefited from the comments, criticisms, and queries of fellow participants and audience members; the pointed encouragements of Jack Katz, Michael Tonry, James Jacobs, and Franklin Zimring were particularly stimulative. Special thanks are due to David Garland, first, for inviting a neophyte to participate in this fateful event and, second, for the extraordinary patience and persistence he mustered in awaiting the final text, which benefited from the editorial vigilance of Megan L. Comfort.

Notes

1 Because males compose over 93 percent of the US state and federal prison population and 89 percent of jail inmates, and because the disciplining of women from the lower class and caste continues to operate primarily through the agencies of the social arm of the American state (namely, welfare and workfare), this article focuses solely on men. But a full-fledged analysis of the distinct causes and consequences of the astonishing growth in the imprisonment of black (and Hispanic) women is urgently needed, among other reasons because the penal confinement of women has immensely deleterious effects on their children (Hagan and Dinovitzer, 1999).

2 It must be stressed, moreover, that this increase in 'racial disproportionality' is notably underestimated since the category 'whites' comprises a significant and growing number of Latinos, as the latter's share of the total inmate population increases over time (and the more so in states that have led the march to mass incarceration, such as Texas, California and Florida).

3 In this, I follow the exhortation of Georg Rusche (1933: 11) in a short but pointed article that sums up the intention of his and Kirchheimer's classic *Punishment and Social Structure*: 'The bond, transparent or not, that is supposed to exist between crime and punishment. . . must be broken. Punishment is neither a simple consequence of crime, nor the reverse side of crime, nor a mere means which is determined by the end to be achieved. Punishment must be understood as a social phenomenon freed from both its juristic concept and its social ends', that is, its official mission of crime control, so that it may be replaced in the complete system of strategies, including social policies, aimed at regulating the poor. But I do *not* follow Rusche in (1) postulating a *direct* link between brute economic forces and penal policy; (2) reducing economic forces to the sole state of the *labor market*, and still less the supply of labor; (3) limiting the control function of the prison to lower *classes*, as distinct from other subordinate categories (ethnic or national, for instance); and (4) omitting the ramifying *symbolic* effects that the penal system exercises by drawing, dramatizing, and enforcing group boundaries. Indeed, in the case of black Americans, the symbolic function of the carceral system is paramount. For a terse application of this approach to the penal containment of immigrants in the European Union today, see Wacquant (1999b).

4 Two features of America's *racial exceptionalism* must be noted briefly here: the United States is the only nation in the world to define as 'black' all persons with *any* recognized African *ancestry*, creating a rigid black/white division between two mutually exclusive communities; second, within the United States, the 'one-drop rule' and the principle of hypodescent (whereby the offspring of any mixed couple are automatically assigned to the inferior category, here blacks, irrespective of their phenotype, upbringing, and other social properties) are applied solely to African Americans, making them the only U.S. ethnic group that cannot merge into white society through intermarriage. This highly peculiar conception of 'blackness' arose in the American South to protect the institution of slavery and later served to solidify the Jim Crow system of segregation (Davis, 1992).

5 Thus also the central place of violence in the black American collective experience and imagination, from Nat Turner, Frederick Douglass and Martin Delany to Ralph

Ellison, Bayard Rustin and Malcolm X (Levine, 1977; Takaki, 1993; Broderick and Meier, 1965).

6 The 'inherent instability of the slave relation' has been demonstrated by Patterson (1982: 336) and that of unfree labor by Kolchin (1987: 359); the congenital incompatibility of caste separation and democracy is the fulcrum of Gunnar Myrdal's (1944) classic analysis of the 'American dilemma' of race (which, *pace* Myrdal, is *not* a value conflict amenable to moral resolution but a structural disjuncture between principles of social vision and vision, maintained or overturned by relations of power).

7 This historical schema should not be read as an ineluctable forward march towards ethnoracial equality. Each new phase of racial domination entailed retrogression as well as progress. And, while it is true that there has been a kind of 'civilizing' of racial domination (in Norbert Elias's sense of the term), it remains that each regime has to be evaluated in light of the institutional possibilities it harbors, not simply by contrast to its predecessor(s).

8 The interaction of slavery and race, and how each transformed the other across the three broad 'generations' of slaves during the 17th and 18th century, the 'charters generations', the 'plantation generations', and the 'revolutionary generations', is well depicted by Ira Berlin (1998).

9 This regime was supported and abetted by the federal government, which acted as a powerful engine for the national legitimation and diffusion of exclusionary racial practices and patterns in the half-century preceding the Civil Rights Act of 1964: every major federal institution, from the US civil service and public employment exchanges to public housing and the armed forces, engaged in the systematic discrimination and ostracization of blacks (King, 1995).

10 In Mississippi, 'the list of disqualifying offenses – which included arson, bigamy, fraud, and petty theft, but not murder, rape, or grand larceny – was tailored, in the opinion of the state supreme court, to bar blacks, a "patient, docile people . . . given rather to furtive offenses than to the robust crimes of the whites"' (McMillen, 1990: 43).

11 As an uprooted people, African Americans have always migrated in search of improved economic opportunities and a less oppressive racial climate. Before World War I, their peregrinations took them throughout the South as well as to the frontier states of the West, in a quest for land as fount of material security. The Great Migration redirected these population streams towards the urban North and amplified them by linking them to industrial wage employment. With the onset of mass imprisonment, lower-class blacks are being forcibly 'migrated' back to the declining rural areas where most state and federal prisons are located.

12 The New Deal helped this parallel city coalesce by (1) further stimulating outmigration from the South via agricultural programs that excluded black farmers and farm laborers; (2) extending public aid to jobless African Americans living in the Northern metropolis (half of Chicago's Negro families were on relief in 1940); and (3) building up its physical infrastructure through public works and the massing of social housing projects in the segregated urban core, while refusing to guarantee loans to blacks seeking residence in white neighborhoods. After the Second World War, federal housing, lending, and transportation policies conspired to keep blacks firmly hemmed in the ghetto.

13 The urbanization of blacks accelerated the 'melting' of mulattos and Negros into a single overarching African-American identity. It also supplied the impetus for the gestation and growth of the gamut of organizations that took up the struggle for racial equality on the national stage, from the gradualist Urban League and National Association for the Advancement of Colored People to the militant Brotherhood of Sleeping Car Porters to the secessionist Universal Negro Improvement Association of Marcus Garvey.

14 A fuller discussion of the homologies between ghetto and prison as institutions of forced confinement of dishonored categories is in Wacquant (2000: 382–5).

15 It is not so much that the black middle class *moved out* of the 'inner city,' as argued by Wilson (1987); rather, it has *grown* outside of the historic core of the ghetto after its heyday. For the black bourgeoisie was miniscule at the mid-century point, and as early as the 1930s it had already established outposts beyond the perimeter of Bronzeville, as Drake and Cayton (1945: 384) point out.

16 On Christmas night of 1988, I attended mass at a Baptist church near the Robert Taylor Homes, the single largest concentration of public housing in Chicago (and, for that matter, in the United States) with a population of some 15,000. Participation was so sparse (about sixty people) that members of the audience had to join the choir impromptu to allow it to wade through its piteous repertoire. The atmosphere upon leaving the cavernous building was one of disaffection and depression. A few months later, the ramshackle structure was boarded up and, by the following Christmas, it had been razed and its lot left vacant.

17 The *Chicago Defender*'s role a 'race paper' has been partially taken up by *The Call*, the official organ of the Nation of Islam, but the latter's circulation is but a fraction of its predecessor's and its impact incomparably smaller.

18 For detailed accounts of the gross and systematic dysfunctioning of these institutions and their impact on residents of Chicago's hyperghetto, see, respectively, Abraham (1992) on public health, Venkatesh (2000) on public housing, Ayers (1997) on the juvenile court, *Chicago Tribune* (1992) on public schools, and Conroy (2000) and Amnesty International (1999) on the police (including reports of more than a decade of rampant torture at Area 2 station on the South Side, involving mock executions, 'Palestinian hangings', electric shocks with cattle prods, burnings with radiators and asphyxiation with plastic bags, in addition to the usual pattern of brutality, unjustified shootings and cover-ups, and the detention and interrogation of children in custody).

19 See the account of Gerstel et al. (1996) on homeless shelters and the vivid description of Chicago's 'SRO Death Row' by Klinenberg (1999: 269–72). Parallels between prison culture and the management of the Armory, New York's biggest homeless shelter, are suggested by Dordick (1997: 126-49)

20 In 1992, the Division of School Safety of the New York City Board of Education had a budget of 73 million dollars, a fleet of ninety vehicles, and over 3,200 uniformed security officers, which made it the ninth largest police force in the country, just ahead of that of Miami. In 1968, this division did not exist. John Devine (1996: 80–2) notes that lower-tier principals now have as one of their major concerns the management of this 'paramilitary force [which] has taken on an independent existence with its own organization and procedures, language, rules, equipment, dresssing rooms, uniforms, vans, and lines of authority'.

21 One must be careful not to romantizice the carceral past: even in the heyday of rehabilitation (corresponding to the full maturation of the Fordist economy and Keynesian state), the prison did not much rehabilitate, owing to the abiding 'priority given to institutional order, discipline, and security' (Rotman, 1995: 295). But the ideal of treatment, the intervention of therapeutic professionals, and the deployment of rehabilitative routines did improve conditions of detention and reduce arbitrariness, cruelty, and lawlessness behind bars. What is more, extensive 'programming' helped achieve internal stability and instilled a forward-looking outlook among inmates.

22 Note the parallel with social research on the ghetto: the field studies of the sixties, focusing on ghetto *institutions* seen at ground level from the insider's point of view, disappeared by the 1970s to be replaced a decade later by survey-based research on the 'underclass', i.e., *population aggregates* constructed from afar and from above via the manipulation of quantitative indicators. Note also that the disappearance of the inmate society from social science partakes at a cognitive level of a distinctively US policy of 'invisibilization' of social problems and problem populations (the same technique is now being applied to welfare recipients). By contrast, ethnographic research on the prison is alive and productive in Europe, especially England and France.

23 The caste-like organization of the Warehouse extends to the management of relations with the outside. At the San Quentin prison near San Francisco, whenever a black (or Latino) inmate is assaulted inside the facility, all African-American (Latino) inmates from that housing unit are automatically barred from visitation and the women who are thus refused entry to see them learn to think of themselves in such categorical terms in their dealings with the prison (personal communication from Megan Comfort, based on ongoing field work in 'the Tube', the enclosed area where prison visitors wait for their visit).

24 'The activities of these violent groups who, in the pursuit of loot, sex, and revenge, will attack any outsider have *completely unraveled any remnants of the old codes of honor* and tip networks that formerly helped to maintain order. In a limited, closed space, such as a prison, threats or attacks like those posed by these groups cannot be ignored. Prisoners must be ready to protect themselves or get out of the way. Those who have chosen to continue to circulate in public, with few exceptions, have formed or joined a clique or gang for their own protection. Consequently, violence-oriented groups dominate many, if not most, large men's prisons' (Irwin, 1980: 192, emphasis added).

25 See, for instance, Hassine (1999: 41–2) first-hand account of the conflict between 'new inmates vs. old heads' in the ghettoized 'prison subcultures' marked by 'their disrespect for authority, drug addition, illiteracy, and welfare mentality', in short, 'all the evils of the decaying American inner city'.

26 The same reasoning applies in big-city jails, which have become so disrupted, violent, and punitive that many detainees hasten to plead guilty in order to be 'sent to state' right away: 'Better do a year in state [prison] than three months in this hell of a jail' is how several detainees at LA's Men's Central Jail put it to me in summer of 1998.

27 'Three Strikes and You're Out', which mandates the lifelong incarceration of

offenders at the edge of their criminal career in response to double recidivism, epitomizes this approach to 'vengeance as public policy' (Shichor and Sechrest, 1996) in its disregard for proportionality and penological efficacy, as well as in its unabashed use of a catchy baseball metaphor that likens crime fighting to a kind of sport.

28 Florida is at the vanguard of the trend to diffuse the criminal justice files of prisoners over the Internet 'in the interest of public safety.' The 'Corrections Offender Network' rubric of its prison administration allows one to run searches by name, race, sex, identifiers (Social Security, passport or alien number, driver's licence) and offense category. It provides not only the usual personal data (name and aliases, birth date, hair and eye color, height and weight, 'scars, marks, and tattoos' with their exact description and location) and criminal justice information (current offense date, offense type, sentence date, case number and prison sentence length, plus an abrievated incarceration history), but also a full-size color picture and the date of release as well as the current address for former inmates out on parole. This site received some 300,000 visits during its first year of operation.

29 As indicated by the disappearance of the term '*ex*-sex offender' in legal, political, and even scholarly discourse, which makes sex crimes the act of a particular *species* of individual, rather than a particular type of legally proscribed *conduct*.

30 'Inasmuch as criminal behavior is associated with [inferior] intelligence and [antisocial] personality, and inasmuch as personality and intelligence have genetic influences on them, then *it follows logically, as night follows day, that criminal behavior has genetic ingredients*' (Herrnstein, 1995: 55, emphasis added). The conceptual sleight-of-hand here lies both in the predicates (that intelligence and antisocial personality, inasmuch as they are themselves coherent variables, are genetically determined), in the vagueness of the terms 'influences' and 'ingredients', and in the locution 'inasmuch as' . . .

31 Not a single source is cited for this rather stunning statistic, despite superabundant notes and references throughout the chapter.

32 This is reaffirmed in the companion article by Brennan et al. (1995: 87–8), who sum up their findings thus: 'Criminal behavior in parents increases the likelihood of nonviolent crime in the offspring. This relationship is due, in part, to genetic transmission of criminogenic characteristics. This genetic effect is stronger for females and is especially important for recidivistic crime'. They also report that perinatal factors (delivery complications), frontal lobe dysfunction, and reduced cerebrospinal serotonin fluid levels are associated with violent crime while EEG slow alpha activity correlates with property crimes! For an up-to-date compendium of gene-based theories of crime and their resurgent popularity in mainstream US criminology, read Ellis and Walsh (1997).

33 It is revealing that these data should come from a survey of the geographic provenance of prisoners carried out by inmates themselves: they sensed at ground level what prison activist and scholar Eddie Ellis (1993: 2; also 1998) calls the 'relation of symbiosis' emerging between the ghetto and the carceral system, even as government officials and social scientists were oblivious or indifferent to it.

34 Hardly a week goes by without the *New York Times* featuring one or several articles reporting on some aspect of prison unrelated to crime control attesting to the seeping

out and normalization of carceral culture: e.g. 'Accessories for the Big House: Corrections Officers Survey the Options for Keeping Inmates in Line' (in the Sunday magazine); 'In Jailhouse Chic, an Anti-Style Turns into a Style Itself' (Fashion rubric); 'Rooms Available in Gated Community: $20 a Day' (Society's Journal); 'Using Internet Links from Behind Bars' (Society); 'A Hard-Case Study Approach to Executive Training' (seminars on communication techniques for executives held inside of Attica, in the Business Section); 'Confined in Prisons, Literature Breaks Out' (in Arts and Ideas) (14 May, 13 June, 10 July, 1, 23 and 26 August, 2000 respectively).

35 That 'race' as a social principle of vision and division (to invoke Pierre Bourdieu's notion) is *made* and therefore contested, as are all social entities, does not mean that it is *eo ipso* infinitely malleable, endowed with a 'fluency', 'inherent instability' and even 'volatility' that would allow it to be reconfigured anew at every historical turn (as argued by Berlin, 1998: 1–3). The welcome emphasis on contention, resistance and change that has been the hallmark of recent populist, 'bottom up' approaches to the historiography and sociology of ethnoracial domination should not blind us to the fact that the ductility and durability of 'race' is highly variable across epochs and societies, depending, precisely, on the nature and workings of the extant 'peculiar institutions' that produce and reproduce it in each particular setting.

36 Two indicators suffice to spotlight the enduring ostracization of African Americans in US society. They are the only group to be 'hypersegregated', with spatial isolation shifting from the macro-level of state and county to the micro-level of municipality and neighborhood so as to minimize contacts with whites throughout the century (Massey and Denton, 1993; Massey and Hajnal, 1995). They remain barred from exogamy to a degree unknown to any other community, notwithstanding the recent growth of so-called multiracial families, with fewer than 3 percent of black women marrying out compared to a majority of Hispanic and Asian women (DaCosta, 2000).

37 Thus the commercial success, based on prurient fascination, of the autobiographical account of the well-named Los Angeles gang member, Monster Kody (Shakur, 1993).

38 Teresa Gowan (2000) reports that white ex-convicts forced to settle in inner-city St. Louis to be close to parole agencies upon being released from Missouri prisons complain that the criminal justice system is 'turning them into blacks'.

39 So much so that they escape even the attention of prison scholars: two days before the conference at which this paper was presented, a race riot pitting some 200 black and Latino inmates broke out at California's high-tech Pelican Bay prison (a maximum-security facility reputed as 'the nation's most-secure' and notorious for being a 'war zone' between African Americans and whites), during which guards killed one prisoner and seriously wounded twelve others. It took 120 correctional officers a full half-hour to quell the frenzied mêlée, despite the use of tear gas, pepper spray, rubber and wooden bullets and two dozen rounds from Ruger Mini-14 rifles. The next day, authorities placed all 33 prisons in the state on security alert ('Guards Kill Prisoner in Brawl at Pelican Bay', *San Francisco Chronicle*, 24 February 2000; 'Inmate Dies and 12 Are Hurt as Riot Erupts in California Prison', *New York Times*, 24 February 2000; 'State Puts all Prisons on Security Alert: Authorities are on Lookout for Signs of Racial Tension after Riot Ended in Shooting Death of an Inmate at Pelican Bay', *Los Angeles Times*, 25 February 2000). None of the

participants to the conference mentioned this disturbance, the single most violent in California prisons in two decades, during the two days of discussions.

40 This is not to say, of course, that all prison upheavals are caused by racial conflict. The typical carceral riot involves a range and mix of grievances, from inadequate food and medical care to arbitrary and repressive management to idleness and lack of rehabilitative programs. But racial divisions and tensions are always a propitious backdrop, if not a major causal factor, of violent incidents, real or perceived, inside of U.S. detention houses (in summer of 1998, the word among detainees of the Los Angeles County Jail was that some facilities had to be avoided at all costs because they witnessed 'a race riot every day').

41 The argument that follows is influenced by Garland's (1991: 219) neo-Durkheimian explication of 'penality as a set of signifying practices' that 'help produce subjectivities, forms of authority and social relations' at large.

42 As when Albert Gore, Jr., declared in his prime-time speech at the Democratic Convention on 20 August of 2000: 'In the name of all the working families who are the strength and soul of America, I accept your nomination for President of the United States', indicating that non-working families and detached individuals, being unfit to be included in the act of political delegation, are not and need not be concerned by the election. The Vice-President uttered the locution 'working families' a record nine times in only 52 minutes and every major speaker that night invoked it repeatedly.

References

Abraham, Laurie Kay (1993) *Mama might be better off dead: The failure of health care in urban America.* Chicago: The University of Chicago Press.

Allen, Francis A. (1981) *The decline of the rehabilitative ideal.* New Haven: Yale University Press.

Amnesty International (1999) *Summary of Amnesty International's concerns on police abuse in Chicago.* London: Amnesty International, AMR/51/168/99.

Anderson, Elijah (1998) *Code of the street: Decency, violence, and the moral life of the inner city.* New York: Knopf.

Ayers, William (1997) *A kind and just parent: The children of juvenile court.* Boston: Beacon Press.

Beck, Allan (2000) *Prison and jail inmates at midyear in 1999.* Washington, D.C.: Bureau of Justice Statistics.

Berlin, Ira (1998) *Many thousands gone : The first two centuries of slavery in North America.* Cambridge MA: Harvard University Press.

Best, Joel (1997) 'Victimization and the victim industry'. *Society* 34(4): 9–17.

Blumstein, Alfred (1993) 'Racial disproportionality of US prison revisited'. *University of Colorado Law Review* 64: 743–60.

Brennan, Patricia, Sarnoff A. Mednick and Jan Volacka (1995) 'Biomedical factors in crime'. In James Q. Wilson and Joan Petersilia (eds), *Crime.* San Francisco: ICS Press, pp. 65–90.

Broderick, Francis L. and August Meier (1965) *Negro protest thought in the twentieth century.* Indianapolis: Bobbs-Merrill.

Camp, C. and G. M. Camp (eds) (1998) *The Corrections Yearbook 1998.* Middletown: Criminal Justice Institute.

Carroll, Leo (1974) *Hacks, Blacks, and cons*. Lexington: D.C. Heath & Co.

Carroll, Leo (1982) 'Race, ethnicity, and the social order of the prison.' In Robert Johnson and HansToch (eds), *The pains of imprisonment*. Beverly Hills: Sage, pp. 181–201.

Clark, Kenneth C. (1965) *Dark ghetto: Dilemmas of social power*. Amherst: University of Massachussetts Press.

Clinton, William Jefferson (1998) 'Saturday radio address'. 25 April 1998 (available on the White House web site).

Chicago Tribune (Staff of the) (1992) *The worst schools in America*. Chicago: Contemporary Press.

Christianson, Scott (1998) *With liberty for some: Five hundred years of imprisonment in America*. Boston: Northeastern University Press.

Conroy, John (2000) *Unspeakable acts, ordinary people: The dynamics of torture*. New York: Knopf.

Cooper, Scott A. (1998) 'Community notification and verification practices in three states' in *National Conference on Sex Offender Registrie*s. pp. 103–6. Washington: Bureau of Justice Statistics.

Cross, Brian (1993) *It's not about a salary: Rap, race, and resistance in Los Angeles*. New York: Verso.

DaCosta, Kim (2000) 'Remaking the color line: Social bases and implications of the multiracial movement'. Ph.D Dissertation Department of Sociology, University of California, Berkeley.

Davidson, Joe (1997) 'Caged cargo: Cashing in on black prisoners'. *Emerge* 23 October: 36–46.

Davis, Angela Y. (1998) 'Globalism and the prison industrial complex: An interview with Angela Davis'. *Race and Class* 40(2/3): 145–57.

Davis, F. James. (1992) *Who is Black? One's nation definition*. University Park: Penn State Press.

Devine, John (1996) *Maximum security: the culture of violence in inner-city schools* Chicago: The University of Chicago Press.

DiIulio, John J. (1991) 'Understanding prisons: The new old penology'. *Law & Social Inquiry* 16(1): 65–99.

Dollard, John (1937) *Caste and class in a southern town*. New York: Doubleday Anchor, reprint 1957.

Donziger, Steven (1996) *The real war on crime*. New York: Basic Books.

Dordick, Gwendolyn (1997) *Something left to lose: Personal relations and survival among New York's homeless*. Philadelphia: Temple University Press.

Drake, St. Clair and Horace Cayton (1945) *Black metropolis: A study of Negro life in a northern city*. New York: Harper and Row, 1962.

Ellis, Edwin (1993) *The non-traditional approach to criminal justice and social justice*. Harlem: Community Justice Center, mimeographed, 8 pages.

Ellis, Edwin (1998) 'An interview with Eddie Ellis'. *Humanity and Society* 22(1): 98–111.

Ellis, Lee and Anthony Walsh (1997) 'Gene-based evolutionary theories in criminology'. *Criminology* 35(2): 229–76.

Esping-Andersen, Gösta (1987) *The three worlds of welfare capitalism*. Princeton: Princeton University Press.

Fellner, Jamie and Marc Mauer (1998) *Losing the vote: The impact of felony disenfranchisement in the United States*. Washington DC: The Sentencing Project and Human Rights Watch.

Fields, Barbara Jean (1982) 'Race and Ideology in American History'. In J. Morgan Kousser and James M. McPherson (eds), *Region, race, and reconstruction: Essays in the honor of C. Vann Woodward*. New York: Oxford University Press, pp. 143–77.

Finley, Moses (1968) 'Slavery'. *International encyclopedia of the social sciences*. New York: Free Press.

Fligstein, Neil (1981) *Going north: Migration of blacks and whites from the South, 1900–1950*. New York: Academic Press.

Frazier, E. Franklin (1932) *The negro family in Chicago*. Chicago: The University of Chicago Press.

Fusfeld, Daniel R. and Timothy Bates (1984) *The political economy of the ghetto*. Carbondale: Southern Illinois University Press.

Garland, David (1991) 'Punishment and Culture: The Symbolic Dimension of Criminal Justice'. *Studies in Law, Politics, and Society* 11: 1911–22.

Gerstel, Naomi, Cynthia J. Bogard, Jeff McConnell, and Michael Schwartz (1996) 'The therapeutic incarceration of homeless'. *The Social Service Review* 70(4): 543–72.

Gilens, Martin (1999) *Why Americans Hate Welfare: Race, Media, and the Politics of Anti-Poverty Policy*. Chicago: The University of Chicago Press.

Gowan, Teresa (2000) 'Excavating Globalization from Street Level: Homeless Men Recycle their Pasts'. In Michael Burawoy et al., *Global ethnography*. Berkeley: University of California Press.

Greenberg, David and Valerie West (1999) 'Growth of state prison populations, 1971–1991'. Paper presented at the Annual Meetings of the Law and Society Association, Chicago, May.

Grossman, James R. (1989) *Land of hope: Chicago, black southerners, and the great migration*. Chicago: The University of Chicago Press.

Hagan, John and Ronit Dinowitzer (1999) 'Collateral consequences of imprisonment for children, communities, and prisoners'. In Michael Tonry and Joan Petersilia (eds), *Prisons*. Chicago: The University of Chicago Press, pp 121–62.

Handler, Joel (1997) *Down with bureaucracy*. Princeton: Princeton University Press.

Harlow, Caroline Wolf (1998) *Profile of jail inmates 1996*. Washington: Bureau of Justice Statistics.

Hassine, Victor. (1999) *Life without parole: Living in prison today*. Boston: Roxbury Publications, 2nd ed.

Herrnstein, R.J. (1995) 'Criminogenic traits'. In James Q. Wilson and Joan Petersilia (eds) *Crime*. San Francisco: ICS Press, pp. 39–64.

Hirsch, Andrew von. (1998) 'Penal theories'. In Michael Tonry (ed.), *The handbook of crime and punishment*. Oxford: Oxford University Press, pp. 659–83.

Hughes, Everett C. (1945 [1984]) 'Dilemmas and Contradictions of Status'. Reprinted in *The sociological eye*. New Brunswick: Transaction, pp. 141–52.

Hunt, Geoffrey, Stephanie Riegel, Tomas Morales, and Dan Waldorf (1993) 'Changes in prison culture: Prison gangs and the case of the "Pepsi Generation"'. *Social Problems* 40(3): 398–409.

Irwin, John (1980) *Prisons in turmoil*. Boston: Little, Brown.

Irwin, John (1970 [1990]). *The felon*. Berkeley: University of California Press, new edition.

Jacobs, James B. (1977) *Stateville: The penitentiary in mass society*. Chicago: The University of Chicago Press.

Jacobs, James B. (1983) 'Race relations and the prisoner subculture'. In *New perspectives on prisons and imprisonment*. Ithaca: Cornell University Press, pp. 61–79.

Johnson, Robert (1996) *Hard Time: Understanding and reforming the prison*. 2nd ed. Belmont: Wadsworth Publishing.

Jones, LeAlan and Lloyd Newman (1997) *Our America: Life and death on the South Side of Chicago*. New York: Washington Square Press.

Katznelson, Ira (1976) *Black men, white cities: Race, politics and migration in the United States, 1900–1930, and Britain, 1948–68*. Chicago: The University of University Press.

Kennedy, Randall (1997) 'Race, law, and suspicion: Using color as a proxy for dangerousness'. In *Race, crime and the law*. New York, Pantheon, pp. 136–67.

King, Desmond (1995) *Separate and unequal: Black Americans and the U.S. Federal Government*. Oxford: Oxford University Press.

King, Roy D. (1999) 'The rise and rise of Supermax: An American solution in search of a problem?'. *Punishment & Society* 1(2): 163–86.

Klinenberg, Eric (1999) 'Denaturalizing disaster: A social autopsy of the 1995 Chicago heat wave'. *Theory and Society* 28(2): 239–95.

Kolchin, Peter (1987) *Unfree labor: American slavery and Russian serfdom*. Cambridge: The Belknap Press of Harvard University Press.

Kotlowitz, Alex (1991) *There are no children here*. New York: Anchor Books.

Krivo, Lauren J. and Ruth D. Peterson (1996) 'Extremely disadvantaged neighborhoods and urban crime'. *Social Forces* 75(2): 619–650.

Lafree, Gary, K. Drass and P. O'Day (1992) 'Race and crime in post-war America: determinants of African American and white rates, 1957–1988'. *Criminology* 30: 157–88.

Lessan, Gloria T. (1991) 'Macro-economic determinants of penal policy: Estimating the unemployment and inflation influences on imprisonment rate changes in the united states, 1948–1985'. *Crime, Law and Social Change* 16(2): 177–98.

Levine, Lawrence (1977) *Black culture and black consciousness*. Oxford: Oxford University Press.

Lieberman, Stanley (1998) *Shifting the color line: Race and the American welfare state*. Cambridge: Harvard University Press.

Light, Ivan (1977) 'Numbers gambling among blacks: A financial institution'. *American Sociological Review*, 42(6): 892–904.

Marks, Carole (1989) *Farewell, we're good and gone: The Great Black Migration*. Bloomington: Indiana University Press.

Martin, Robert J. (1996) 'Pursuing public protection through mandatory community notification of convicted sex offenders: The trials and tribulations of Megan's Law'. *The Boston Public Interest Law Journal* 26: 26–56.

Martin, Steve J. and Sheldon Ekland-Olson (1987) *Texas prisons: The walls came tumbling down*. Austin: Texas Monthly Press.

Massey, Douglas, and Nancy Denton (1993) *American apartheid: Segregation and the making of the underclass*. Cambridge: Harvard University Press.

Massey, Douglas and Zoltan L. Hajnal (1995) 'The changing geographic structure of black-white segregation in the United States'. *Social Science Quarterly* 76(3): 527–42.

Mauer, Marc (1997) 'Racial disparities in prison getting worse in the 1990s'. *Overcrowded Times* 8(1): 8–13.

McMillen, Neil R. (1990) *Dark journey: Black Mississippians in the age of Jim Crow.* Urbana: University of Illinois Press.

Melossi Dario (2000) 'Changing representations of the criminal'. *British Journal of Criminology* 40(2): 296–320.

Miller, Jerome G. (1997) *Search and destroy: African-American males in the criminal justice system.* Cambridge: Cambridge University Press.

Morgan, Edmund S. (1975) *American slavery, American freedom: The ordeal of colonial Virginia.* New York: W.W. Norton.

Morris, Norval (1995) 'The contemporary Prison, 1965–present'. In Norval Morris and David Rothman (eds), *The Oxford history of the prison.* New York: Oxford University Press, pp. 226–59.

Myrdal, Gunnar (1944 [1962]) *An American dilemma: The Negro problem and modern democracy.* New York: Harper Torchbook.

Oshinsky, David M. (1996) *Worse than slavery: Parchman farm and the ordeal of Jim Crow justice.* New York: Free Press.

Page, Josh (2000). 'Eliminating the enemy: A cultural analysis of the exclusion of prisoners from higher education'. M.A. paper, Department of Sociology, University of California-Berkeley.

Patillo-McCoy, Mary (1999) *Black picket fences: Privilege and peril among the black middle class.* Chicago: The University of Chicago Press.

Patterson, Orlando (1982) *Slavery as social death.* Cambridge: Harvard University Press.

Pens, Dan (1998) 'Federal prisons erupt'. In Daniel Burton-Rose, Dan Pens and Paul Wright (eds), *The celling of America: An inside look at the U.S. prison industry.* Monroe, Maine: Common Courage Press, pp. 244–9.

Petersilia, Joan (1999) 'Parole and prisoner reentry in the United States'. In Michael Tonry and Joan Petersilia (eds), *Prisons.* Chicago: The University of Chicago Press, pp. 479–529.

Philipps, Susan A. (1999) *Wallbangin': Graffiti and Gangs in L.A.* Chicago: The University of Chicago Press.

Powdermaker, Hortense (1939 [1993]) *After freedom: A cultural study of the Deep South.* Madison: University of Wisconsin Press, new ed.

Rifkin, Jeff (1995) *The end of work: The decline of the global labor force and the dawn of the post-market era.* New York: Tarcher and Putnam.

Rotman, Edgardo (1995) 'The failure of reform: United States, 1865–1965'. In Norval Morris and David J. Rothman (eds), *The Oxford history of the prison.* New York: Oxford University Press, pp. 169–97.

Rusche, Georg. (1933 [1980]). 'Labor market and penal sanction: Thoughts on the sociology of punishment'. In T. Platt and P. Takagi (eds), *Punishment and penal discipline.* Berkeley: Crime and Justice Associates, pp. 10–17.

Sampson, Robert J. and Janet L. Lauritsen (1997) 'Racial and ethnic disparities in crime and criminal justice in the United States'. In Michael Tonry (ed.), *Ethnicity, crime, and immigration: Comparative and cross-national perspectives.* Chicago: The University of Chicago Press, pp. 311–74.

Shakur, Sanyika (1993) *Monster: The autobiography of an L.A. gang member.* New York: The Atlantic Monthly Press.

Shichor, David and Dale K. Sechrest (eds) (1996) *Three strikes and you're out : Vengeance as public policy.* Thousand Oaks: Sage Publications.

Simon, Jonathan (2000) 'The "Society of Captives" in the era of hyper-incarceration'. *Theoretical Criminology* 4(3): 285–308.

Spear, Allan H. (1967) *Black Chicago: The making of a negro ghetto, 1890–1920.* Chicago: The University of Chicago Press.

Sugrue, Tom (1996) *The origins of the urban crisis: Race and inequality in postwar Detroit.* Princeton: Princeton University Press.

Sykes, Gresham (1958 [1974]) *The society of captives: A study in a maximum security prison.* Princeton: Princeton University Press.

Sykes, Gresham and Sheldon Messinger (1960) 'The inmate social system'. In Richard Cloward et al., *Theoretical studies in the social organization of the prison.* New York: Social Science Research Council, pp. 6–10.

Takaki, Ronald T. (1993) *Violence in the black imagination.* Oxford: Oxford University Press (expanded and revised edition).

Tolnay, Stewart E. and E.M. Beck (1992) '*Racial violence and black migration in the American south, 1910 to 1930'. American Sociological Review* 57(1): 103–116.

Tonry, Michael (1995) *Malign neglect: Race, class, and punishment in America.* New York: Oxford University Press.

Useem, Bert and Peter Kimball (1989) *States of siege: U.S. prison riots, 1971–1986.* New York: Oxford University Press.

Venkatesh, Suhdir (2000) *American project: The rise and fall of a modern ghetto.* Cambridge: Harvard University Press.

Wacquant, Loïc (1989) 'The Ghetto, the state, and the new capitalist economy'. *Dissent (Fall)*: 508–20.

Wacquant, Loïc (1998a) 'Negative social capital: State breakdown and social destitution in America's urban core'. *The Netherlands Journal of the Built Environment* 13-1: 25–40.

Wacquant, Loïc (1998b) 'Inside the zone: The social art of the hustler in the black American ghetto'. *Theory, Culture, and Society* 15(2): 1–36.

Wacquant, Loïc (1998c) ' "A Black City Within the White": Revisiting America's Dark Ghetto'. *Black Renaissance – Renaissance Noire* 2(1): 141–151.

Wacquant, Loïc (1999a) *Les Prisons de la misère.* Paris: Editions Raisons d'agir (English trans. forthcoming as *Prisons of Poverty*, Minneapolis, University of Minnesota Press, 2001).

Wacquant, Loïc (1999b) ' "Suitable enemies": Foreigners and immigrants in the prisons of Europe'. *Punishment & Society* 1(2): 215–23.

Wacquant, Loïc (2000) 'The new "peculiar institution": On the prison as surrogate ghetto'. *Theoretical Criminology* 4(3), Special issue on 'New Social Studies of the Prison': 377–89.

Williamson, Joel (1986) *A rage for order: Black-white relations in the American south since Emancipation.* New York: Oxford University Press.

Wilson, William Julius (1980) *The declining significance of race*. Chicago: The University of Chicago Press, 2nd edition.

Wilson, William Julius (1987) *The truly disadvantaged: The inner city, the underclass and public policy*. Chicago: The University of Chicago Press

Woodward, C. Vann (1971) *American counterpoint: Slavery and racism in the North-South dialogue*. Boston: Little, Brown.

Wideman, John Edgar (1995) 'Doing time, marking race.' *The Nation* 261 (30 October): 503–505.

Yates, Jeff (1997) 'Racial incarceration disparity among states.' *Social Science Quarterly* 78–4 (December): 1001–10.

8   Going straight

The story of a young inner-city ex-convict[1]

ELIJAH ANDERSON

Of all the problems besetting the poor inner-city black community, none is more pressing than that of interpersonal violence and aggression. It wreaks havoc daily with the lives of community residents and increasingly spills over into downtown and residential middle-class areas. Muggings, burglaries, carjackings, and drug-related shootings, all of which may leave their victims or innocent bystanders dead, as well as drug-related shootings are now common enough to concern all urban and many suburban residents. The inclination to violence springs from the circumstances of life among the ghetto poor – the lack of jobs that pay a living wage, the stigma of race, the fallout from rampant drug use and drug trafficking, and the resulting alienation and lack of hope for the future.

Simply living in such an environment places young people at special risk of falling victim to aggressive behavior. Although there are often forces in the community which can counteract the negative influences, by far most powerful being a strong, loving, 'decent' (as inner-city residents put it) family committed to conventional social values, the despair is pervasive enough to have spawned an oppositional culture, that of 'the streets,' whose norms are often consciously opposed to those of mainstream society. These two orientations – decent and street – socially organize the community, and their coexistence has important consequences for residents, particularly children growing up in the inner city. Above all, this environment means that even youngsters whose home lives reflect mainstream values – and the majority of homes in the community do – must be able to handle themselves in a street-oriented environment.

This is because the street culture has evolved what may be called a code of the streets, which amounts to a set of informal rules governing interpersonal public behavior, including violence. The rules prescribe both a proper comportment and the proper way to respond if challenged. They regulate the use of violence and so supply a rationale which allows those who are inclined to aggression to precipitate violent encounters in an approved way. The rules have been established and are enforced mainly by the street-oriented, but on the streets the distinction between street and decent is often irrelevant; everybody knows that if the rules are violated, there are penalties. Knowledge of the code is thus largely defensive; it is literally necessary for operating in public. Therefore, even though families with a decency orientation are usually opposed to the values of the code, they often reluctantly encourage their children's familiarity with it to enable them to negotiate the inner-city environment.

At the heart of the code is the issue of respect – loosely defined as being treated 'right' or granted the deference one deserves. However, in the troublesome public environment of the inner city, as people increasingly feel buffeted by forces beyond their control, what one deserves in the way of respect becomes more and more problematic and uncertain. This in turn further opens the issue of respect to sometimes intense interpersonal negotiation. In the street culture, especially among young people, respect is viewed as almost an external entity that is hard-won but easily lost, and so must constantly be guarded. The rules of the code in fact provide a framework for negotiating respect. The person whose very appearance – including his clothing, demeanor, and way of moving – deters transgressions feels that he possesses, and may be considered by others to possess, a measure of respect. With the right amount, for instance, he can avoid 'being bothered' in public. If he is bothered, not only may he be in physical danger but he has been disgraced or 'dissed' (disrespected). Many of the forms that dissing can take might seem petty to middle-class people (maintaining eye contact for too long, for example), but to those invested in the street code, these actions become serious indications of the other person's intentions. Consequently, such people become very sensitive to advances and slights, which could well serve as a warning of imminent physical confrontation.

This hard reality can be traced to the profound sense of alienation from mainstream society and its institutions felt by many poor inner-city black people, particularly the young. The code of the streets is actually a cultural adaptation to a profound lack of faith in the police and the judicial system. The justice system is often viewed as a hostile imposition rather than a social institution that serves the community – a perception that is reinforced by massively disproportionate imprisonment rates for young black men and drug sentencing laws that seem designed to create this racial disparity. And the police are most often seen as representing the dominant white society and not caring to protect inner-city residents. When called, they may not respond, which is one reason many residents feel they must be prepared to take extraordinary measures to defend themselves and their loved ones against those who are inclined to aggression. Lack of police accountability has in fact been incorporated into the status system: the person who is believed capable of 'taking care of himself' is accorded a certain deference, which translates into a sense of physical and psychological control. Thus the street code emerges where the influence of the police ends and personal responsibility for one's safety is felt to begin. Exacerbated by the proliferation of drugs and easy access to guns, this volatile situation results in the ability of the street-oriented minority (or those who effectively 'go for bad') to dominate the public spaces.

These are the circumstances in which so much urban violence occurs. What we have is an absence of civil society, a situation in which retributive violence – an eye for an eye and a tooth for a tooth – in the service of payback is common. The decent people are under pressure, and in altercations and disputes they often have to put their bodies on the line. They cannot rely on the civil authorities because civil law does not have much impact here, unless people are being incarcerated or going before the criminal justice system. It is in that vacuum that street justice emerges as a way to deal with civil infractions and violations of disrespect. Rob's story is a case in point. A young man who has been through so much in the inner-city black community, he has effectively been tried and tested by the code of the street.

Ten years ago, at age 17, Robert was arrested and sentenced for the aggravated assault of a rival drug dealer. Having been convicted as a juvenile, he has now served his time. When he returned to the old neighborhood from prison, many people who had known him before his conviction believed that he would settle some old scores and revive his old drug gang, that things would get hot in the 'hood. Some of his old friends approached him with gifts, welcoming him back into the fold. Among these offerings was a pistol, ostensibly for his protection, which Robert flatly refused. He had decided in prison that he did not want to go that route again. He simply wanted some space, to catch up on 'the haps' and to spend time with his girlfriend, Thomasina. He wished to find a way to earn money legitimately. Nevertheless, from the moment he set foot on his old turf, the people there expected to see some action.

When Robert was arrested, charged, and convicted, he had already developed a strong name on the street. Many considered him a big-time drug dealer, and he was one of the most feared people on the streets of the community. It was assumed that he would 'get' anyone who crossed him. This reputation allowed him to go about the neighborhood unmolested. To be sure, people sometimes tested him, but this only made Robert stronger, for he took great delight in meeting the tests people set for him. He was a man, and in this environment nothing was more important than his manhood. Nevertheless, when he was incarcerated, his status and identity underwent a fundamental change. On the street his status remained high, but in prison in rural Pennsylvania he encountered white prison guards who treated him very badly. They called him 'nigger' on an almost daily basis, planned Ku Klux Klan meetings in his presence, assigned him to 'shit' work, and in other ways rode and harassed him all the while, hoping he 'would strike out at one of them so they could extend [his] time.' Robert says, 'I was smart enough to avoid their traps, but many other black guys fell for it.'

For the most part, he maintains, prison was 'good for me. It made me think and reassess my life.' In prison he became aware of his inability to read and the deficiencies of his vocabulary and decided he had an opportunity to rectify these problems. He had his friends and relatives send him books. He read and studied the dictionary, the Koran, the Bible, and other works, all from cover to cover. By the time he was released, he had gained a new attitude. He could see that a 'game was being run' on the community. In prison most of the inmates were black or Hispanic, while most of the guards were white men from the surrounding rural areas. He felt that the guards and prison staff were being supported, if not subsidized, by 'people like me.' The streets in his neighborhood fueled the prison engine by providing young men who actively played their roles in a grand scheme. He knew he had to change himself and his community, and he committed himself to this end.

Since his release from prison Robert has shunned his previous materialism and become a somewhat ascetic individual – calmer, more thoughtful. Many of his former friends looked at him strangely, because they do not see the Ruck (his street name) they knew. He was always intelligent and motivated – this is what made him an upcoming leader in the drug trade – but now he was applying these traits not to living out the code of the street but to making the transition to a life of decency. This confused his old friends, because prison usually enhances one's prestige on the street, particularly in terms of code values like toughness, nerve, and willingness to retaliate for transgressions.

Yet Robert returned from prison to put his old street way of being behind him. Subsequently he joined with three other young men – David, Tyrone, and Marvin, all desiring to change – to do what they could to support one another in turning their lives around. The young men grew up together in the local neighborhood, where they had their share of fights and run-ins with the law. Each of them has his own history, but there are common threads. They have all survived grinding urban poverty. They have endured the gamut of problems – welfare, single-parent households, emotionally and physically abusive fathers – and, like Robert, gravitated initially to the street, which provided them with family of a sort. On the street and in the gangs, they experienced a certain cohesion, bravado, and coming of age. Obtaining a high level of street knowledge from all of this, they understood the code very well. Nevertheless, something was missing from their lives. Their awareness of this prompted them to raise searching questions about their futures – where they would be in five, 10, or 15 years. Would they be simply more casualties of the street? Could they really attain the 'good life'? What were the impediments to such a goal? Whenever they would get together, they would discuss such issues. Robert was usually the main catalyst for this kind of talk.

After a few months of sitting around on one another's stoops discussing and critiquing the system and their roles in it, they decided to begin to take some concrete steps toward change. In this regard they summoned the decency from within themselves. They worked to move away from the lives of petty criminal activity, including hustling and drug dealing. They wanted to see themselves one day as solid pillars in their community. But how could they get on the road to that end? They decided to approach a well-known community activist named Herman Wrice.

For many years Herman has been a very active old head in the impoverished inner-city community. The old head was once the epitome of decency in inner-city neighborhoods. Thanks to a vibrant manufacturing economy, he had relatively stable means. His acknowledged role in the community was to teach, support, encourage, and, in effect, socialize young men to meet their responsibilities regarding work, family life, the law, and common decency. Young boys and single men in their late teens or twenties had confidence in the old head's ability to impart practical advice. Very often he played surrogate father to those who needed his attention and moral support.

But as meaningful employment becomes increasingly scarce for young men of the neighborhood and the expansion of the drug culture offers opportunities for quick money, the old head is losing prestige and authority. Streetwise boys are concluding that his lessons about life and work ethic are no longer relevant, and a new role model is emerging. The embodiment of the street, this man is young, often a product of the street gang, and indifferent, at best, to the law and traditional values.

Traditional female role models, often paragons of decency, have also suffered decreased authority. Mature women, often grandmothers themselves, once effectively served the community as auxiliary parents who publicly augmented and supported the relationship between parent and child. These women would discipline children and act as role models for young women, exerting a certain degree of social control. As the neighborhoods grow ever more drug infested, ordinary young mothers and their children are among the most obvious casualties. The traditional female old head becomes stretched and overburdened; her role has become more complicated as she often steps in as a surrogate mother for her grandchildren or a stray neighborhood child.

These women universally lament the proliferation of drugs in the community, the 'crack whores' who walk the neighborhood, the sporadic violence that now and then claims innocent bystanders. The open-air drug sales, the many pregnant girls, the incivility, the crime, the many street kids, and the diminished number of upstanding (as the residents say) role models make it difficult for old and young alike to maintain a positive outlook, to envision themselves beyond the immediate situation. As neighborhood deterioration feeds on itself, decent law-abiding people become increasingly demoralized; many of those who are capable leave, while some succumb to the street.

Herman, who recently passed away, worked hard to close down crack houses and to frustrate drug dealers. Having lived in this community for so long, he was deeply invested in cleaning it up. He felt strongly that the drug trade and the lack of jobs are the bane of the community's existence. Herman was highly visible in the community and went the extra mile in fighting drug dealing, to such an extent that from time to time his life was threatened. But he had great courage, which is highly respected on the street, and strong motivation. In his crusade Herman organized decent people in the community, including old heads, grandmothers, grandfathers, law-abiding youths, and their parents, to participate in antidrug vigils and marches in the community.

Often they selected specific drug corners or drug houses and drew attention to them by demonstrating outside in the street. At their marches, now organized by others, the police are usually present. Together they have closed down many drug corners and crack houses, not only in ghetto areas of Philadelphia but throughout the nation as well. Herman became something of a media figure as a result of the television coverage of his activities. Indeed, he was the nemesis of hustlers and drug dealers. He knew many of the neighborhood's young men for many years as well as many of their mothers, fathers, and other family members. His death is a profound loss to the community. Not only did he help resolve some of these problems in Philadelphia, but nationally as well.

So Robert and the other young men viewed Herman as approachable; they reasoned, correctly, that he would lend them a sympathetic ear. Therefore, on a Tuesday afternoon in July 1997, the four of them went to him with their plan for turning their lives around. They simply requested some time to talk. Herman listened. They told him, essentially, 'We'd like to change. Can you help us?' Their approach was so unusual that Herman was at first incredulous and somewhat suspicious. After so many years of working with young people in the community, of harassing drug dealers and closing them down, was he now seeing some real success for his efforts? He speculated that the drug trade was becoming increasingly dangerous and competitive and that this was why these young men wanted out. Yet he remained uncertain and perplexed. The young men's request 'blew my mind,' he says. Were they on the level?

'If you're serious about wanting to improve the neighborhood, you can start by cleaning up this lot,' he said, pointing to an overgrown and trash-filled vacant lot. His command was a test, and the young men may have known this, but they agreed to clean up the lot. The task required a couple of days' work, but the boys accomplished what they started. Herman was impressed, though still not totally convinced that they were serious. He therefore showed them another, bigger lot to clean up as well. This task took them even longer, but they did finish it.

Again they returned to Herman, who was more impressed though still not fully convinced. He knew they had been drug dealers, whom he sees as businessmen 'but with a terrible product,' and wondered whether they might become entrepreneurs. Could they sell fruit on a local street corner instead of drugs? Could this then grow into a larger market, contributing eventually to revitalizing the community? If so, Robert and the others might be visible role models of hard work, an example to younger people.

With this in mind he said to them, 'OK, meet me down at the [food distribution] docks at five tomorrow morning.' He was testing and probing, for he did not want to be taken in. His knowledge and understanding were that committed drug dealers don't just get up at 5 o'clock in the morning and present themselves for honest work. But these young men surprised him; they appeared promptly at 5 o'clock, and Herman presented his plan for them to become fruit sellers, pointing out how this effort, while small, could grow into something much larger. The boys listened intently. Herman can be a very persuasive person. They hung on his words. They appeared hungry for an opportunity to go legitimate, to make a difference in their own community.

Once Herman decided to help them, he gave them about $800 for materials and lumber to construct a fruit stand, which had to be built in compliance with the Philadelphia Licenses and Inspections (L&I) codes. Given the young men's inexperience, their first attempt was not very successful; in fact, the stand blew over in the wind. But Herman took them to the Italian Market, an open-air market full of wooden stands, and had them get the advice of people who knew about building stands. Robert and the other young men then went back and built another stand and painted it white as mandated by L&I. L&I also required them to bring the whole thing downtown for inspection. Herman intervened again and arranged through the district police captain to have the inspector come to them.

At first the young men purchased fruit from the docks, took it back to their community, and set up shop on a busy thoroughfare. People did begin purchasing fruit and vegetables from them. The boys were heartened by how easy it seemed to start up something legitimate. But Herman also told them about other important requirements of becoming small businessmen: issues like licenses and inspections, bookkeeping, and taxes. The young men were undaunted and attempted to rise to the occasion. At this point Herman approached various professors at the University of Pennsylvania, including myself. One professor at the Wharton School invited the young men to attend one of his seminars, making them the focus of a class on small-time entrepreneurship.

The class involved the nuts and bolts of starting up a small business. In the classroom Robert and the others encountered young white and black students of the Wharton School, not to mention a professor who was interested in them and their future. They were all ears, listening attentively and taking copious notes. The students and the professor provided them with much needed advice, but they also gave them accounting and tax books. The young men took it all in and left the class with their minds brimming with ideas about business. In addition, they occasionally attended my class on urban sociology, learning from, but also contributing to, the discourse. It seemed as though their dreams were being realized, if as yet only in a small way; they were gaining positive reinforcement for making constructive changes in their lives, and they were also learning something worthwhile.

Ever since the young men have had the stand up and operating, Robert has been the most consistent worker. He is serious and focused, the one who gets the fruit every day, stocks the shelves, and sells it in all kinds of weather. Having also acquired an aluminum hot dog stand that he began operating across the street, he literally runs back and forth between the two stands. In addition, he is what people in the community would call 'free-hearted,' sometimes giving away food when people ask for it, telling them to pay him when they get the money. His generosity cuts down on profits, but he still clears 100–200 dollars a day. Now just a shadow of his former large-living, materialistic self, Robert is resigned to making do with relatively little. At the stand he calls passersby over and enjoins them to buy something or, if they cannot do that, simply to contribute something 'to the cause.' And people do.

Robert's popularity and reputation in the community account in part for the group's success. His neighbors, friends, and relatives generally want to see him succeed. But the group has its detractors, most often among old friends who are still involved in the drug trade. When these people see Robert standing on the corner selling fruit, they mock him and the others. At times they flash their considerable wads of cash, or 'cheese,' as they call it, and laugh, putting Robert and his partners down as 'little Hermans.' While a term of derision in the minds of street toughs and hoodlums, 'little Hermans' is a complimentary term in the minds of many upstanding men of the community, men who are now old heads 'raised' by Herman and who remember with pride when they were little Hermans. Many of these men today work to follow the lead of Herman, in trying to revitalize their community and to rid it of drugs, violence, and other social scourges. When labeled little Hermans by their street peers, Robert and the others pretend to be unfazed, but they are in fact challenged and encouraged to settle on their new identity, trying out the role of 'upstanding young men' of their community and, in fits and starts, learning to appreciate the positive connotations of the term 'little Hermans.' But serious as they are about turning their lives around and serving the community and its children as positive role models, the boys are beginning to confront the truth that this is not an easy or simple process.

For instance, as Robert and the boys experience success, they face the problem of how to make the transition from underground hustling activities to legal entrepreneurship – or, as Robert puts it, from 'underground ghetto-nomics to above-ground economics' – and attain a semblance of organization. While Robert takes his role very seriously and usually does exactly what is required, he cannot always motivate the others to be as consistent in doing their parts. Still, he rarely complains. The group seldom engages in casting blame or trading recriminations. One major operating principle the group has developed is that people do 'what they are strong at.' Robert knows he is strong at selling and at public relations. The others have their strengths as well. Two are still in high school. It may on the surface look as though the others are simply using Robert – getting over on him – but he does not see things this way. He contends that they are all working together toward the common goal of improving their lives and, by extension, their community.

From time to time minor conflicts and arguments over strategy arise, but they tend not to become very serious. The young men have a high threshold for physicality; they might raise their voices at one another, but then it stops. When explaining why they never get physical, they say, 'We grew up together, and we're like brothers.' Of course, their old ideology of alienation from mainstream society is a complicating factor in their transition. To be sure, many decent people may work two or three jobs to make ends meet or pick up some kind of more or less legal hustle, join forces with their relatives, or barter and trade favors and services with their neighbors and friends. People associated with the criminal element, on the other hand, tend to justify their criminal behavior by reference to racism, which they and their friends and neighbors face daily. Some of them remember the racism they have endured from whites and from the black 'system operators,' who are seen as standing in and acting as proxies for the white power structure. And the criminal justice system intensifies the sense of *in*justice through its drug laws and patterns of arrest and sentencing, all of which are seen as disproportionately targeting blacks.

Accordingly, many of those who remain part of the underground economy are quite embittered, if not profoundly alienated from the wider system, believing that this system is absolutely unfair to black people. Rather than feeling connected to the wider society and emulating it, they suspect and distrust anyone associated with mainstream institutions. They often demand that other blacks show solidarity with them. This orientation can – and does to some extent for Robert – inhibit a full conversion to participation in the world of L&I, Wharton, and legitimate, visible forms of entrepreneurship.

Robert's ambivalence became apparent one afternoon in early January 1998, while I was standing with him at his hot dog stand, watching him sell hot dogs. A customer approached once every 10 or 15 minutes. In between customers Robert was also manning the fruit stand across the street and engaging in conversation with friends who happened by there as well. Because of his status on the street, younger and older fellows alike would often come by for advice.

Suddenly, a city L&I truck pulled up. Out hopped a black man of about 50 in the company of a 45-year-old black woman. They demanded to see Robert's license for the hot dog stand. Now, Robert had acquired the 1998 license, but had neglected to carry it on his person. In fact, he had misplaced the paperwork for the 1998 license and only had the sticker for 1997, which was displayed on his stand. He pointed out the sticker to the man, but the inspector insisted, 'I need the current license.'

When Robert could not produce the license, the inspector, clearly not inclined to give him a break, became gruff. Robert tried to explain that he had been there for a while and that he did in fact have his license but had lost it. The man was unmoved; he simply said, 'This will be a lesson to you to get your license.' I tried to intervene, explaining the situation, and asked if he could not just give Robert a warning. 'This *is* a warning,' he snapped, and I said nothing more. After a little more tense conversation between the two, Robert turned to me and said, 'See how hard it is to fit into this system?' Then he muttered under his breath, 'System operator,' referring to the black man. The inspector overheard the comment, and the tension escalated.

Robert next invoked the name of the district police captain, who had been quite supportive of him and is a strong advocate of community policing. But this apparently carried no weight with the inspector, who proceeded to lecture Robert some more on the need for paperwork. Finally, he filled out a report form, which he wanted Robert to sign immediately. 'Here, sign this,' he said. 'I got to read it first,' said Robert. After a few seconds, the inspector became impatient, and said, 'All right, all right,' taking the clipboard and form and writing at the bottom where Robert's signature was to go, 'Refused to sign.' Robert then became outright angry, complaining about not having had enough time to read the form. People passing by looked over at what appeared to be the beginning of a commotion. A crowd was beginning to form. The inspector would not discuss the matter further, telling Robert he would have to go downtown now to deal with the matter. In the meantime, the inspector said, 'You must cease operations right now, and if I see you operating, I'll confiscate it [the stand]. I've got a hook on this truck,' he added, pointing to the back of his truck.

Robert stood fuming and frustrated. Clearly, he saw the inspector as picking on him – a young black man trying to abide by the system, trying to go straight, but getting no support from people he thought should be helping him the most: other black people who should know all about the racism of the system and so should collude with him against it. He could not understand why this man would not give him a break.

This alienation from 'the system' and the belief that blacks have to mobilize against it helps to legitimate – for its participants – the code of the street, settling scores personally, going for oneself. The inspector sees himself as just doing his job. But Robert has his doubts. He feels that, because of politics and racism, the inspector would never go to the Italian Market and 'pick on them, because he'd lose his job in two seconds. You don't see him coming after the Koreans either. He just gon' pick on another black man.' Robert wants the inspector to be what is often called a 'race man,' but the inspector wants to see himself as a 'professional.' So he goes by the book and demands that Robert obey the rules and hold to the notion 'that race doesn't enter into it.' Robert views it very differently, though; he thinks the inspector is betraying his race.

Most people like Robert who are trying to make the transition from street to decent, to negotiate the wider system, eventually run up against this problem. Robert wants the system to be racially particularistic, to recognize him as an individual with his own problems and needs for special treatment and collusion against the system, but the system does not always cooperate.

On the street, in his old life as a drug dealer, a person like Robert could, and did, demand that others 'make way' for him. In his street world he had a particular reputation, or name, and a history of resorting to violence to make sure that they did. He carried a gun. In giving all that up, he has stepped into a world where he has no particular status – where L&I does not fear him or want to please him. And because he carries no gun, his old friends on the street do not need to make way for him either. He has thus entered a kind of limbo with regard to his status and the rules that govern the management and outcome of conflicts involving him.

An illustration of his loss of power on the street came up recently when Robert was putting away his hot dog stand for the evening, locking it up in a fenced lot. While he was doing this, his backpack, which contained his licenses and other paperwork, was lying on the ground. While his back was turned, someone took the backpack. When he finished, Robert noticed the theft and became livid. Nobody would rob a drug dealer, he felt, for fear of being shot in retaliation, but 'they' robbed him. In Robert's analysis, the people who took the bag knew they had a guardian angel in Herman because 'they knew Herman would talk Robert out of doing something foolish to retaliate.'

As Robert told me the story, I pointed out that the thief could simply have been a crack addict who made no such calculations. Robert admitted that he did not know, but he said, 'Even crack addicts have sense [know how far they can go with whom]. It makes you wonder, Is it better to be loved or feared?' In this comment Robert seemed to question his new orientation.

Yet his analysis is revealing in that it shows his awareness that as he makes his transition to a decent life he is losing something very important on the street – credibility, props (deference), and, ultimately, protection. The whole point of the street posture is to let people know, 'If you mess with me, there will be consequences. Don't count on the law. Don't count on the cops. It's me and you.' That is the essence of the street code. Robert's experience can be held up and studied as an example in microcosm of the difficulty of making the transition from the street to the decent world of law-abiding people who commit themselves to what might be seen as a code apart from the code of the street, a code of civility.

The problem for Robert is that as he leaves his old life and moves toward his new life, he is also entering what Victor Turner has called a 'liminal status,' becoming somewhat marginal to both groups. In this sense he also becomes weakened as a player in the neighborhood. Furthermore, the fact that Robert is now on parole means there are certain rules he absolutely must follow. If he engages in any form of violence, he risks returning to jail. He knows this, and the others know it as well. The code is a way of surviving in the toughest neighborhoods, neighborhoods like Robert's. To survive in this community, one must be able to wield the credible threat of violence. It is not that the person must always engage in violent acts; rather, he must be able to threaten violence at some point to keep the 'knuckleheads' in line. But to live by this code is almost certainly to run afoul of the conditions of parole. Since a threat ignored must be carried out to maintain credibility, Robert cannot threaten violence without jeopardizing his own freedom. On the other hand, he cannot survive in his environment without maintaining his credibility. There is thus a tension between the demands of the code and the demands of parole, the result of which is a high probability that parole will be revoked (see Marc Mauer, this volume).

Assuming this, some of the young men will try and test Robert, probing to see just what they can get away with in their dealings with him. Over the months since his release from jail, Robert has been tested a number of times, from both sides of the fence. A probation officer recently placed him in handcuffs, only to let him go and apologize. Robert was provoked and very disturbed, for he could see no reason for such treatment, and later the officer could not give a good reason for it either. But the incident allowed Robert to see just how vulnerable he now was to the whims of individuals charged with upholding the system.

More recently, Robert has been forced to confront the tension between the street and the decent world even more directly. He has accepted a business proposition from a woman in the neighborhood, Ms Newbill. For many years Ms Newbill has been operating a carryout restaurant on the corner across from Robert's fruit stand. Lately, however, drug dealers have taken to hanging around, intercepting Ms Newbill's customers. Part of what makes the carryout attractive for the drug dealers is that people hang out there: it is busy with traffic, and the dealers can blend in with the young people who are simply standing on the corner, and even sell drugs to some of them.

While Ms Newbill was there alone, this is what they did. Police driving by could not always distinguish between the drug dealers and the kids just hanging out. In fact, adapting to the code, otherwise law-abiding and decent youths at times develop an interest in being confused with those who are hard-core street, because such a posture makes them feel strong and affords them an aura of protection, even allowing them to 'go for bad' – or pretend they too are tough.

Because of the presence of drug dealers, Ms Newbill's business declined, since few people wanted to run an obstacle course to buy sodas and hamburgers. When she complained about this to the dealers, their response was to rob her store at gunpoint. They also vandalized her automobile, which she parked outside the store. Wanting no further trouble, she had an inspiration. She offered to lease the deli section of the business to Robert for $800 per month in the hope that his presence, as a person with respect and props, could deter the drug dealers. Robert has accepted the challenge. He feels it is a good deal, just the opportunity he has been looking for to become a legitimate businessman and not just a street vendor. On his first day he made $91. If he can maintain that level of profit, he thinks, he can make a go of the business.

This involvement has given Robert an even bigger stake in the corner the store occupies, across the street from his fruit stand. He, Ms Newbill, and the drug dealers all know this. One of the many ironies here is that in his previous life Robert established himself as a drug dealer on this very corner and, to this day, feels he can claim some 'ownership' rights to it. In fact, he introduced to the drug trade the young dealers with whom he is now competing for the corner. And, invoking his 'rights,' he had told them that they must take their drugs off his corner, because they harm his legitimate business, that by continuing to sell, they are disrespecting him, or dissing him. Yet they still want to sell drugs on the corner and say they are entitled to do so because 'this is where [they] grew up.' Robert answers that they must be responsible young men and not defile their neighborhood. He also points out to them that such 'defilement' hurts his own business, and thus must cease.

Before Robert was incarcerated, his was a big name in the neighborhood. He was an enforcer for a drug-dealing gang. This role gave him great props on the streets, indicating that he was not to be messed with. But now, as was pointed out above, he can be only a shadow of his former self, because such displays of violent behavior could get him arrested and reincarcerated. Having publicly come out as a little Herman, and a legitimate businessperson, he finds himself in a dilemma: does he revert to his street self in pursuit of decent goals?

It is a predicament that Robert must confront on his own. He knows it, and his antagonists know it. They all know that the police are not the main players here, the ones to 'get cool' with; rather, the 'beef' is between Robert and the drug dealers. These are the people with whom he must now achieve a new understanding. They are testing his mettle, probing for weakness, to see if he is the same old Ruck. Much suggests to them that he is not. Above all, he is now on parole and thus must watch his step in dealing with people the way he would have dealt with them 'back in the day,' or the old days; moreover, his close association with Herman is something of a liability on the street.

Robert has been going through a gradual transformation, shedding his 'old skin' and identity of Ruck and taking on his new identity of Robert, or Rob. His former street cronies constantly address him by his street name of Ruck, while the decent people of the community, people he is getting to know better, address him more consistently as Robert.

If Rob resolves the current tension and passes the test, he will be much stronger than he was before, garnering juice, or respect, and credibility from others he meets on the street. Bear in mind, Rob already has credibility and respect from many of the decent people who know him and what he has been up against; many are cheering for him, the celebrity of the neighborhood. It is the street element, specifically the local drug gang, which he must now impress. For his part, Herman understands that he must not fight this battle for Rob, that Rob must fight it for himself. After all, he will not always be with Rob. Choc is Rob's main opponent in the contest for the corner in front of Ms Newbill's. He grew up and has been living in the area for a long time, and, as was indicated earlier, Rob helped raise him and introduce him to the drug trade. Choc's mother still lives in the area, just a few doors away from Rob's store.

Soon after taking control of the store, Rob confronted Choc about his drug-dealing activities. He said, 'Listen, Choc, this has to stop. If you want to sell drugs, go somewhere else. You not gon' do it here. Go sit on your mother's step and sell. Don't sell in front of my business.' Choc responded, 'Why you want to do that [keep us from selling drugs here]? You know how it is. I got to eat. I got to make a living, too. Why you want to be so hard?' Rob answered that he also had to make a living and that the drug dealers were hurting his business. They could sell somewhere else; they did not have to sell on his corner. Choc responded that this is where his mother lives: 'I grew up here, so I can do what I want. I'll die for this [corner], 'cause I got to eat. And ain't nobody gon' stop me from eating.' Rob asked, 'Is that how you feel?' Choc bellowed, 'Yeah!' 'All right, I'm gon' talk to your mama about it and see if she feel the same way.'

Many people in the neighborhood are aware of the present tension around the corner by Ms Newbill's. A beef has been created and infused with a certain social significance. People want to know what is going to happen next. Will Rob back down? Or will the boys back down? Either way, the result carries implications for the community and the local status order. Core elements of the code of the street are heavily in play: can I take care of myself without going to the authorities? Do I have enough juice or personal power to do what I want? The metaphor of a chess game is not lost, as both Rob and Choc consider their next moves, with everyone anxiously looking on. Ostensibly, it is between them and nobody else. In fact, it is over who is going to rule the community in the long run – the decent folks or the street element. The struggle over the corner may be viewed as simply one battle in a war.

In trying out strategies for winning, Rob offered a scenario of what he might do in regard to Choc. He said, 'I'm gon' go tell his mother, that if I crack him in his head he won't be selling drugs there. Now, there are three corners he can't sell on: where I got the fruit stand, where Ms Newbill's place is, and in front of the library or gym. He can go over to the vacant lot where the gas station used to be. I'll tell him, "You can sell over there because my customers don't come that way," but he knows that place is in the open, and Captain Perez [leader of local district] will get him if he do that. "You can't sell on any other corner. But since you are gonna sell anyway, go over and sell on the vacant gas station lot." ' Rob knew that setting up business there would put Choc in the open so the captain could see him, and everyone knew that the captain was not to be trifled with.

Choc then sent five others of the local community to warn Rob, as a way both of getting the message back to Rob and of obtaining feedback on the situation and drumming up support: 'Rob is gonna find himself with some problems' was a common sentiment. These five people, one by one, came to Rob his first day on the job at Ms Newbill's and told him what Choc had said – 'that he will find himself in some problems.' And they would inquire of Rob, 'What's going on?' Or 'You closing down drug corners, now?' Or 'Choc feels some type o'way about all this [he's mad].'

Herman and I were at Ms Newbill's on Rob's first day as the proprietor of his new business there. Rob made us cheesesteaks and then came and sat with us. It was clear that he was not himself. He was somewhat agitated, and his street antennae were on high alert, as he glanced back and forth at the front door, studying everyone who entered. Suddenly he said, 'Did you see that? Did you see that?' Herman asked, 'What?' 'She nodded her head, gave a signal to somebody,' replied Rob. We looked up and saw an older woman standing in line to pay for some soap. She was facing the street. We noticed nothing out of the ordinary. But Rob was very concerned. He seems to have thought the woman might be alerting someone outside that we were here: if they wanted us, here we were. This turned out to be nothing.

People entered and left. One person after another warmly greeted Herman, including a man who planted a kiss on the side of his face, with obvious affection and appreciation. Herman answered politely, indicating what we were up to that day: 'We're having a Little League practice this evening at six. You got any equipment, a ball, a bat, anything?' The man answered affirmatively: 'Yeah, I got something for you. How long you gon' be here?' 'Until you get back,' answered Herman. The man then left the store and in about 10 minutes returned with a baseball bat and a ball. We were very pleased, for the youngsters with whom we were to practice this evening needed this equipment to start up their games.

Soon we received our food and soft drinks. People continued to enter and leave. It was clear that our presence was the support Rob needed. He relaxed, and we had easy talk for the next hour and a half, at which point we left. Every minute we were there, we were putting the word out that drug dealing would not be tolerated on this corner. Herman felt strongly that the young men who were coming and going were letting others know that we were there and that we were committed to being there. And that was what Rob needed on his first day at Ms Newbill's.

After one man left, Herman said of him confidently, 'Yeah, he know Rob will hurt that boy [Choc], so why mess up Rob's future by sending Rob back to jail for killing this nut. He's putting Rob's word out, that Rob is here to stay.' The man was a crack addict named Johnny Brown, a mechanic – 'the best there is when he can stay off that stuff.' Brown is like a neighborhood courier who knows the latest about the neighborhood: 'He know everything, including the shooting last night.' He will also get the word to the neighborhood that another day has passed and that Rob has not been chased out. Everyone is watching, expectantly, taking in the drama. The atmosphere is something like that of *High noon*, in part because there were shootouts on this busy, lucrative corner in the past. The stakes, financial and social, are high.

Moments later Maurice's brother Tip (a crack addict) comes in, approaches Rob, and asks, 'Do you want me to get rid of him, ol' head? I know you, ol' head.' In conversation the use of the term 'ol' head' is most often an address of respect, but may also be slightly derisive, depending on the social context. Although the address does not always go by age, anyone over 40 years old is considered to be past his prime and generally not as tough as the younger men. Reverent younger men may gently put such people in their place by calling them 'ol' head.' Rob says of Tip, 'I didn't need his help. 'Cause then Tip would have been on the corner. In other words, you can't "ask a devil to get rid of a devil, because then all you get is another devil."'

The code of the street says, in certain circumstances, that each person will test the next person, probing to take his measure, in order to know how to behave toward that person. The people who survive respond by showing their tough sides. If they can do that, they deserve to be left alone. Herman comments, 'Rob is like a test tube baby. He is an ongoing experiment, and we got to save this one.' Herman's role, as it has been all along, is to help Rob through the obstacle course toward civility and decency. Herman can often be heard from the sidelines, coaching, 'Now, don't go and bust the man in his face. There is always a better way [than violence]' – this is his constant message.

Because of his relationship with Herman – and Herman's relationship with the police – Rob now and then converses with the local police, who recognize him when they see him on the streets. On one recent afternoon Rob encountered a policeman, who said, 'How you doing, Rob?' The local drug dealers see this, too, and their reaction might be 'Aw, he's rattin' to the cops.' This relationship with the police brings Rob respect and derision at the same time. His goal is to be completely on his own, to establish himself as a decent person in the community with the props of such a person, along with the props of the street life: toughness and decency, which are not easy to manage and to combine. But Rob must do so if he is to exist in the community with the status he would like. Without his knowledge of the code of the street, he would be in more peril. Possessing it is knowing to some degree what to do in what circumstances, and what not to do.

At this point Rob has figured out his next move with the drug dealers, but he does not know how it will work out. He is reluctant to bring Captain Perez into it, for doing so would hurt his long-term status and reputation on the street. Perez might come in with too much police power and authority, and that would lead the others on the street to say, 'Aw, he had to bring in the police. Aw, he's just a pussy, he went and got them to help him.' Not to involve the police will give Rob more 'heart' on the corner, on the street, where standoffs like this must be settled 'man to man.'

According to the code, the man goes for himself, takes up for himself, and calls on no one else to fight his battles. Whether he is successful or not in dealing with the situation man to man, the outcome will become known around the neighborhood, and his status on the street will be affected. To have to resort to the cops or anyone else is to be judged a chump, to have lost heart. He loses 'stripes,' or respect, because he cannot deal with the threat by the street code. Practically speaking, the police cannot be present all the time. Hence real and enduring protection depends on having a name, a reputation, and credibility for being able to defend what is rightfully one's own, even to the point of engaging in physicality; in a word, the person must get with the challenger, get in his face, and deal with him.

What Rob did was to go see Choc's mother and threaten Choc through her. Standing at the Little League field that evening, he explained to me that he told her that her son's drug dealing in front of the store was hurting his business and that if it did not stop, he would be forced to 'handle his business.' 'So I'm just lettin' you know.' 'Don't worry about [it], Ruck, I'm gon' talk to him,' responded Choc's mother, Mrs Harmon. 'I'm just lettin' you know,' Rob repeated, ''cause I been knowin' y'all for a long time. And I didn't want to just move out like that, without talking to you first. He said he's "willing to die for the corner."' Unlike some other mothers, Mrs Harmon did not deny her son's involvement in the drug trade. She owned up to his dealing drugs in front of the store, expressed her own exasperation with it, and indicated she would handle it.

Telling Choc's mother has turned out to be a deft move on Rob's part because it increases the number of people who can work to defuse the situation. Choc's mother has strong emotional reasons to prevail on her son. It also gives Choc an excuse for capitulating, for, even though he may feel manly and able enough to overcome Rob, he knows he is disturbing his mother. Now he can give in but still save face by telling his boys, 'I did it for my mother.' For the time being, Rob's strategy seems to have worked. The boys have stopped selling drugs on Ms Newbill's and Rob's corner. Things have cooled down.

To reiterate, Rob was seen by the boys on the street to be in a weak position both because he was on parole and so had to watch his step and because he had affiliated himself with Herman, whom they view as square, as an informer, as a policeman – 'And they can't do anything about it,' says Herman. As Rob undergoes his tests, trials, and tribulations, a chorus of old heads cheers him on. For although the old heads do not condone selling drugs, they do observe the code of the street: to be worthy of respect, to be convincing, to be credible on the street, is to display heart, nerve, and manhood at once. Correspondingly, through his actions and words Rob lets the dealers know in no uncertain terms that he is ready to do what it takes to be his own man, to put his own physical self in the gap, and to go back to jail if he must for standing his ground. On these issues the local old heads and Rob converge; they all understand that in this environment such an orientation is the mark of a 'real' man.

Rob still confronts major challenges. The test he went through is only one among many he will face in the future. He resides and operates in a community in which most of the residents are decent or trying to be. But there is also a street element that is less decent, poorly educated, alienated, and to some extent angry; finally, there is a criminal element that is not only street-oriented but often also in the business of street hustling and drug-related crime.

Rob has to navigate this environment, not simply as an ordinary person, not as a drug dealer, but as a legitimate businessman operating a carryout. That means that from time to time he has to meet with all kinds of people, some of whom are involved in scams, trying to shoplift, to sell him stolen goods. Every day will bring another test. He will be tried by drug dealers because his corner is so valuable; it represents capital. As an issue of urban turf, somebody must run that corner: either the police or the drug dealers. In this case, for the time being, Rob is running it. But a new drug gang could come to town, make dibs on this corner, and challenge him. And this time he may not know the man's mother.

Thus far Rob is surviving, and his capital has grown. His business is expanding. Word has gotten around that he is serving food at a decent price and declaring that he is not putting up with the drug activity on the corner. The neighborhood has breathed a sigh of relief, and now people visit the store in large numbers. One man likened the situation to 'sunshine after the rain, and now that the sun is out, the people have returned.' Rob likens it to there being 'a new sheriff in town,' and his presence signals a new day for the 'Stop and Go.' Before the standoff between Rob and the drug dealers, many community residents, particularly the decent people, stayed away. But since he has won – at least for the time being – they have returned. The whole situation is public. Rob has in effect retaken the corner, and his accomplishment affects not just that corner but the whole neighborhood as well. For several blocks around, a sphere of influence has been created that Rob controls and the drug dealers are keeping out of. If the community could take back more such corners, perhaps some real progress could be made in shifting the balance of power from the street-oriented people to the decent people.

The task is difficult because Rob is navigating an environment of so many alienated people, some of them without hope, some of them ready to try to pull him down – for as he rises, they may feel a sharp drop in their own self-esteem. As he gains more legitimate clout, however, his influence spreads through the neighborhood and he becomes a role model for those who lack direction or have fallen into the street life: he has visibly pulled himself up and thus offers them a profoundly different way out of the street. His example shows this way can work.

Yet it is a fine understanding of the code of the street that enables Rob to survive the many physical standoffs that characterize ghetto street life. It is by deftly interpreting and abiding by the rules of the code that he is able to get through his days and nights, to manage the respect necessary to keep the drug dealers, scam artists and others at bay, or in line. At the same time, he must function in the decent world as well, in the world of legitimate business practice – licences, tax laws, and the like. The inner-city success story therefore requires the ability to code-switch, to play by the code of the street with the street element and by the code of decency with others. Rob can do that, and in the process he works at setting an example for other young people. In addition, he is helping organize a Little League team and has plans for a Cub Scout den, the kinds of groups that build up the community's institutions. Rob has thus become an old head for today – both creating opportunity and getting people to see the opportunity and taking responsibility for helping themselves.

Rob never really wavered over whether or not to go back to a life of crime, but the problem was whether he would know how to go about going straight. It was lucky for him to have Herman and me to guide him through the process. We were able to teach him the dominant codes, the codes of civility and decency, as opposed to the code of the street, and this has advanced his human capital. He has expanded his horizons and that has helped him avoid going back to the street. According to Rob, however, the street continues to hold extremely valuable lessons, not just for navigating the ghetto streets but for life as well, and he would not consider raising his children without teaching them those lessons.

Presently Rob is employed in a major university in the field of computer technology, and he has recently received a promotion to full-time status. He now counts judges, professors, doctors, major businesspeople, journalists, and schoolteachers among the people he knows and can call upon. Before him he sees even more opportunities for growth. He has begun to bring qualified people from his old neighborhood into his work environment. He is in fact mentoring others, trying to steer them in the right direction, as Herman and I mentored him. Since Herman's passing, Rob has become more of a social activist, trying to fill Herman's shoes and play the role he always played in the community. He has been to Africa twice. He has been to conferences where he has met prominent people. And he sees his mission as that of helping disadvantaged people not just in the United States but in other regions of the world. To that end, he is working on plans with his supervisor to start a training program that would both empower young people and teach them skills marketable in today's high-tech economy. Rob has shown himself to be quite understanding with the younger men he has picked up to mentor and is able to show them a better way.

While going straight has not been a simple journey for Rob, it has been a profoundly edifying and life-changing one that has benefited both him and others, including friends and family. In this sense, he has become a fount of human capital interested in building up the social capital of the community In addition, Rob came to my classes at Penn and lectured my students, an experience that taught him as much as it taught them. All in all, Rob has taken up the mantle. In the process, he has learned a lot, he has matured a lot, and he continues to grow.

The other boys with whom Rob began are now envious of him as they look at his success and how far he has moved from them. They look up to him and wonder how he does it. He is miles ahead of them now, and they are sorry they did not continue. His job gives him benefits and a steady income so he has no trouble getting the material things he wants, within reason. Rob is so far beyond his peers now that going back to the street is not an option. It ceases even to be thinkable.

In conclusion, by focusing on the case of Rob, I implicitly emphasize his individualism and his ability to negotiate 'the system' because of the human capital he has come to possess. This in turn implies that the structure does not determine or even significantly affect his life chances. In fact, however, the structure does provide him and others like him with limited life chances and opportunities. But it only allows a certain proportion of individuals to succeed and therefore also requires that a certain proportion fail. Hence, although Rob's success seems to validate the structure, by implication blaming those who do succeed, in fact many people in his position do fail for structural reasons. We must not confuse the success of some with the possibility for all to so succeed or with the existence of an open and fair occupational structure. Surely some will succeed if they find a way to have access to social capital and the right kinds of opportunities. But inevitably, many will continue to fail, and the class structure will endure.

Ultimately, what this reflects is the structure/agency paradox. There is neither complete structural determination nor free agency. Therefore, what we need are analyses that depict the contradictory lived experiences of people who find themselves in similar situations, analyses that neither assume limitless agency, thereby blaming the victim, nor rely on simplistic formulations of social reproduction through structural determination. Success brings class mobility to a fortunate few. Yet their very success serves to reproduce or legitimate the racialized class and status structures that continue to oppress those who either do not encounter the same opportunities or choose not to 'sell out' in order to achieve the dominant society's version of success.

In that racialized class and status structure, the system of mass imprisonment plays an increasingly important part – with effects that are, despite Rob's experience, overwhelmingly negative for the individuals and communities involved.

Note

1   This piece derives from my recently published book, *Code of the street: decency, violence, and the moral life of the inner city* (New York: Norton, 1999), which was based on four years of fieldwork in inner-city neighborhoods about Philadelphia, especially the hypersegregated communities at ground zero characterized by profound and persistent poverty. The quoted statements are taken from my own ethnographic research.

9 Bringing the individual back in

A commentary on Wacquant and Anderson

JEROME MILLER

The articles of Loïc Wacquant and Elijah Anderson are in a tradition that I fear is fast leaving us – not only in criminology but also in law. As well as commenting on these articles, I want to comment upon the unintended consequences of the research methodologies that have come to characterize contemporary criminological research. Both of these articles by implication offer a challenge to much of the current wisdom in that regard.

A couple of years ago, someone asked well-known social theorist and linguist Noam Chomsky why he was so seldom seen in the mainstream media – particularly on television. This seemed particularly curious since so many of his views had unusual salience in contemporary American society. Chomsky replied by describing a conversation with ABC/CNN political commentator Jeff Greenfield. Greenfield suggested to Chomsky that he was unlikely to be booked on a program like 'Nightline' because, in effect, he was 'from Neptune.' He explained this comment by telling Chomsky that his views on contemporary matters – regardless of their validity – were too far outside the box for a discussion on a popular program like 'Nightline.' This was because the TV format would not allow Chomsky the time necessary to lay out the context necessary for his views to be understood by the average viewing audience. Minus the context he would, in effect, be seen as someone 'from Neptune.' The comment carries personal resonance as I have tried to address the development of criminal justice practice in recent years. Indeed, as the years have passed – and as any semblance of consensual validation of my own views fades, I find myself less taken with Chomsky's dilemma than with William Burrough's observation that at times he thinks that he must have arrived from another planet but has forgotten the message. Articles such as these assure me that I am not a lone alien in my own land.

Professor Anderson's article is in a tradition now sadly, pretty much abandoned by contemporary sociology and criminology. It demonstrates a way of plumbing serious public issues through the use of the single case – in this instance the life-experience of 'Robert.' It is the way of the hedgehog rather than the fox.

Professor Anderson's article bespeaks hours of participant observation, spanning months. It attempts to shed light on the life of one young black man – 'Robert.' We see some of his world, his friends (and enemies), his job, etc. What distinguishes this research from most contemporary articles is the fact that Prof. Anderson does not shy away from dealing with the inconstant and unpredictable realities that tend ultimately, to defeat many of the findings of routine positivist approaches. Ultimately, Anderson brings us face to face with that Great Satan of contemporary criminological research and criminal justice practice – i.e. the *meaning* that a particular action might carry for the individual in a given society.

Let me briefly read to you a passage about the centrality of this kind of thinking to research. In their classic study of *The Polish peasant* W.I. Thomas and Florian Znaniecki postulated the startling premise that not only was the 'life history' a necessary prerequisite for the study of man, it was the *only* one upon which we should be permitted to draw conclusions. As they put it, 'whether we draw our materials from sociological analysis, from detailed life-records of concrete individuals or from the observation of mass-phenomena, the problems of sociological analysis are the same' (Thomas and Znaniecki, 1927: 1832–4).

They held that even in the search for abstract laws the 'life-records' of individuals were superior to any other kind of data. As they put it

> ... personal life-records, as complete as possible, constitute the perfect type of sociological material, and that if social science has to use other materials at all it is only because of the practical difficulty of obtaining ... a sufficient number of records ... and of the enormous amount of work demanded for an adequate analysis of all the personal materials necessary ... (Thomas and Znaniecki, 1927)

(Parenthetically, it should be noted that in our information age such technological bars to quality life-history research no longer exist. Rather, we are confronted with ideological objections and political bars to this kind of knowledge.)

In a comment that today would truly seem to emanate from Neptune, Thomas and Znaniecki concluded that if the researcher is 'forced' to use mass-phenomena 'without regard to the life-histories of the individuals who participate in them, it is a *defect*, not an advantage' (1927) The great 'Chicago School' of sociological method emerged out of this tradition. It was the tradition of George Herbert Mead, Clifford Shaw, and other giants of American sociology.

In a recent psychological reiteration of this research stance, Jerome Bruner, a founder of cognitive psychology, recently made historical note of the fact that this field was not established to simply provide better technologies for control – where it seems to be presently headed. Rather, it was an 'all-out effort to establish *meaning* as the central concept of psychology – not stimuli and responses, not overtly observable behavior, not biological drives and their transformation, but *meaning*' (Bruner, 1990: 4).

It calls to mind the false predictions of many legal scholars in the 1980s that positivist research unfettered by such messy concerns as states of mind or differing individual environments would herald the 'end of ideology' in implementing criminal justice policies. The facts of the offense would be the sole determinant of sentencing.

This is truly wrongheaded – both as research and as a social policy. As political philosopher Eric Voegelin held, facts are there for one main purpose – to illuminate meaning.

We know now that the British political philosopher Quentin Skinner was more than a little correct when he commented that the first victim of social-science positivism and by implication of legal positivism, is the so-called 'end of ideology' argument.

'[T]o claim that politics is a purely technological affair, and thus that ideology must have come to an end,' writes Skinner, 'has the effect of grounding the stability and even the legitimacy of the state on its capacity to maintain a high level of technological success.' It amounted, he said, 'to little more than an ideological reading of consensus politics . . .' (Skinner, 1985: 8).

Professor Wacquant's important article demands of us that we look not only at the economic issues but also at crucial symbolic issues. He confronts the 'end of ideology' argument as a rationale for positivism most persuasively. He effectively deconstructs the 'givens' of most contemporary criminological research – 'givens' that we have ignored at our peril.

He questions the kind of thinking in criminal justice that is premised upon a method-ology that gave us 'body counts' and 'pacification' as the best measures of our progress in Vietnam. Indeed, as that national experience came to a predictably dismal end, the same approaches, and in some cases, the same researchers that had previously been associated with the Defense Department and its private contractors were turned loose on criminal justice.

As the numerous Right-wing 'think tanks' around the nation joined the fray, we got no better research – but they did come up with immeasurably better marketing. It gave us a whole new set of slogans around which to rally a national crusade against crime – 'selective incapacitation,' 'three strikes,' 'broken window theory,' 'sentencing guidelines,' 'zero tolerance,' and 'supermax' prisons. Ultimately, we have ended in saddling the country with a national criminal justice system that is more racially driven than we could have imagined.

Professor Anderson's article stands in contrast to these trends. It is an uncomfortable reminder that we have otherwise succeeded only too well in shutting out the *narrative* – from our theories, our research, and our courts.

It has been dismaying over the past 20 years of testifying as an expert witness in a few hundred criminal cases to see the narrative increasingly marginalized in state courts while it has all but disappeared in federal courts – particularly insofar as those proceedings involve poor and minority defendants. Not surprisingly, however, the narrative con-tinues to survive in courts among upper and upper-middle class defendants and for some specific categories of institutionally 'sympathetic' defendants, e.g. police – so long as the cases are tried in non-minority venues.

Obviously this carries profound implications for the individual defendants involved. However, it suggests an even worse prospect for the progressive development of crimi-nal law and criminal justice policies.

The political philosopher Jürgen Habermas placed these matters in perspective when he noted that when the divide between the 'haves' and 'have-nots' in a society grows ever wider (and more racially defined), researchers are called upon to provide the appropri-ate rationales for the social Darwinism which follows.

We saw the first inklings of this in the early 'pick and choose' work of Herrnstein and Wilson, *Crime and human nature*, with its subtle racist implications. We saw it in a less disguised form in Herrnstein and Murray's tome *The bell curve* – a book that spoke what is clearly unspoken in large elements of American society by selling 400,000 copies in its first 60 days.

Certainly, the present racial and ethnic makeup of our prisons and jails – with 54 percent of all new admissions to federal and state prisons being black and with another 22 percent being Latino-Hispanic – cries out for an explanation that will let the criminal justice system and the larger society off the hook. Social Darwinist explanations usually suffice.

The former head of the US Civil Rights Commission and professor of Law and history at the University of Pennsylvania Mary Berry, sees the narrative as crucial to the development of law. It is really a matter of whose story carries the day. In her book on this subject entitled *The pig farmer's daughter and other tales of American justice*, she quotes this passage from William Pickens in 1933:

> For generations in this country when a Negro came into court facing a white opponent, he had to settle not only the question involved in the charge against him as an individual, but also all the traditional charges against his race – in fact the whole race question. Like Socrates before his accusers, he had to face a jury which was influenced not only by the evidence just presented, but also by the 'evidence' that had been taught to them in their infancy, in their growing up, in literature, taverns, shops, and from a million other sources. (Berry, 1999: 80)

Berry sums matters up this way:

> I now know that everyone has stories, including lawyers, judges, and jurors. Stories provide a frame of reference that determines what each of us believes is true about the law. They also shape law and how it is enforced. . . . Whose story counts in legal decisions rests heavily on who controls political and economic power, in a process that is circular and progressive. The stories of the powerful are the only ones that count, and the counting further enhances the power of the tellers in the economic and political arena. The exclusion of their stories reflects the historical silencing of African Americans. (Berry, 1999: 80)

I might add that in an atmosphere of mandatory sentencing and a 'do the crime do the time' atmosphere we guarantee that silence is, for want of a better word, amplified. This is a sorry state for our democracy.

Elijah Anderson's 'story' of Robert is an attempt to bring other realities into our consideration of the 'criminal.' For that, he meets a crucial need in contemporary criminological research. Having said all this, I must take small issue with some of the premises that are implicit in his article.

Robert's prison experience – characterized by bad treatment, being subjected to daily racial slurs by guards, assigned to do 'shit' work, and being goaded to 'strike out' so that his sentence might be extended – is presented as having convinced him that 'he did not want to go that route again.' It is on its face, an argument for deterrence – the harsher the better.

At best, it is a demonstration of how one young man derived meaning from a needlessly hostile, out-of-control, and openly racist environment to which our society assigned him and in which he was held captive. It speaks more to issues like 'identification with the aggressor,' or to developing survival skills for an outside society which, for African American males, is often not unlike the prison.

Professor Wacquant speaks articulately to this issue in proposing that we consider

Moses Finley's distinction between 'societies with slaves and slave societies.' He suggests that we view the criminal justice system within another context – noting that 'the same social relations premised on a caste division, social withdrawal, a defended built environment, and depacification' now pervade both the 'hyperghetto' and the prisons.

It is in precisely this sense, I do not feel that Professor Anderson gives enough weight to the influences of prison on the code of the streets. It is no accident that most of the known violent gangs in California developed in the institutions of the California Youth Authority or the California prisons. Leadership is confirmed by a stint in prison. The walk, the 'pose,' the language, the argot, the dress, the focus of one's eyes, and the studied indifference all bespeak prison.

In this sense, when Robert goes to an adult prison as a teenager it is difficult to know which attitudes emanated from the prisonized culture on the streets and what emanated from what Professor Anderson terms Robert's 'previous materialism.' Street code values like 'toughness, nerve, and willingness to retaliate for transgressions' are often born of, and usually enhanced by, the prison experience. The 'code of the streets' and what prison sociologists have termed 'the convict code,' have been so fully intermixed that it is now difficult to tell them apart.

These are dicey issues needing to be sorted out if we are to develop sound criminal justice policies. Stomping on the lawbreaker will certainly stop his or her behavior for the time being. I doubt – if the recidivism statistics of prisons hold any weight – that such stratagems hold equal promise in the long haul. The irony of Robert's prison experience was that it must have cost in excess of one-quarter million dollars. One would hope for more return on that kind of investment than a fruit stand.

I must also take issue with the comments of Professor Wacquant that 'racial division and the predatory culture of the street, centered on hypermasculinist notions of honor, toughness, and coolness (summed up by the imperative of "respect") have entered into and transformed the social structure and culture of jails and prisons.'

I do not believe that the convict code has been swamped by the code of the street. It is precisely the reverse. Because of pandemic incarceration of young African American men, street culture has been swamped by the convict code. It has taken hold as a devastating disproportion of young African American men and teenagers are subjected to what has become, in effect, America's chosen 'rite of passage' for them. It begins with the stop and arrest. It entails the formalized ritual of the booking, the mug shot, the body-cavity search, the jailing, the court hearing, and finally, the decision to release (usually conditioned by the availability of a modest amount of money). As befits a true rite, it is presided over by a robed representative of the larger society – the judge. It is finalized with the striking of his gavel.

The 'code of the streets' has great meaning in this context. It is indispensable to survival in those facilities we have determined are necessary to deter or treat the 'criminal.' Indeed, those markers we routinely employ to ferret out the psychopaths among us, are the very same qualities that a maximum security prison demands of its inmates.

It is why, if the anthropologist Jay Haley (1978) can refer to most mental hospitals as 'hothouses' for schizophrenia it is even more appropriate that we see prisons and jails as 'hothouses' for nurturing psychopathy.

Loïc Wacquant's comments on the 'criminalization' of poverty are particularly compelling and salient. His references to 'horizontal expansion or carceral hyperinflation' are crucial if we are going to understand the phenomenon elsewhere labeled as 'spreading the net of social control' – something addressed in great depth by Michel Foucault (1977).

With the ever growing acceptance by the larger society of such slogan concepts as 'zero tolerance' and 'broken window theory' we can expect the 'criminalization' of the majority of black men to continue and accelerate.

Another development is taking place around 'carceral hyperinflation' as the bulk of state and federal prison inmates change from white to black and brown. A whole range of treatment providers – psychiatrists, psychologists, and social workers have adjusted their diagnoses and treatment modalities to meet the demands of this new reality. They have been only too willing to give the criminal justice system what it wants and is willing to pay well for – professional validation of pre-existing practices – no matter how demeaning, brutal, or disorienting to the individual inmate.

Not unlike the 'code of the streets' the 'tough on crime' code has infected the ideology, theories and practice of the so-called 'helping professions.' One can perhaps best see this change in the number of psychiatrists and psychologists who routinely testify for the prosecution. They are providing what they are paid to provide for their keepers.

One could, of course, make a similar argument regarding professionals who testify for the defense. In the past, that may have been somewhat true. However, in this new era of 'consequences' and disparagement of personal history, such services are pretty much confined to the domain of the wealthy client. The poorer individual is less able to buy a thorough life-history and complete diagnostic workup. He or she is left to the ministrations of the system. If matters are more serious he or she will be assigned to one of the many 'forensic units' established by the states in one or another of its state hospitals for the criminally insane. They are generally quite willing to provide the prosecution with the labels necessary to proceed with the most punitive recommendations available for accused adults and juveniles alike.

It was such a unit that recently held 11-year-old Nate Abraham in Michigan fit for trial as an adult on first degree murder – a case in which I testified and in which the prosecution was seeking a life sentence.

The political scientist Eric Voegelin put these diagnostic trends in another context. 'Material reality' he said,

> is, in a sense static, and the progress we can make in its exploration is the progress in the dissection of a corpse that holds still; the realm of man and society is relatively much more alive and the degrees of understanding will be determined by the amplitude of the idea of man that is at the disposition of a scholar . . . (Voegelin, quoted in Cooper, 1999)

It seems to me that many of the current crop of researchers in criminology have little room for 'the living individual' at all.

The kinds of research we are losing are precisely those that allow these confounding, chaotic, frustrating realities some primary place in all our conclusions. All in all we must maintain some role for the element of passion that likely got us involved in this work at the beginning.

This year we will reach 1 million black men in our prisons and jails. This sad reality speaks less to the abiding presence of crime than it does to the twisted ideas of man held by those who control the stories. In summary, may I ask the reader to consider for a moment some remarks of G.K. Chesterton. In his meditation on St Francis of Assisi, Chesterton notes that

> In a word, we talk of a man who cannot see the wood for the trees . . . a man who did not want to see the wood for the trees. He wanted to see each tree as a separate and almost sacred thing . . . not all of a piece like a picture but in action like a play. A bird went by him like an arrow; something with a story and a purpose, though it was the purpose of life and not the purpose of death. (Chesterton, 1954)

Chesterton's comment suggests that we might well read the disturbing term of Loic Wacquant – 'Deadly Symbiosis' – within a somewhat larger context. The problem reaches well beyond current criminal justice practices to the symbolic heart of our culture – and in that sense it encroaches upon those aspects of American life that contain the potential for the undoing of our democratic experiment.

References

Berry, M.F. (1999) *The pig farmer's daughter and other tales of American justice: episodes of racism and sexism in the courts from 1865 to the present.* New York: Knopf.

Bruner, J. (1990) *Acts of meaning.* Cambridge, MA: Harvard University Press.

Chesterton, G.K. (1954 [1924]) *St Francis of Assisi.* Garden City, NY: Doubleday & Company (copyright George H. Doran Company, 1924).

Cooper, B. (1999) *Eric Voegelin and the foundations of modern political science.* Columbia & London: University of Missouri Press.

Foucault, M. (1977) *Discipline and punish: the birth of the prison,* trans. Alan Sheridan. New York: Pantheon Books.

Haley, J. (1978) Personal communication with author.

Skinner, Q. (1985) *The return of grand theory in human sciences.* Cambridge: Cambridge University Press.

Thomas, W.I. and Znaniecki, F. (1927) *The Polish peasant in Europe and America, vol. II.* New York: Knopf.

10 Imprisonment rates and the new politics of criminal punishment

FRANKLIN E. ZIMRING

ONE GROWTH ERA OR THREE?

Figure 1 divides the last 75 years of the 20th century into two discrete segments. Between 1925 and 1973, there was very little fluctuation from a mean level, that averages between 110 and 120 per 100,000 and never varies by more than 30 percent up or down from that. After a low of 93 per 100,000 in 1972, the rate of imprisonment has increased in 26 consecutive years, growing during this time from 93 to 452 per 100,000, or just under fivefold in a quarter century. What had been a non-volatile and cyclical phenomenon becomes very volatile and non-cyclical.

The visual evidence suggests that the acceleration of prison populations was a unitary phenomenon, a process that starts in the early or middle 1970s, picks up steam in the early 1980s, and just keeps going. And history may very well regard the last quarter of the 20th century in unitary terms. But it seems that three different patterns of

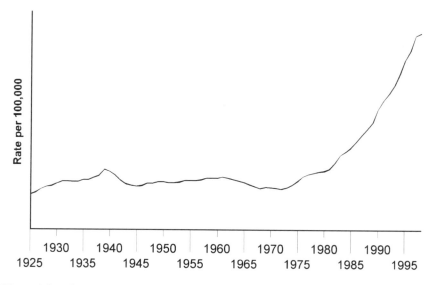

•Figure 1 Imprisonment rate per 100,000 population, United States, 1925–98

substantive emphasis have accompanied this steady upward progression at different times in the 26-year push. From 1973 to the mid-1980s, the emphasis was on general increases in the commitment of marginal felons to prison, with few clear patterns by type of crime or by type of offender (Zimring and Hawkins, 1991: Ch. 5). During the period from about 1985 to 1992, the substantive emphasis shifted to drugs, and the growth of drug commitments and drug sentences far outpaced the rate of growth of other offense commitments.

The third period is the subject of my focus in this article, the period of time when imprisonment rates defy gravity and continue to grow even as crime rates are dropping. This is the high point of what I shall call the new politics of punishment, of Megan's Law and Three Strikes and You're Out and Truth in Sentencing. Here the shift in emphasis is from 'lock 'em up' to 'throw away the key,' and I believe (without currently sufficient evidence) that lengthening of sentences has begun during this period to play a much larger role in sustaining the growth of prison population. In the six years from 1992 to 1998, the imprisonment rate grew from 313 to 452 per 100,000, or 139 per 100,000. To put that in context, the total prison population was 139 per 100,000 as recently as 1981. So what we have added in a six-year period is another United States prison system the size of the 1981 total to the 1992 mass which was already a United States high.

I believe a new politics of criminal punishment has played a major role in the events of the past eight years in the United States and will play an important part in determining future policy. In this article, I want to highlight three characteristics of the new political attitudes and then make some guesses about how the new political landscape might limit the range of decarceration.

THREE CHARACTERISTICS OF THE NEW POLITICAL LANDSCAPE

Three characteristics of the recent politics of punishment that deserve special attention are: (1) the loose linkage between the symbolic and operational content of punishment laws, (2) the zero sum rhetoric supporting punishment proposals, and (3) the paradoxical politics of distrust in penal legislation.

Loose linkage

First, the matter of loose linkage. There are two quite different public purposes served when legislation concerning criminal punishment is enacted. One purpose is the symbolic denunciation of crime and criminals, a statement of condemnation that enables the political community to make its detestation of crime manifest in legal form. A second and distinct public purpose is to effect change in the operations of punishment systems – to change the behavior of courts, prisons, or parole authorities. For most members of the public, the symbolic functions of penal legislation are the most important aspect of new legislation. For this reason, there need not be any profound linkage between symbolic legislation and large changes in the punishment output of operating criminal justice systems.

This loose linkage between symbolic and operational impacts has traditionally allowed new criminal laws to bark much louder than they bite, to satisfy the need for symbols of denunciation without making much difference in the penalties meted out to most offenders. But recent events have shown that the loose connection between symbolic and operational impact can work both ways. Both the United States federal system and California passed laws labeled 'Three Strikes and You're Out' in 1994. By late 1998, the United States federal statute had resulted in 35 special prison sentences while the California law had produced more than 40,000 sentences under its terms (Zimring et al., 1999). Laws serving the same symbolic functions can have vastly different operational impacts in different settings.

The federal law was traditional in that it barked louder than it bit. The California law actually bit louder than it barked because 90 percent of its enhanced prison sentences were given not to people with two prior strikes convictions, but to offenders with only one prior strike. The law was 10 times as broad as its label.

When citizens are more concerned with the symbolism than with the operational impact of penal laws, the same rhetorical appeals can lead to very different operational law reforms. In such cases, the practical impact of new penal laws will be determined more by who controls the planning and drafting process and what they want than by the level of public support for labels like 'three strikes'. And those who wish to maximize impact can ride slogans a long way. The California version of Three Strikes has resulted in nine times as many prison terms as all of the 26 other three strikes laws in the United States combined. The chronically loose linkage between symbolic and operational impact will lead to high stakes competition for control of legislative drafting as a recurrent phenomenon in the politics of modern criminal justice.

The zero sum fallacy

A second feature of the recent politics of punishment also concerns the relationship between the symbolic and the operational aspects of penal law. The rhetoric in support of new punishment proposals in current politics often seems to assume that criminals and crime victims are engaged in a zero sum contest. If the criminal justice process is imagined as a zero sum game, anything that hurts offenders *by definition* helps victims. If the competition between victims and offenders is really like a football score, then any detriment to the offender team helps the victim's score.

The zero sum assumption is a convenient method of avoiding questions about exactly how (and how much) measures that hurt criminal offenders might also help their victims. In a zero sum universe, there is a law of equivalent benefit. Anything that hurts the other team by definition helps the competition in equal measure. In a zero sum setting, all a citizen must do to choose punishment policy is decide whether she prefers victims or offenders. The zero sum assumption is open-ended and seemingly universally applicable.

The problem here, of course, is the non-logic of the assumption. If victims of violent crime are given public funds to compensate their economic loses, does that benefit automatically hurt criminal offenders? Of course not, because there is no real zero sum relationship. But assuming such a relationship generates a justification for endless cycles of increased infliction of suffering on counterfeit utilitarian grounds. I suspect that what happens here is that the symbolic aspects of a status competition where the denunciation of offenders might be seen as supporting the social standing of crime victims is carried over to assumptions that the actual hurt of punishment creates equal and opposite reactions in victims.

The paradoxical politics of governmental distrust

The punishment of criminals is at root an exercise of governmental power. It might therefore seem reasonable to suppose that citizen support for harsh measures against criminals would increase with increasing levels of citizen trust in government, and that citizen support for excessive punishments would decline when levels of confidence in government fall off. In this reading, support for harsh punishment would be a disease of excess confidence in state authority. But support for mandatory penalties and Truth in Sentencing actually increases with additional distrust of parole officials, distrust of judges, and with distrust of the governance of punishment by professionals.

Distrust in government can raise the stakes in criminal punishment. Citizens worry that judges will identify with offenders and treat them with inappropriate leniency. A bad judge in this view is one prone to coddle criminals and thus act against the interests of the citizenry. The way to guard against such governmental weakness is to force the imposition of stern penal measures. What makes the government untrustworthy in this rhetoric is the danger that it might side with the criminals and thus against the interests of the ordinary citizen.

The mandatory punishment term is the way to insure against such weakness. But the mandatory term is a huge expansion of punishment, rendering excessive outcomes in many cases to assure sufficiency of punishment in a very few that might otherwise escape their just deserts. Such huge inefficiency is the hallmark of Three Strikes and You're Out in California and of Truth in Sentencing generally. What links Megan's Law (where citizens rather than police get information on sex offender addresses) to Three Strikes and to Truth in Sentencing is the politics of distrust. Megan's Law is distrust of police, Three Strikes and mandatory sentences are distrust of judges, and Truth in Sentencing is distrust of parole authorities.

POLITICAL LIMITS ON DECARCERATION

The independent power of this new political cast on prison populations is difficult to determine in the 1990s. The counterfactual control we would need is a United States from 1992 onward without a political climate aimed at increasing imprisonment. But there is nothing evanescent about this new political emphasis, no reason to expect it to spend itself in the near future, and every reason to believe that political pressures that have added to hyper-incarceration will also provide resistance to downward movements in prison populations. How great a counter-pressure this political climate will amount to is not something that can be precisely measured.

My current guess is that undoing even this last six years of the United States incarceration boom will be more than difficult, more than improbable, under the political conditions that currently determine punishment policy. In one respect, this gloomy prediction contradicts the common-sense physics of prison population. Surely what went up so very recently can come down as well. How can it be that even 1992 levels of incarceration seem out of reach? This is not a prediction based on statistical study of any long-standing dynamic processes associated with prison populations. It is instead a guess about the politics of the matter, about links that have been created between political processes and imprisonment levels, and that cannot be easily undone. In six years, the United States has grown a second prison system with an extra incarceration rate per 100,000 larger than the United States had at any time between 1900 and 1980. This run up was a policy change but I would not want to say *only* a policy change.

Just as the American incarceration explosion was unprecedented, so too would be the reduction in prison rates and numbers that we would need to get back to 1992 levels. Cutting a prison system by 139 per 100,000 in times of governmental stability has never ever been done. To imagine any such policy reversal can be achieved sailing into the political winds of recent years is difficult indeed.

A decade ago Gordon Hawkins and I wrote a book on the scale of imprisonment and there was no chapter in it on politics (Zimring and Hawkins, 1991). Perhaps this was not an oversight. It is probable that the politics of criminal punishment now play a much more important role in determining prison populations than in earlier eras. Here, too, however, there is no obvious path to reversing the political momentum that has created closer links between politics and rates of imprisonment. Putting distance between state politics and the creation of state level imprisonment policy should obviously be a high priority in efforts to restrain and to reverse the growth of incarceration.

References

Zimring, F.E. and Hawkins, G. (1991) *The scale of imprisonment*. Chicago, IL: University of Chicago Press.

Zimring, F.E., Kamin, S. and Hawkins, G. (1999) *Crime and punishment in California: the impact of three strikes and you're out*. Berkeley, CA: Institute of Governmental Studies, University of California, Berkeley.

11 Unthought thoughts

The influence of changing sensibilities on penal policies

MICHAEL TONRY

What we see, think and believe often depends as much on when we stand as where. This is true about trivial things – many people who were once enamoured of bouffant hairdos, bellbottoms or polyester pantsuits have a hard time imagining that was ever true and a harder time picturing themselves so garbed. That is not surprising. Fashions change, tastes evolve and few people are immune to influence in such matters; what once we liked, we now dislike. And anyway such things are ephemeral and not very important. However, we are just as susceptible to influence about subjects that are important and about issues that are timeless. Periods of romanticism and classicism in the arts, for example, have alternated throughout human history, as have periods of tolerance and intolerance of homosexuality and of religious pluralism, and people's views and beliefs oscillate with them. In western countries, the pendulum swings between conservative and liberal politics are so regular as to be a cliché. And the same thing is true in recent centuries in relation to punishment, with moralistic ideas about retribution and deserved punishments alternating with instrumental ideas about problem-solving and human fragility.

This is one of several related articles that attempt to propose ways in which understanding of long-term trends in crime, punishment and public sensibilities can aid in efforts to understand our own time, and to avoid making mistakes we will later regret. No doubt, for example, contemporary use of capital punishment, indiscriminate private possession of handguns and mass incarceration of black men will some day be widely deplored and deeply regretted. One article (Tonry, 1999a) assesses the persuasiveness of four explanations for why incarceration use quadrupled in the United States between 1972 and 2000. The first is that crime rates rose steadily from the late 1960s, remain much higher now than they were then and increased imprisonment was an almost mechanistic consequence. The second is that public attitudes toward crime and criminals steadily hardened and punishment policies followed (see Roberts and Stalans, 1997). The third is that conservative politicians used crime as a 'wedge issue' to separate working and middle-class voters from the Democratic Party, purposely raising public anxieties and then proposing harsh polices as if in response (Edsall and Edsall, 1991; Beckett,

1997). The fourth is that America's political fragmentation into one-issue interest groups, coupled with government's loss of political legitimacy, has made crime one of only a few issues politicians can use to mobilize widespread support, and not surprisingly they have used an instrument at hand in exactly that way (Caplow and Simon, 1999). That article concludes that most of those explanations have some merit, but that a deeper explanation is required for why those forces operated so powerfully in our time and not in others.

A second article (Tonry, 1999b) attempts to explain adoption of particularly repressive contemporary crime policies (federal 'real offence' sentencing, Virginia's use of youth as an aggravating factor in sentencing) and policy proposals (Kahan's (1998) disintegrative shaming) in terms of cyclical patterns of heightened intolerance of crime and criminals. The question asked is why policies have been adopted or credibly proposed in the past 15 years that would have been unthinkable a generation earlier and will become unthinkable again. The answer offered is that a series of moral panics about particular problems, amplified and extended by modern mass media, has interacted with a cyclical period of high intolerance of crime. Each exacerbates the effects of the other, and together they create an environment conducive to adoption of symbolic and expressive policies without much attention being paid to foreseeably damaging direct and collateral effects.

This article is in some ways the converse of the preceding one. It examines issues and ideas that are conspicuously absent, almost forgotten, in some periods even though they are powerful or ubiquitous in adjacent ones. Contextual influences of a moment or a decade influence not only what we do think and believe, but what we do not.

Here is how this article is organized. The first section examines evidence of the influence of changing secular conditions on sensibilities and of changing sensibilities on beliefs. Examples are drawn from a number of realms but the emphasis is on drug use and crime. The second section then looks quickly at two issues absent from normative and policy debate in the 1990s – preventive detention and prosecutorial sentence appeals – and more fully at the absence of just deserts in the Model Penal Code development process in the 1950s and at the absence of researchers', or anyone else's, interest since the 1960s in the recidivism of first-time prisoners.

CYCLES AND SENSIBILITIES

Beliefs and attitudes about punishment, religious pluralism and sexual tolerance are fundamentally different from preferences for polyester pantsuits. In the 21st century AD, as in the third century BC, and at most times in between, thoughtful people have understood the polar cases, the alternatives that range between them, the practical and principled arguments that can be made for one position or another, and the inexorability of the processes by which one set of beliefs displaces another. Unfortunately, all that tends to get forgotten by most but not all people in the heat of an historical moment. Apostates are killed (Erikson, 1966; Johnson, 1976), homosexuals are tyrannized (Boswell, 1980), cruel punishments are imposed (Foucault, 1977; Bennett et al., 1996). Such things happen because many or most people in an era come to share perceptions and beliefs that justify them, unmindful that their perceptions and beliefs may be wrong and that they themselves in a few years may see them to have been wrong.

In one representative realm, literature and the arts, Grant Gilmore described typical fluctuations:

> We have become used to the idea that, in literature and the arts, there are alternating rhythms of classicism and romanticism. During classical periods, which are, typically, of short duration, everything is neat, tidy and logical; theorists and critics reign supreme; formal rules of structure and composition are stated to the general acclaim. During classical periods, which are, among other things, extremely dull, it seems that nothing interesting is ever going to happen again. But the classical aesthetic, once it has been formulated, regularly breaks down in a protracted romantic agony. The romantics spurn the exquisitely stated rules of the preceding period; they experiment, they churn around in an ecstasy of self-expression. At the height of a romantic period, everything is confused, sprawling, formless and chaotic – as well as, frequently, extremely interesting. Then, the romantic energy having spent itself, there is a new classical reformulation – and so the rhythms continue. (Gilmore, 1974: 102)

Historian David Musto has described similar cycles in American attitudes toward alcohol and drug use (1973, 1987a, 1987b). At least three times since the beginning of the 19th century, the United States has moved from periods of widespread, tolerated recreational use of alcohol and drugs to puritanical periods of uncompromising prohibition. The first period of intolerance began in the 1820s and culminated in prohibition of alcohol in eight states by the 1850s (Gusfield, 1963). The temperance movement of the late 19th century led to national Prohibition; more generalized intolerance of drug use and users produced the first major federal narcotics laws, the Harrison Act of 1914 and the Marijuana Tax Act of 1937. The first signs of the contemporary period of intolerance appeared around 1970, when the Nixon administration declared its war on drugs. Intolerance of drug use took firm hold in the early 1980s and the United States remains in its grip.

According to Musto, peoples' normative beliefs about drug use also vary with phases in drug-use tolerance cycles. For example, live-and-let-live attitudes prevail in periods of relative tolerance, like the 1820s, 1880s and 1960s. In the late 19th century, for example, cocaine and opium (and derivatives) were widely used in patent medicines, most addicts were conventional, law-abiding people, predominantly women, and cocaine was widely seen as a harmless recreational drug. In the 1960s marijuana was widely and openly used; it and many hallucinogens were seen by many as recreational drugs that were less harmful than alcohol. In the 1970s, before attitudes had hardened, President Carter called for federal decriminalization of private marijuana possession. A few years earlier Peter Bourne (not then but later Carter's primary drug policy advisor) wrote that cocaine 'is probably the most benign of illicit drugs currently in widespread use. At least as strong a case could be made for legalizing it as for legalizing marijuana' (Musto, 1987b: 277). Promotion of neither of those positions is imaginable in the contemporary White House.

Musto has several times written of the seeming anomaly that prohibitionistic sentiments become strongest and drug policies harshest after drug use has begun to decline (e.g. 1987a). At various periods, drug use comes into vogue, use increases and dangers of abusive use become evident. Then, as Daniel Kagan has summarized Musto's argument

> Soon the trend reverses; drug use starts to decline faster and faster. Public opinion turns against drugs and their acceptability begins to evaporate. Gradually, drug use becomes associated,

truthfully or not, with the lower ranks of society, and often with racial and ethnic groups that are feared or despised by the middle class. Drugs become seen as deviant and dangerous and become a potent symbol of evil. Trailing behind this decline come large-scale legislative and law enforcement efforts . . . aimed at curtailing drug sales and use through energetic prohibition and enforcement and ever-harsher punishments against sellers and users. During this period, public opprobrium intensifies into outright fear, hatred of drug dealers and users, and a burning anger and intolerance toward anyone and anything associated with drug use. (Kagan, 1989: 10)

During periods of relative tolerance, traditional American notions of individualism and personal autonomy allow individuals to make their own choices about drug use, drug use is widely seen as only mildly deviant, or not deviant at all, and people feel able to argue on the merits for the benefits and pleasures of drug use, for individuals' moral rights to make their own choices and against state intrusion into those choices. In periods of intolerance, drug use is widely seen as deviant and few people feel comfortable risking moral disapproval or stigmatization by arguing in favour of drug use or tolerance of drug users. Musto notes that

in the decline phase of drug use . . . we tend to have an overkill, that is to say people become so righteous and so zealous that we can have excesses in the name of fighting drugs. There is very little opposition to draconian policies because no one wants to stand up for using drugs. (1987a: 43)

The important thing about the Gilmore and Musto accounts, for the purposes of this article, is that they tie sensibilities and beliefs to recurring segments of cyclical patterns. Gilmore observes that, during classical periods, rules of composition and structure are stated 'to the general acclaim'. Formalism, in other words, is not foisted upon a society or an era, but embodies aesthetic qualities that people value, or believe they value, which is almost the same thing. Musto observes that excesses occur during the decline phase because 'people become so righteous and so zealous'.

It is a truism that our upbringings, past experiences, material circumstances and immediate environments shape the way we see and understand the world. People tend not be conservative until they have things to conserve, and so the frequent pattern that youthful radicals become middle-aged moderates and elderly conservatives. Or, the somewhat different Chinese developmental stereotype that people are Confucianist while young, Realist in maturity and Taoist when old. And history is full of stories of whole societies overwhelmed by fear or insecurity to do or tolerate horrible things that later appear unthinkable.

It is one thing, however, to acknowledge that our interests and experiences influence our wants and beliefs, and quite another to urge, with some of the sillier postmodernists, that what we see depends solely on where we stand. Since one standpoint is as good as any other, we cannot see anything (or we can see many things, but no perception is any more 'privileged' or any less contingent than any other). That may be a plausible position to adopt in relation to aesthetic assessments of bellbottoms or bouffant hairdos, but not in relation to fundamental normative issues over which human beings have been puzzling for millennia. Human beings have been round the bend and come back enough times that we should be able, by learning from history, to escape being condemned to repeat at least the worst excesses. Witches and heretics have burned sufficiently often, to later regret, that there is no need to burn them again in order again to be able to regret it. That lesson should have been learnt for good by now and, at least in most western countries, probably has been. Similar lessons could and should be learned about tolerance of human sexual diversity, experimentation with and use of intoxicants and punishment of wrongdoers. In this article the subject is the punishment of offenders.

UNTHOUGHT THOUGHTS

Lots of examples could be offered of issues and ways of thinking that are common in particular times and conspicuously absent in others. I mention two, preventive detention and prosecutorial sentence appeal, quickly and then devote more sustained attention to two others. The first is the near absence in the decade-long development of the Model Penal Code of more than passing mention of desert, proportionality, retribution or placating the public mood as important aims of punishment or sentencing. The second is a curious disappearance from corrections research of interest in the recidivism of people released after serving a first prison term. Both are like Holmes's non-barking dog. The absence of issues may offer important clues. And, if those times were blind to some things and acutely aware of others, we are likely to be just as vulnerable to collective selective awareness.

The disappearance of debate over preventive detention and prosecutorial appeals

In the year 2000, battles over preventive detention and prosecutorial sentence appeals are distant memories and no one seems in principle opposed to either. Due process liberals, judges and just about everyone else has been socialized by the ethos of our time into accepting that the public safety arguments for both are self-evident. 'Twasn't so before and likely some day won't be again.

In the 1970s, there were heated and extended political fights over preventive detention. Due process champions for years successfully opposed federal adoption of legislation that would permit persons accused of crime to be confined before trial because of dangers they might present to public safety. Defendants are presumed innocent, the argument went, and pre-trial confinement is allowable only to assure defendants' presence at trial; detention for any other reason except in the case of capital crimes is an unconstitutional invasion of citizens' liberty interests. Crime-control conservatives by contrast argued that the presumption of innocence is merely an evidentiary presumption and citizens' interest in public safety justified restrictions on the liberties of dangerous alleged offenders. The battle raged for years but finally the conservatives won and in 1973 Congress enacted the District of Colombia preventative detention law (D.C. sect. 23-1322-23-1331).

Here's another example of a long-forgotten but sharply contested issue of principle. Before sentencing guidelines, appellate review of sentences in the USA was close to nonexistent. The existence of sentencing rules or guidelines, however, implied the right of defendants to appeal sentences they believed were inconsistent with applicable guidelines (Frankel, 1972). But if defendants were to be allowed to appeal sentences they believed too harsh, should not prosecutors be allowed to appeal sentences they believed too soft? The principal arguments were two: procedural symmetry, what is fair for the defendant is fair for the prosecution; and substantive symmetry, if the defendant has a cognizable interest in avoiding too much punishment the state has a reciprocal interest in assuring enough. There was one principal argument against: the state should not be able to win on appeal what it could not win in court. Just as, under double jeopardy doctrine, an acquittal absolves a factually guilty defendant of the jeopardy of a second prosecution, so an anomalously slight sentence should insulate from the risk of a harder one. The state gets but one bite at the defendant's apple, and the presumptions all run in favour of the defendant's autonomy and liberty interests. There was extended and spirited disagreement. Most criminal procedure scholars predicted that prosecutorial appeal would not withstand constitutional scrutiny. In *United States* v. *DiFrancesco*, 449 US 117 (1980), it did, and the issue has disappeared.

One might suggest that the two preceding examples merely illustrate stare decisis in action. Litigants have accepted that the courts have ruled, and life has moved on. That could be, but not necessarily. There are many normatively contested subjects about which people do not lambishly accept authoritative court decisions. Abortion, affirmative action and capital punishment offer examples. The difference may be that these are such deeply contested normative issues that proponents of polar positions are less likely to be worn down by the general ethos of an era, or there may be no ethos. Issues imbued with less primal emotions may be more susceptible to the social and cognitive forces Musto (1973), Gilmore (1974), Johnson (1976) and many other historians describe.

Desert and the model penal code

It can be eye-glazingly tedious to encounter another recital of the mainstream theories of punishment – retributive, consequential, hybrid, expressive – and the various ways they can be sub-partitioned. Precursors, foreshadows and full statements of core ideas can be found in 3rd-century Athens, and they have echoed and accreted throughout the centuries. This is a subject about which little that is new is likely to be found under the sun. Every post-Enlightenment period has its matched pair of preventive and moralizing debaters – Jeremy Bentham and Immanuel Kant, John Stuart Mill and James Fitzjames Stephen, Herbert Hart and Lord Patrick Devlin, Norval Morris and James Q. Wilson. And yet, the Model Penal Code, 15 years in the making, never mentions desert, retribution or proportionality in its text or original commentary, and echoes of such ideas only occasionally appear in the transcripts of the American Law Institute (ALI) meetings at which successive drafts were discussed.

The following paragraphs describe and quote from ALI discussions of such things as purposes of punishment, presumptions against imprisonment and for parole release and related subjects. First, though, to give a fuller picture of how far 1950s' ideas about punishment were from mainstream contemporary views, I describe the Code's major punishment provisions. The main themes are that offenders' prospects for law-abidingness are nearly always relevant to decision making, that officials should have broad discretion in making those decisions and that prison should be used as little as possible. A fourth theme could be offered – that public safety considerations should always govern decisions, in effect a co-equal goal with offender rehabilitation – but allusions to public safety often feel as if they are offered by rote and the Code's provisions clearly give primacy to the first three themes.

The American Law Institute is an establishmentarian organization of lawyers, judges and law professors. It has a self-perpetuating nominated membership and for much of its life has been preponderantly composed of members of major urban commercial law firms. At least in legal circles, one might suppose that 'prestigious' were part of the organizational name, as in 'X is a member of the prestigious American Law Institute'. It was established early in 1923 with a law reform purpose and special emphasis on systematizing and rationalizing state laws (Goodrich and Wolkin, 1961; Hull, 1990; American Law Institute, 1998; Elson, 1998). Each American state and the federal government has its own legal system, and this led to the very real problem for businesses operating in national markets that legal provisions concerning basic features of contract, tort, insurance and personal property law varied significantly from state to state. Initially ALI concentrated on descriptive statements or 'restatements' of existing law, as in the Restatement of the Law of Contracts, or on more prescriptive synthetic proposals for improvement, as in the Uniform Commercial Code. Particular ALI projects are carried out under the aegis of committees, and under the direction of 'reporters', but proposals receive official ALI imprimatur only upon positive votes of the membership at annual meetings.

The Model Penal Code, conceived in the 1940s, exemplified later and even more prescriptive attempts to develop model codes which, if successful, might serve as the bases for comprehensive refashioning of state laws. Columbia Law School professor, Herbert Wechsler, in retrospect the most influential American criminal law scholar of his century, was the Chief Reporter for the Model Penal Code. The key drafters of the Code's sentencing and corrections provisions, and the oversight committee, included leading law professors, judges, prosecutors, psychiatrists, mental health specialists and corrections professionals. Sanford Bates and James V. Bennett, for example, successive reformist heads of the US Bureau of Prisons, and Paul W. Tappan, sometime head of the US Parole Board, and comparable state officials, were active participants. Over a 10-year period, from 1953 to 1962, drafts of various proposed sections of the Code were discussed at ALI annual meetings and final approvals were given in 1961 (sentencing and corrections) and 1962 (the rest).

I describe ALI and its processes to highlight that it is about as establishmentarian as an organization can be. Its centre of gravity in the elite commercial bar implies institutional conservatism. Its deliberative processes are ponderous and unwieldy and, at day's end, require that the text of a proposed model criminal law pass muster with an ALI membership composed largely of judges and business lawyers. In other words, it is not an organization predisposed to cutting-edge ideas or radical innovation. Curiously, though, the provisions of its Model Penal Code are so radical by contemporary standards as nearly to be unimaginable. In retrospect, it is striking how much attention was given to the perceived need to accommodate offenders' treatment needs and prospects and how little attention to notions of 'deserved punishment', 'just deserts' or public opinion. The following paragraphs set out the principal sentencing, parole release and good time provisions (ALI, 1954, 1956, 1960; ALI Proceedings, 1954, 1956, 1960, 1961).

Purposes of sentencing

The first official draft, from 1962, lists eight 'general purposes of the provisions governing the sentencing and treatment of the offender'. The first three are: 'To prevent the commission of offenses; To promote the correction and rehabilitation of offenders; To safeguard offenders against excessive, disproportionate or arbitrary punishment' (ALI, 1962: 2–3). Nowhere is mention made of 'imposing deserved punishment', 'acknowledging the seriousness of the crime', 'expressing public outrage' or anything similar.

Authorized prison sentences

The first proposed draft divided all felonies into three classes. Judges set minimums and maximums were prescribed by statute. For first-degree felonies, the minimum was one to 20 years and the maximum was life. For second-degree felonies, the minimum was one to three years and the maximum 10. For third-degree felonies, the minimum was one to two years and the maximum five (tentative draft 2, ALI, 1954). In other words, a judge could impose a one-year minimum sentence, no matter how serious the offence.

Authorized probation sentences

The first proposed draft authorized judges to sentence any person to probation, including those convicted of murder and other first-degree felonies potentially punishable by a life sentence, when the judge 'deems that his imprisonment is unnecessary for protection of the public'. To make certain no one could misunderstand, the commentary explains that the draft 'is based upon the view that suspension of sentence or probation may be appropriate dispositions on conviction of *any* offense' (tentative draft 2, ALI, 1954: 34, emphasis added) unless a mandatory sentence of death or life imprisonment is prescribed.

Reconsideration of sentences

The first proposed draft made every prison sentence 'tentative' for the first year and authorized the corrections commissioner to petition for resentencing. The commentary explains that judges have limited opportunity to study the offender and that corrections officials may decide that the judge 'proceeded on the basis of misapprehension as to the history, character or physical or mental condition of the defendant' (ALI, 1954: 57). Herbert Wechsler explained during the ALI deliberations:

> This is a really fundamental provision of the draft. One of the great arguments against judicial sentencing has always been that the judge must decide too much, too soon . . . Even with a good pre-sentence report there has been a limited opportunity to study the offender . . . (ALI Proceedings, 1954: 143)

Mitigation of sentences

The first proposed draft authorized judges, when they believed the offence of conviction authorized sentences that were too harsh under all the circumstances of the case, to sentence an offender convicted of any felony, as if convicted of a lower-degree felony or a misdemeanour (tentative draft 2, ALI, 1954). Wechsler explained that the provision was 'really a kind of introduction of equity, the basic Aristotelian idea of equity into law that every generalization – and law must be general – has unstatable qualifications that must be acknowledged when the case arises' (ALI Proceedings, 1954: 92).

Good time

The first proposed draft directed that prisoners receive six days' good time for each month served on good behaviour, and that corrections officials could award another six days per month for 'especially meritorious behaviour or exceptional performance of his duties' (tentative draft 5, ALI, 1956: 81). The good time credits would apply to (and thus advance) both the minimum to be served before parole release eligibility and the maximum to be served before mandatory release.

Parole release

The first proposed draft made prisoners eligible for parole release on completion of their minimum sentences less any applicable good time, and created a presumption in favour of release when prisoners first became eligible. Prisoners were required to be released when they had served their maximum sentences (net of good time) (tentative draft 5, ALI, 1956).

Public sentiments

The Model Penal Code created no mandatory sentences or probation ineligibility provisions (except concerning life sentences and the death penalty). The final draft, however, acknowledged that public opinion might sometimes be relevant. In a provision creating a presumption against imprisonment and for probation in every case, the final draft added a new criterion, 'a lesser sentence will depreciate the seriousness of the defendant's crime', among the reasons for disregarding the presumption and ordering a term of imprisonment (ALI, 1962: 106). A similar provision was added to a list of considerations that might justify disregarding the presumption that prisoners be released at first parole eligibility. Wechsler explained in 1961, however, that the language was not meant to direct a judge to respond to public sentiment about a particular crime, but instead to consider deterrent processes:

> [W]hat really is of concern to the court in relation to deterrence is not the stiffness of the disposition of this particular man, but that the disposition not have a general effect on the community which tends to depreciate the gravity of the crime and thus imply a license to commit it. (ALI Proceedings, 1961: 340)

The tone of the discussions on the relevance of public opinion was set by Corrections Commissioner (and former judge) Anna M. Kross of New York. She worried that

> sentencing power [would] . . . remain in the hands of a judge who at the time is in the first place influenced by the temper of the people. He is worried about what they are going to say about him. He is worried about what the newspapers are going to print. His judgment, no matter how well adjusted and how sound and how sane and how honest he is, necessarily is affected. He is only human. (ALI Proceedings, 1954: 75)

Only one speaker spoke of public opinion in terms resonant of our time. Judge James Alger Fee of California, after telling of his father's life as a judge in frontier Oregon, observed

> There is one place where I do not agree at all with some of the sentiments that have been expressed here. I think that local thought on the subject of penalty is one thing you should

recognize because it is to the community eventually and the local community, not some United Nations or Federal community – that you are really responsible. It is the people that make and enforce the law, and it is community sentiment that backs up a law. (ALI Proceedings, 1954: 78)

Others acknowledged the existence and force of public opinion, but as something to be managed or evaded, not as something to be respected. Judge Gerald F. Flood of Pennsylvania, for example, preferred to place powers in judges' than administrators' hands because judges were better able to withstand the force of public opinion:

[S]omeone has to take up the shock of the community outrage and community pressure. And I think that Dr [Thorsten] Sellin [about to go to California for ALI to study California practices] will find (it was a visit to California that changed my mind, really) the community pressure is less able to be resisted by a Board than it is by a Judge. A Judge is elected for a long period, and he can much more easily resist pressure than can a Board which can be thrown out of office by a Governor the next morning. (ALI Proceedings, 1954: 79)

Wechsler noted the problem, but in an oddly circumscribed way. The minimum sentence provision allowed judges to set minimums as long as 20 years for first-degree felonies such as murder. Wechsler explained this as a response to public passions:

It often happens that crimes of violence are shocking crimes and are perpetrated by individuals who three or four years later do not, to the people who study them, seem to present the kind of threat for the future that the particular act that they committed suggests. But the public remembers the act. Therefore we thought that in this area where by hypothesis public indignation as to the offense in the sense of need for a general deterrent penalty would be very strong, it would be prudent to give the Judge power at the time of sentence to satisfy the community that this person would be taken out of currency for a substantial period of time. (ALI Proceedings, 1954: 74)

And so the Code provided (though as eventually adopted the 20 years was dropped to 10). It strikes me as noteworthy that Wechsler described the public demand in terms of 'a general need for a deterrent sentence' rather than in terms of retributive or expressive needs. It also strikes me as noteworthy that judges could (but need not) impose up to a 20-year minimum for a first-degree felony (but only up to three years for any other), but could also impose probation in the same case, and could reconsider any prison sentence at any time within a year of imposition.

I write this article in a time when powerful ideas like 'truth in sentencing', 'do the crime, do the time' and 'just deserts' have great influence. They are not new ideas. Cesare Beccaria would have found the concepts though not the phrases familiar. Herbert Wechsler, and many of the judges, lawyers and law professors with whom he worked, would have been familiar with the writings not only of Beccaria but also of Kant, Hegel, Stephen and many other proponents of ideas that are only very weakly discernible in the Model Penal Code. That so talented a group of law-reformers, working within so inherently conservative and establishmentarian a setting as the American Law Institute, produced and won approval of a document so uninfluenced by powerful and influential ideas, should make us wonder what similarly powerful ideas are being ignored in our time.

'Prison works': recidivism of first-time prisoners

One striking sign of the differences in penal ethos between our and earlier times is in the way we think, speak and write about prisoner recidivism. Two robust recidivism findings were evident in the 1960s and today. I overstate them for effect, because inevitably methodological qualifications warrant mention, but they nonetheless express an important contrast.

First, answering a question researchers often asked in the 1950s and 1960s, *of people released from a first prison sentence*, two-thirds do not return to prison. Prison works, in the sense that most people sent there do not want to go back and organize their future lives so as not to go back.

Second, answering the question researchers asked in the 1980s and 1990s, *of people released from prison in a given year* or as part of a representative release sample or cohort, considerably more than half return to prison. Prison does not work, in the sense that most people released from prison do not manage to conduct law-abiding lives and to refrain from the kinds of unlawful behaviour that leads to apprehension, conviction and imprisonment.

Both statements can be true because they are statements about different groups of people. The first statement refers to people in prison for the first time. Some have done things, including violent things, which are situational and out-of-character, and they would be subsequently law-abiding whether or not they are sent to prison. Some may be essentially conformist people with prosocial values who behaved criminally and are shamed or shocked by their imprisonment into law-abidingness. Some may be young offenders who committed crimes but were not too badly damaged by their prison experiences and after release found love, work or God and aged out of their offending years, as most young offenders do. And some, a minority, are so developmentally disadvantaged, or so predisposed to deviance, or so committed to a life of crime that they return to crime and in due course to court and prison.

The second statement refers to all people released from prison in a representative sample of releasees. This means they include a small fraction who are being released from prison for the first time, and if the first statement is true have about a one-third likelihood of returning to prison, and a much larger fraction who have been released from prison before, and have a much higher likelihood of returning to prison. The clearest example of this is found in data on return to prison for all persons released from Florida prisons between 1 July 1986 and February 1992. Of those with no prior incarcerations, 31.6 percent returned to prison compared with 42 percent of those with one prior incarceration and 52 percent of those with four or more (Florida Legislative Office of Program Policy Analysis and Government Accountability, 1995: exhibit 9).

Because recidivism and reincarceration of first-time prisoners have not received much attention for three decades, data on the subject are not readily available, but other data support strong inferences. For example, a BJS survey of arrest data for all prisoners released in 1983 from prisons in 11 states found that, within three years, 62.5 percent were rearrested for a felony or serious misdemeanour, 46.8 percent were reconvicted and 41.8 percent were returned to prison or jail (Beck, 1989). However, of those releasees with only one prior arrest at the time of the study (that which led to the incarceration), 38.1 percent had been rearrested within three years compared with 63.2 percent for the entire sample and in excess of 75 percent for the half of the group who had been arrested six or more times (Beck, 1989: table 11). Similarly, of all adult Minnesota prisoners released in 1992, 59 percent were rearrested within three years, 45 percent were reconvicted and 28 percent were reimprisoned for a new offence (Minnesota Legislative Auditor, 1997: figure 3.2). However, of those with no criminal history (no prior adult felony convictions and not more than one minor petty misdemeanour), 39 percent were rearrested and only 24 percent were reconvicted (Minnesota Legislative Auditor, 1997: table 3.6).

None of this should be surprising. Research on age and crime shows that crime participation rates for property crime peak in the mid-teens and for violence in the late teens and that most criminally active people desist by the early twenties (Farrington, 1986). Research on criminal careers shows that the probability of rearrest given one arrest is not high but that the probability rises monotonically with each subsequent arrest, reaching 80 percent by the 6th arrest (Farrington, 1979; Blumstein et al., 1986). Putting the two findings together should make it self-evident that most people sent to prison, and hence released, will be persistent offenders, and accordingly that on average people released from prison will present relatively high risks for recidivism.

Is it not odd though, that in our time, we have forgotten the lower-risk first-timers, and do not even think in our research to ask separately about them? Social scientists who self-select to study criminals and prisoners are not especially known for their conservatism or Republicanism and yet, in our time, they have forgotten that the question they ask, 'What percentage of prisoners fail?', provides an answer that supports the penal policies of our time, while the answer to a different question about first-time prisoners would not.

This is the last of the non-barking dogs described in this article. Taken together, the various forgotten and overlooked issues described above should suggest a collective partial amnesia, which is striking, given the universality of the underlying issues and principles.

Building futures on pasts

It may be impossible in these final paragraphs to avoid appearing sententious, but that is a risk I comfortably take. The lessons of this article are simple and suggest that much that we do in the name of public safety is cruel and excessive, ruining lives for no good reason, and will in time be deeply regretted. Thoughtful, decent people, and the governments that variously follow and lead them, should know better than to strike in anger, to do things they will later regret, to treat others cruelly for no good reason. This is no less true of the punishment of offenders than of the burning of apostates or the scourging of homosexuals.

Looking at how human beings in other times have been affected by the oscillations of regularly recurring normative cycles should help us to recognize where there be dragons, and at least to reduce the excesses and cruelties that otherwise are likely during periods of deepest intolerance and moralism.

We live in a time when the broad waves of sensibility that Musto suggests are associated with the moralism of a period of declining drug use, and that are likely also associated with times of declining crime rates, have provided an especially receptive climate for the calls of moral entrepreneurs and cynical politicians. They in turn are responding to the hysteria and tendency to overreaction associated with moral panics, all in a de-stabilised era of massive social and economic change.

US crime policy for nearly two decades has been driven much more by ideology, emotion and political opportunism than by rational analysis of options and reasoned discussion. It is as if a continuous moral panic has prevented policy makers from stepping back and taking stock of what they have been doing.

Human beings have the capacity to resist or divert powerful emotional forces. Evidence can be found in folk wisdom by which decent people try to govern their daily lives – things like, 'Don't take it out on your child' or 'sit down and count to 10'. Aphorisms like these are commonly part of our personal ethics because we know that things that make us angry or depressed often make us irritable and at danger of overreacting or taking out our upset on whoever is close at hand, and that is not fair. The child or spouse or employee who is abused because of other things happening in the abuser's life has been treated unfairly. It happens more often than most people like to admit, but gives rise to guilty feelings later, to resolutions not to let it happen again and to aphorisms like those quoted.

What is right in private lives is also right in public life. Moral panics, cyclical patterns of moral intolerance and anxieties associated with fundamental social changes increase inclinations for adoption of harsh, inhumane and ill-considered crime policies. Knowing that, policy makers should try all the harder to separate the ephemeral and emotional from the lasting and reflective. Most elected officials, it seems reasonable to guess, do try in their private lives to manage their outbursts of emotion and their displacements of anger. If they did so in their public lives, contemporary American crime policies would look very different.

References

Alschuler, A.W. (1978) 'Sentencing reform and prosecutorial power', *University of Pennsylvania Law Review* 126: 550–77.

American Law Institute (ALI) (1954) *Model Penal Code: tentative draft no. 2*. Philadelphia, PA: American Law Institute.

American Law Institute (ALI) (1956) *Model Penal Code: tentative draft no. 5*. Philadelphia, PA: American Law Institute.

American Law Institute (ALI) (1960) *Model Penal Code: tentative draft no. 12*. Philadelphia, PA: American Law Institute.

American Law Institute (ALI) (1962) Model Penal Code (*proposed official draft*). Philadelphia, PA: American Law Institute.

American Law Institute (ALI) (1998) *The American Law Institute seventy-fifth anniversary 1923–1998*. Philadelphia, PA: American Law Institute.

American Law Institute (ALI), Proceedings (1954) *31st annual meeting. The American Law Institute. Proceedings*. Philadelphia, PA: American Law Institute.

American Law Institute (ALI), Proceedings (1956) *33rd annual meeting. The American Law Institute. Proceedings*. Philadelphia, PA: American Law Institute.

American Law Institute (ALI), Proceedings (1960) *37th annual meeting. The American Law Institute. Proceedings*. Philadelphia, PA: American Law Institute.

American Law Institute (ALI), Proceedings (1961) *38th annual meeting. The American Law Institute. Proceedings*. Philadelphia, PA: American Law Institute.

Beck, A.J. (1989) *Recidivism of prisoners released in 1983*. Washington, DC: US Department of Justice, Bureau of Justice Statistics.

Beckett, K. (1997) *Making crime pay: law and order in contemporary American politics*. New York: Oxford University Press.

Bennett, W.J., DiIulio, J.J. and Walters, J.P. (1996) *Body count: moral poverty – and how to win America's war against crime and drugs*. New York: Simon & Schuster.

Blumstein, A., Coteen, J., Roth, J. and Visher, C. (1986) *Criminal careers and 'career' criminals*. Washington, DC: National Academic Press.

Boswell, J. (1980) *Christianity, social tolerance, and sexuality*. Chicago, IL: University of Chicago Press.

Boutellier, H.J. (2000) *Crime and morality: the significance of criminal justice in post-modern culture*. Dordrecht, Netherlands: Kluwer Academic.

Caplow, T. and Simon, J. (1999) 'Understanding prison policy and population trends', in M. Tonry and J. Petersilia (eds) *Prisons*, vol. 26 of *Crime and justice: a review of research*, edited by M. Tonry. Chicago, IL: University of Chicago Press.

Cox, E. (1877) *Principles of punishment as applied to the criminal law by judges and magistrates*. London: Law Times Office.

Edsall, T. and Edsall, M. (1991) *Chain reaction: the impact of race, rights, and taxes on American politics*. New York: Norton.

Elson, A. (1998) 'The case for an in-depth study of the American Law Institute', *Law and Social Enquiry* 23: 625–40.

Erikson, K.T. (1966) *Wayward pilgrims: a study in the sociology of deviance*. New York: John Wiley.

Farrington, D.P. (1979) 'Longitudinal research on crime and delinquency', in N. Thomas and M. Tonry (eds) *Crime and justice: an annual review of research, vol. 1*. Chicago, IL: University of Chicago Press.

Farrington, D.P. (1986) 'Age and crime', in M. Tonry and N. Thomas (eds) *Crime and justice: an annual review of research, vol. 7*. Chicago, IL: University of Chicago Press.

Florida Legislative Office of Program Policy Analysis and Government Accountability (1995) *Policy review of reincarceration in Florida's prisons administered by the Department of Corrections*. Tallahassee: Florida Legislature.

Foucault, M. (1977) *Discipline and punish: the birth of the prison*, trans. Robert Hurley. New York: Pantheon.

Frankel, M. (1972) *Criminal sentences: law without order*. New York: Hill & Wang.

Garland, D. (1996) 'The limits of the sovereign state: strategies of crime control in contemporary society', *British Journal of Criminology* 36(4): 445–71.

Gilmore, G. (1974) *The death of contract*. Columbus, OH: Ohio State University Press.

Goodrich, H.F. and Wolkin, P.A. (1961) *The story of the American Law Institute 1023–1961*. St Paul, MN: American Law Institute.

Gusfield, J.R. (1963) *Symbolic crusade: status politics and the American temperance movement*. Urbana, IL: University of Illinois Press.

Hull, N.E.H. (1990) 'Restatement and reform: a new perspective on the origins of the American Law Institute', *Law and History Review* 8: 55–000.

Johnson, P. (1976) *A history of Christianity*. New York: Atheneum.

Kagan, D. (1989) 'How America lost its first drug war', *Insight* 20 November: 8–17.

Kahan, D. (1998) 'Punishment and incommensurability', *Buffalo Law Review* 1: 691–708.

Lappi-Seppälä, T. (2000) 'Sentencing and punishment in Finland: the decline of the repressive ideal', in M. Tonry and R.S. Frase (eds) *Sentencing and sanctions in western countries*. New York: Oxford University Press.

Minnesota Legislative Auditor (1997) *Recidivism of adult felons.* St Paul, MN: State of Minnesota, Office of the Legislative Auditor.

Morris, N. (1974) *The future of imprisonment.* Chicago, IL: University of Chicago Press.

Musto, D. (1973) *The American disease: origins of narcotic control.* New York: Oxford University Press.

Musto, D. (1987a) 'Remarks', in J. Roth, M. Tonry and N. Morris (eds) *Drugs and crime: workshop proceedings.* A Report of the 1986 National Academy of Sciences Conference on Drugs and Crime Research. Washington, DC: National Academy of Sciences.

Musto, D. (1987b) *The American disease: origins of narcotic control,* Expanded edn (orig. 1973). New York: Oxford University Press.

Reitz, K.R. (2000) 'The disassembly and reassembly of US sentencing practices', in M. Tonry and R. Frase (eds) *Sentencing and sanctions in western countries.* New York: Oxford University Press.

Roberts, J. and Stalans, L. (1997) *Public opinion, crime, and criminal justice.* Boulder, CO: Westview Press.

Rothman, D.J. (1980) *Conscience and convenience.* Boston, MA: Little, Brown.

Tonry, M. (1999a) 'Why are US incarceration rates so high?', *Crime and Delinquency* 45: 419–37.

Tonry, M. (1999b) 'Rethinking unthinkable punishment policies in America', *UCLA Law Review* 46(1): 1–38.

Törnudd, P. (1997) 'Sentencing and punishment in Finland', in M. Tonry and K. Hatlestad (eds) *Sentencing reform in overcrowded times: a comparative perspective.* New York: Oxford University Press.

Walker, N. (1999) *Aggravation, mitigation, and mercy in English criminal law.* London: Blackstone.

12   Facts, values and prison policies

A commentary on Zimring and Tonry

JAMES B. JACOBS

The first part of Professor Franklin Zimring's article presents an important hypothesis that could and should itself be an article: that the US prison expansion of the last quarter century can be understood as three separate expansions, each driven by different independent variables. In presenting this hypothesis, Zimring focuses on national-level data and does not, as he has done elsewhere (Zimring and Hawkins, 1991) examine whether the hypothesis holds for each region and state. According to Zimring, the first expansion (1973–85) was caused by the influx of low-level offenders who previously would have received non-incarcerative sanctions. The second expansion (1985–92) is accounted for by the imprisonment of drug offenders who previously would not have gone to prison because either (Zimring does not specify) they were not offending at such a high rate or, more likely, they were not being arrested as frequently. (If it is just a greater propensity to incarcerate low-level drug offenders who previously would have received probation, then phase 2 would collapse into phase 1. If it is just a greater propensity to incarcerate drug offenders for longer terms, then phase 2 would collapse into phase 3.) The third expansion (1992–present) is the consequence of requiring offenders to serve more time. The hypothesis is quite plausible but, as Zimring, himself notes, it needs to be fleshed out and supported by empirical evidence. For example, does the increase in time served apply to all categories of offenses and offenders or just to certain subgroups?[1]

In the second part of his article, Professor Zimring seeks out the causes of the most dramatic prison expansion, which occurred from 1992 to the present. Zimring identifies three political developments (variables) to account for this extraordinary growth of imprisonment. The first is that politically or rhetorically the interests of victims have come to be defined in terms of the suffering of offenders. This is presented as pure hypothesis; no data, facts, or even anecdotes. Zimring does not say who defines victims and offenders as locked into a zero sum game or how this has changed over time. Is it true that, since 1992, more people, more members of key elite groups, or more legislators define doing something positive for victims as doing something negative to offenders?

At this point, Zimring shifts gears and offers a short and unflattering critique of victims' advocates who campaign for tougher sentencing laws. He sees no logical link between harming offenders and helping victims. It is not true logically or empirically, he points out, that more severe treatment of offenders provides equivalent (or indeed any) benefits to victims. There is not much to quarrel with here. I am sure that there is some irrationality in this, as arguably with practically all public policy, but undoubtedly some victims' advocates believe that more severe sentences serve the interests of their constituents through added incapacitation, deterrence, and retribution. That does not mean that they see crime and justice policy making as a zero sum game in which every pain imposed upon defendants bestows an equivalent benefit upon offenders. Indeed, there are victims rights advocates who support all kinds of alternatives to incarceration projects.

According to Professor Zimring, a second political development that contributes to the post-1992 prison explosion is an increasingly strong linkage between 'get tough' ideological (symbolic) concerns and policy implementation. He points out that the link is not always and everywhere strong. Politicians can claim credit for passing tough legislation which, in fact, turns out to be much less tough. Our traditional sentencing laws and practices are a good example. The legislature passed and judges imposed draconian sentences, but only a fraction of those sentences was ever served. The politicians got the political credit without having to pay the budgetary price. Have things changed since 1992? Zimring thinks they have, but his primary example is California, which may be exceptional in terms of populist politics and use of ballot initiatives to implement policy. He points out that California's 'three strikes law' affects more offenders by far than any other three strikes law in the country. But that very point means that the political variable he has isolated here – the strengthened link between symbolic politics and criminal justice policy – has not occurred everywhere in the country. For example, Congress, with much fanfare, passed federal three strikes legislation with the same symbolic message, but with impact on a very small number of defendants (see Austin et al., 1999).

Zimring's third political variable is the expansion or intensification of popular distrust in government. He believes that, since 1992, there has been a quantum increase in distrust of government that is reflected in legislation seeking to curb discretionary actions that heretofore ameliorated the impacts of tough criminal justice legislation. At this point, this also is a conjecture. Is there more distrust in government and particularly criminal-justice-specific governing than there was prior to 1992? Maybe so. Maybe that explains the proliferation of Megan's laws. Zimring's contribution, once again, is to have raised the question, not to have answered it.

The third part of Zimring's article argues that it will be difficult to significantly reverse the post-1992 prison explosion, say to the prisoner level of the pre-1992 period (which was still the highest in US history), and that such a reversal is therefore unlikely to occur. Zimring points out that never in history has anything like that kind of decarceration occurred, and he cannot see any political possibilities that would produce that result.

Admittedly, it is difficult to imagine what kind of political shifts would have to take place to produce such a massive decarceration. Of course, we are only too aware these days that criminologists are not good at predicting decreases. Even now we are scrambling to explain the extraordinary decrease in violent crime. How could the NYC murder rate decline by two-thirds in less than a decade? Still, Zimring makes a good point. We have constructed and entrenched a massive penal state, and it would be a major undertaking to dismantle it to any significant extent.

Make no mistake, Professor Zimring believes that there are too many people in prison; so does Professor Tonry and virtually all the academics who work on this subject. However, it is not clear whether this is only a 'values issue' for criminologists, or whether they have an objective methodology for determining the right and appropriate number of people in prison. Zimring's previous work suggests that no such methodology exists, and that we currently lack even a jurisprudence of the scale of imprisonment, let alone an objective norm of social health.

Professor Michael Tonry's article is explicitly about values. It would not be an exaggeration to say that Tonry believes our current prison policy to be evil: 'Much that we do . . . is cruel and excessive, ruin[s] lives for no good reason. . .' (Tonry, this volume, p. 161). These are strong, deeply felt sentiments, shared by the majority of liberal criminologists and often stated and restated as scientific facts rather than as beliefs, opinions, sentiments, values, and ideology. Tonry offers no evidence or even argument in support of this serious charge against contemporary American society. He does not seek to convince us that the current level of imprisonment is morally unjustifiable and repugnant. Rather, Tonry assumes that readers will find his conclusion obvious. He urges us not to accept the penal status quo as inevitable, reminding us that social, intellectual, and political history is full of shifts and swings in styles and values. His prediction that the contemporary cruelty 'will in time be deeply regretted' aims to give comfort, boost morale, and reinforce commitment to a certain liberal and humane ideology. It is also a claim to the moral superiority of his preferred sentencing policies.

Should we regard Professor Tonry's critique of the present predicament as anything other than an intuitive value judgment? I am not persuaded that there is a methodology that allows us to determine objectively whether the level of US incarceration is 'excessive,' that is to say, greater than is necessary to achieve its intended effect. (Are we to take Tonry to mean that all excessive sentences are ipso facto 'cruel?') There is certainly no objectivity to the judgment that it is 'cruel' – such an evaluation is inevitably subjective and comparative. 'Cruel' compared to what?

Why do Tonry and many other liberal penologists think that current policy is cruel and excessive? Presumably there are many prison inmates whom Professor Tonry thinks should have received a non-incarcerative sanction. It would help to have an analysis of the crimes and criminal record of a large sample of defendants sentenced to prison, perhaps in a single jurisdiction. It would be interesting to have Professor Tonry sort these defendants into two groups: (1) those whom he believes should not have been sent to prison, and (2) those whom he believes rightly deserved a prison term. We could ask him to next divide this second group, those rightly sent to prison, into two more groups: (1) those sentenced excessively, and (2) those sentenced fairly. Ideally, we could then scrutinize the motives, intentions, conduct, consequences, records, and excuses of defendants he assigned to category No. 1. Could more conservative raters provide rational (persuasive?) reasons why some or all of these defendants were rightly sentenced to prison? Then we could repeat the same exercise with respect to length of sentence. I think we would find that disagreement could not be resolved by social science facts or specialized expertise. How could we resolve a dispute, for example, about whether a first-time robber deserved to be sentenced to one year in jail? Before calling his one year jail sentence 'cruel and excessive,' we would at a minimum need to know how long that defendant will actually serve and how long he would serve for the same offense in different countries. Suppose we found that the average time served for rape is 60 months (see Brown et al., 1999). Put aside the point that many sentences have resulted from plea bargains in which additional and sometimes more serious counts have been dropped. How would we go about determining whether this is too severe, much less cruel and excessive? Practically everyone thinks rape is a serious crime and that some prison time is warranted. It seems to me that it would be hard to carry the argument that making rapists serve 60 months is per se cruel and excessive, especially those with prior criminal records.

There are a lot of difficulties in coming up with accurate data on time served for federal and state prisoners. The best government study of time served that I know of, found that 'based on admissions data for 1992 to 1994, violent State prisoners had an average sentence of about ten years and were expected (i.e. projected) to serve slightly less than 5 years on average' (Beck and Greenfeld, 1995). Granted that we would need to examine what is meant by 'violent,' I do not find these numbers on their face to make out a prima facie case of 'cruel and excessive.' No doubt shockingly severe individual sentences could be found, but so could shockingly lenient sentences.

Comparative time served data, holding criminal conduct and prior criminal record constant is very hard to come by (Lynch, 1988, 1993, 1995; Pease, 1994). I do not believe that criminologists have the data to back up the constantly repeated assertion that American offenders serve hugely greater sentences than similarly situated offenders in other countries.[2] It is very difficult to obtain time served data for US state prisoners. Moreover, plea bargaining confounds the data that are obtained, e.g. did the robber who served 24 months actually commit armed robbery? Furthermore, data are never broken down for prior criminal record, i.e. it would not make sense to compare time served by US robbers who average 3.0 previous felony convictions with a European sample of robbers who average 0.5 previous felony convictions.[3]

Professor Tonry is probably on more solid footing (and has more widespread support) when it comes to drug offenses. Unlike violent offenses, such as rape, there is not a strong consensus about how severely drug possessors and traffickers should be punished. Indeed, a small minority, including many intellectuals, believe that possession and trafficking in mind-altering drugs should not be illegal at all and therefore that any punishment is cruel and excessive. Even people who do not support drug legalization probably differ quite a bit in comparing the seriousness of drug crimes with other crimes.

Professor Tonry rightly points out that US current mass incarceration should not be thought of as inevitable. Prevailing values in a national population vary from generation to generation, and are contested by groups and individuals within the same generation. That is why there is debate on penal policy. I found his review of the ALI's (Model Penal Code) sentencing provisions useful and interesting. It is remarkable how differently that generation's legal elites thought than their successors 30 years later.

Professor Tonry, more elsewhere than in this article, has focused on and sharply denounced the rhetoric and policies of conservatives, mostly Republicans, in seizing on the crime issue to rally political support by appealing to fear and resentments. I think his critique applies to the 'liberal' Democrats as well. Indeed, the massive increase in incarceration (Frank Zimring's 3rd phase) that took place from 1992 to the present, tracks the years of Bill Clinton's presidency. I recently heard Harvard Law School professor, Philip Heymann state that the huge increase in federal inmates convicted of drug offenses has mainly occurred since the beginning of the first Clinton administration. Heymann pointed out that '[d]rug prosecutions have increased from 15,000 in the middle of President Reagan's second term to 60,000 now; and [offenders] are getting longer sentences' (Heymann, 2000). As he pointed out, it would be a major 'reform' undertaking just to go back to the drug imprisonment level that existed at the height of the Reagan Administration. President Clinton has strongly supported expansion of federal and state death penalties, retraction of federal habeas corpus, the drug war, and prison construction. Would Professor Tonry hold Clinton as guilty as Reagan and Bush in exploiting the political potential of these issues? And if there is such continuing bipartisan consensus at the political level, does not this suggest widespread public support for them too?

Notes

1 The following data support the phase 3 hypothesis. For all federal offenders, the mean time served in FY '85 was 14.9 months, FY '88 was 18.7 months, FY '91 was 21.7 months, FY '94 25.1 months, FY '95 was 28.5 months, and in FY '96 28.2 months. *Sourcebook on criminal justice statistics.* I have not found any systematic data on time served by state prisoners other than Allen Beck and Larry Greenfeld, *Violent offenders in state prison: sentences and time served*, Bureau of Justice Statistics, US Department of Justice, Office of Justice Programs, July 1995.

2 James Lynch argues that with respect to time served for serious offenses, European criminal justice does not look much different from US criminal justice. See James Lynch, 'Crime in international perspective', in J.Q. Wilson and J. Petersilia (eds) *Crime.* San Francisco, CA: ICS Press.

3 In actuality, because of plea bargaining, the real offense on average is likely to have been more serious. Allen Beck and Larry Greenfeld, '*Violent offenders in state prison: sentences and time served*, Bureau of Justice Statistics, US Department of Justice, Office of Justice, July 1995. A full discussion of 'cruel and excessive' would require an examination of the 'conditions' and 'terms' of confinement.

References

Austin, J., Clark, J., Hardyman, P. and Henry, D.A. (1999) 'The impact of three strikes and you're out', *Punishment & Society* 1(2).

Beck, A. and Greenfeld, L. (1995) *Violent offenders in state prison: sentences and time served*. Bureau of Justice Statistics: Selected Findings.

Brown, J., Langan, P. and Levin, D. (1999) *Felony sentences in state courts*. Bureau of Justice Statistics: Bulletin.

Heymann, P. (2000) 'Cautionary note on the expanding role of the US attorneys' offices, summary of proceedings', keynote address at the National Symposium on the Changing Role of US Attorneys' Offices in Public Safety, Arlington, Virginia 14–16 November.

Lynch, J. (1988) 'A comparison of prison use in England and Wales, Canada, the United States and West Germany: a limited test of the punitiveness hypothesis', *Journal of Criminal Law & Criminology* 79(1): 180–217.

Lynch, J. (1993) 'A cross-national comparison of the length of custodial sentences for serious crime', *Justice Quarterly* 10(4): 639–60.

Lynch, J. (1995) 'Crime in international perspective', in J.Q. Wilson and J. Petersilia (eds) *Crime*. San Francisco, CA: ICS Press.

Pease, K. (1994) 'Cross-national imprisonment rates: limitations of method and possible conclusions', *British Journal of Criminology* 34: 116–30.

Zimring, F.E. and Hawkins, G. (1991) *The scale of imprisonment*. Chicago, IL: University of Chicago Press.

13   The private and the public in penal history

A commentary on Zimring and Tonry

ALEX LICHTENSTEIN

Michael Tonry argues that appeals to retribution and reformation have alternated in the penal history of the West in general, and the US in particular. Periods of 'moral panic,' like our own today, precipitate crime policy driven by 'ideology, emotion, and political opportunism,' only to be superseded by calmer periods of crime control characterized by 'rational analysis' and 'reasoned discussion.' I wish I had such dialectical faith, or agreed that the historical record offered such cause for optimism. Unfortunately, Foucault's aphorism that 'prison "reform" is virtually contemporary with the prison itself' remains on the mark (Foucault, 1977). My own research on the racialized history of punishment in the American South suggests that brief moments of reform did more to refine and justify retribution than to alleviate suffering or rationalize punishment, and that regrets about previous penal practice have served more often than not to underwrite current horrors (Lichtenstein, 1996a). So, for example, the southern chain gang, widely regarded today as an abhorrent, racist, atavistic throwback to what Frank Tannenbaum called the 'Darker Phases of the South' was in fact on the cutting edge of modern, reformative, progressive penology when instituted as a humane alternative to convict leasing (Tannenbaum, 1924; Lichtenstein, 1993). Death penalty 'reform' today means abandoning the chair in favor of the needle, moving from the age of industry and electricity to the age of medicine and pathology. Current debates and anxiety about forensic certainty may constitute a stopgap against executions for now, as in Illinois,[1] but with forensic refinement may come an increased efficiency in the 'machinery of death,' reducing discomfort for the executioners as much as the executed. So too some reformers who sought to stamp out the practice of lynching in the first decades of the 20th century assured white southerners that a more effective, swift, and just application of legalized executions might render the mob unnecessary, and allow whites to control blacks without degrading themselves in the process (Brundage, 1993; Oshinsky, 1996; Wypijewski, 2000).

It is true that the sort of judicial discretion embodied in the American Law Institute's Model Penal Code might appear remarkably 'radical' from today's standpoint, as Tonry points out. The specter of the late Rose Bird haunts the profound shift in sentencing procedures over the past two decades, for her 1986 recall from the California Supreme

Court by popular referendum marked the inability of judges to insulate themselves from the tide of retributive sensibilities that has swept all penal policy before it since (Fried, 1999).[2] Yet, from another angle, the legal establishmentarians of the 1950s were quite *conservative*. Like many intellectuals and professionals of the time, they sought to shift public policy into the hands of an allegedly knowledgeable, scientific, and rational elite that 'knew better,' and away from the passions of the uneducated masses. If you are like me, this observation should send you running to your bookshelf to dust off that disused copy of something from the Frankfurt School. This mindset brought us discretionary sentencing – and it also brought us, courtesy of the Best and the Brightest, Viet Nam. And, I might add that while the process of punishment – the over-reliance on incarceration, the destruction of judicial discretion, a penal code rooted in retribution – has long overturned the assumptions of the Model Penal Code, actual reform of prison *conditions* was another matter. In all likelihood, most state prisons – especially, but not exclusively, in the South, which still has the highest incarceration rate in the country – were far *worse* places to do time in the 1950s or 1960s than they are even today. It did take the scrutiny of conscientious members of the Federal bench to enact genuine prison reform, but the civil rights and prisoners' rights movements made an enormous difference as well. This, not the Model Penal Code, was radical.

I would propose that in the realm of sensibilities about punishment we think not so much in terms of oscillation between rehabilitation and retribution, reform and reaction, expertise and emotion, but of a struggle between the public and the private faces of punishment. As both Tonry's and Zimring's articles suggest, when it comes to popular consumption of ideologies of crime control, punishment tends to be driven by symbolism – and usually a symbolism playing to the emotional desire for retribution for a private wrong rather than an offense against the state. Hence the 'zero sum model' of punishment noted by Zimring. Zimring observes, however, that the symbolic function of criminal law can sometimes have dire operational consequences, as with California's Three Strikes law. The 'loose linkage' between the symbolic and operational functions of the criminal law depends as well on a further bifurcation. Criminal justice as process, made visible to the average law-abiding citizen and his or her private concerns and fears by popular culture, political posturing, and on occasion, victimization, is severed from punishment itself, carried out in the abstract name of the public by the state but rendered invisible behind penitentiary walls.[3]

Zimring seems puzzled by the paradox of increased support for harsh punishment at a time of suspicion of the state. But his normative assumption that '[t]he punishment of criminals is at root an exercise of governmental power' (Zimring, this volume, p. 148) seems unwarranted. In fact, historically, many Americans have always maintained a very *weak* faith in the state's capacity to punish transgressors of community mores with due efficiency or retributive cruelty. They have expressed a deep suspicion of the adequacy of state-based punishment especially in times and places that criminality and the desire for social order have been racialized and harnessed to the project of white supremacy.[4] Naturally, such distrust has had a regional dimension as well, cropping up most frequently in the South, a section persistently bedeviled by high degrees of personal violence and elevated crime rates, anxieties about racial control, and the highest incarceration rates in the country, if not the world (Ayers, 1984; Butterfield, 1995).[5]

For argument's sake, let us begin with the exact opposite assumption from Zimring's – that historically, in the USA 'the punishment of criminals is at root an exercise of private power.' What if the history and evolution of crime policy reflects the struggle on the part of rationalizing 'experts' to overcome forms of punishment more traditionally rooted in the patriarchal family, the ownership of slaves, vigilantism, and employer–employee contract relations than in state sanctions? Indeed, operating from this counter-assumption erases the conundrum identified by Zimring. For when confidence in the state declines the citizenry takes criminal justice matters into its own hands. Of course in a modern society vigilantism is no longer openly tolerable, but a wide latitude for the use of force by the police might be; lynching is displayed as an atavism of the faded past, but the death penalty is wildly popular, indeed almost totally beyond political challenge; and as state capacity for punishment reaches its fiscal limits in response to the cry for law and order, the privatization of prisons and prison labor fills the gap (Christie, 1993; Lichtenstein and Kroll, 1996; Lafer, 1999; Parenti, 1999; Featherstone, 2000). The expanded state capacity for retributive justice, then, actually becomes a proxy for an enhanced nostalgic ideal of private punishment.

Taken together, Tonry's and Zimring's articles imply that a brief period of post-Second World War rationalization of criminal justice, exemplified by the crafting of a humane, flexible penal code by a coterie of experts, has now been supplanted by a populistic embrace of the symbolism of punishment. Harnessed to a nostalgic longing for private retribution, and driven by emotion (and the pandering of politicians) this trend has driven incarceration rates to unprecedented levels over the past two decades. Granting this narrative – and I remain skeptical about the contrast between penal reform and penal reaction on which it partially rests – this view still deserves to be placed in some sort of long-range historical context. To begin with, we might ask not only what has driven Professor Zimring's graph off the charts since 1980, but why 20th-century incarceration rates show such remarkable *stability* prior to that, during a period in American history that saw a cataclysmic economic collapse, three wars and subsequent demobilizations, a massive population transfer from the rural South to the urban North, and the turmoil of the 1960s. Incarceration rates, while not impervious to these events, did not seem to respond to them dramatically either, or at least not immediately. A second, related question, would be to look back to the 19th century and ask if such a historic rupture in incarceration patterns has any precedents.

Undeniably the sheer scale of incarceration today *is* unprecedented, and frightening precisely because of its absolute novelty. But the sudden transition from a relatively stable pattern of incarceration to a rapid increase is not unprecedented. Let me take the example I am most familiar with, and one, which I happen to think, illustrates my contention that punishment in America is first and foremost a private phenomenon. If we look at the pattern of imprisonment that emerged in the American South in the aftermath of the Civil War and Reconstruction I think we can find some important hints about what drives sudden rapid increases in incarceration in the United States, and why such increases do prove immune to reform or retrenchment.

Prior to the 1860s the slave states of the South maintained very stable and small incarceration rates (Ayers, 1984). As is well known, the southern prison population remained almost entirely white, as slaves were subject to private forms of justice meted out by their owners. In the wake of the emancipation of 4 million African-Americans, however, the southern criminal justice system underwent a massive transformation (Lichtenstein, 1996a; Mancini, 1996; Oshinsky, 1996; Myers, 1998; Shapiro, 1998). First, there was a large increase in the absolute numbers of people sentenced to prison. To take just one example, in Georgia in 1871, at the tail end of Radical Reconstruction, there were only 385 prisoners; two and a half decades later that number had increased six-fold to 2357. In 1871 the overall incarceration rate in Georgia was 38 per 100,000; by 1896 it was roughly 100 per 100,000, having reached the plateau that characterized national rates of incarceration throughout the first three-quarters of the 20th century. (In 1998 Georgia's incarceration rate reached 492.) It is worth noting, however, that Georgia's incarceration rate for *whites* in 1896 was approximately 15 per 100,000 (the corresponding figure for blacks was 150 per 100,000), suggesting either a massive racial bias in the pattern of imprisonment or else the unlikely prospect that the state's white population was the most law-abiding citizenry in human history (Lichtenstein, 1996a).

This, of course, reflects the other crucial dimension of the increase in imprisonment in the South in the last quarter of the 19th century: crime control quite explicitly targeted emancipated African-Americans. With the overthrow of Radical Reconstruction and the reassertion of white supremacy in the South, blacks found themselves at the mercy of southern courts for offenses both petty and grand. Like today the net of criminal justice was cast widely in order to criminalize a whole battery of behaviors associated with blacks, while allowing whites to slip through. But the increase in incarceration did not entail only more convictions for newly defined crimes, but longer convictions as well. Like today, offenses that once would have incurred short sentences of a year or two suddenly merited five or 10 years. And, like today, anyone who objected to the resort to the penitentiary for previously minor offenses, to the lengthy sentences meted out, or to the conditions prevailing in the South's convict camps, was told that the grave dangers posed to the social order by the criminal class warranted such a drastic response (Cable, 1907 [1883]).

Yet this rapid increase in incarceration took place under the auspices of an extremely weak state (Woodward, 1951; Wallerstein, 1987); in fact, the wave of punishment depended on and to some extent even exacerbated feeble state capacity. Criminal justice in the South constituted a highly localized matter, dependent on sheriffs and judges elected at the county level, subject to grand juries convened from among the local white citizenry, and driven by the fee system, which made both sheriff and judge financially interested in convictions. Moreover, there was no actual penitentiary in many southern states, or at best only a shell of one: the vast majority of southern prisoners were leased out by the state to dozens of private entrepreneurs who were allowed to profit from the prisoners' labor and absorbed responsibility for feeding, incarcerating, and controlling them (Lichtenstein, 1996a).

Private exploitation came to fill the vacuum left by the 'virtual penitentiary,' which represented the state's hollowed out capacity to punish. This notorious convict lease system transformed the southern penal system from a fiscal burden upon the state into a revenue generator. Despite its extraordinary and well-known cruelties, for over 40 years most white southerners happily acquiesced in this regional penal practice because it accorded with their racial assumptions, relieved the state of the fiscal and administrative burden of penality, and stimulated private profit in key economic sectors like railroad construction, coal mining, and lumber production (Lichtenstein, 1994, 1996a; Mancini, 1996; Shapiro, 1998). Here, indeed, was a penal system driven by 'emotion, ideology, and political opportunism,' in Michael Tonry's words.

Instructive as well, however, is the penal 'reform' that replaced the convict lease system with chain gangs during the Progressive Era, which at least in theory eliminated private punishment in favor of renewed state control of prisoners and their labor. Did this represent a flowering of modern, reformist sensibilities and humane penal practice? Was it the 'rational analysis' and 'reasoned discussion' that its advocates proclaimed? A closer look at the advent of the chain gang may lend weight to the idea that the deep structures of American punishment cleave to penal notions derived from the private rather than the public sphere. The destruction of leasing and the embrace of the chain gang brought together a populist critique of leasing, the restoration of local control over the labor of prisoners and the intervention of rational penal expertise, without in any way severing punishment from its crucial role in racial control – perhaps, indeed, further legitimizing it (Lichtenstein, 1993).

At first glance the successful attack on convict leasing appears to be the state's reassertion of its power to punish over the private interests that had wrested it away in the name of profit. In fact, it more nearly represented an assault by popular interests – farmers, workers, and other ordinary citizens – against state collusion with a corrupt privatized system of punishment that benefited a few. Rather than send county convicts to the state 'penitentiary,' where they would be distributed to the lessees, the chain gang allowed localities to retain control over the prisoners convicted in their jurisdiction. There they were put to work improving local roads. Ironically, state oversight and control of the penal system actually was diminished by the decentralized nature of the chain gang system (Steiner and Brown, 1927). Under leasing, Georgia's convicts labored under control of a handful of powerful corporations; on the chain gang, the penal labor system was administered by over 150 separate county organizations with the scrutiny of only three state inspectors (Lichtenstein, 1993, 1996a).

As a political reform then, the chain gang was a 'populist' measure instituted not in the name of humanity but as a more equitable allocation of the fruits of the penal labor of African-Americans, who still constituted 80–90 percent of state prison populations in the South. As an administrative and legal measure, its champions held the chain gang up as a rational, efficient, and humane form of penal control – at least for southern blacks. It would train them to hard labor and discipline, be fiscally responsible, and even penally reformative (Whitin, 1912). Moreover, Progressive penal reformers in the South were quite explicit in their claims that chain gangs would relegitimize a system of racial control that had fallen into disrepute because of the corruption and brutality of convict leasing (McKelway, 1909). When privatized forms of racial control proved inadequate, or appeared illegitimate, as with lynching and leasing, the state stepped in as a proxy for the private power to punish.

With the exception of the 1960s, political mobilization on behalf of prisoners, rather than on behalf of the effectiveness of punishment itself, has rarely had much effect on penal regimes. Historically, patterns of increased incarceration and harsh forms of punishment have been deflected in one of three ways: by a crisis of legitimacy, by fiscal constraints, or by the inadvertent weakening of racial disparities in their effects (these often are reinforcing). The chain gang itself eventually succumbed to reforms when it was 'whitened' in its composition, exposed by a Hollywood film that focused on one of its white victims, and became fiscally untenable during the Great Depression (Burns, 1994 [1932]; Lichtenstein, 1995). Today's criminal justice process, from who gets arrested, to who gets charged with what, to the process of plea-bargaining, and access to a good defense, still has deeply racialized outcomes that are not all traceable to the shibboleth that more blacks go to prison because more blacks commit crime (Tonry, 1995; Cole, 1999). Yet some of the more egregious forms of racial disparity have been eroded; we are not going back to the days of white incarceration rates of less than 20 per 100,000. When the state of Alabama re-established the chain gang a few years ago they made sure that each coffle chained together three blacks with two whites, in exact proportion to their numbers in the state prison system (Lichtenstein, 1996b). Still, one cannot examine imprisonment in the USA without concluding that it is intimately bound up with larger patterns of historic and contemporary racial inequality, discrimination, and repression. Indeed, I would argue that stable incarceration rates appear in periods of white racial hegemony and a stable racial order, such as that secured by slavery in the first half of the 19th century or Jim Crow during the first half of the 20th. Correspondingly, sudden rises in incarceration, especially of minorities, tend to appear one generation after this racial hegemony has been cracked, as in the first and second Reconstructions of emancipation and civil rights.

Even while mass imprisonment has a profound impact on whites, who also go to prison today in record numbers, the public's acquiescence to a very expensive penal policy remains driven by a private fear of crime that remains stubbornly associated in the minds of many whites with people of color. Whether there is a limit to the social costs *whites* are willing to incur for this policy, as there was eventually with the chain gang in the first half of this century, is an open question. Imagine what the results would be if the impact of mass incarceration on whites was comparable to its effect on blacks. If nearly 10 percent of all white people were placed under correctional control tomorrow, would there be a national outcry? Of course there would. But today's penal policies are not likely to produce this kind of nonracialized police state. Their character is instead to be found in America's intertwined histories of prisons, penal reform, and racism.

Notes

1 In late January 2000, Governor Ryan of Illinois suspended that state's use of the death penalty, citing faulty verdicts. See *New York Times*, 1 February 2000: A1.

2 Rose Bird (1936–99) was appointed Chief Justice of the California Supreme Court by liberal governor Jerry Brown in 1977. Her opposition to the death penalty and solicitude for the rights of defendants earned her the enmity of the state's growing conservative movement. She was removed from the court in 1986 by popular vote.

3 A most trenchant comment on this dynamic can be found in Wright (1999).

4 A harsh reminder of this is to be found in the recent exhibit of lynching photographs, published as a 'catalog' under the title of *Without sanctuary* (Allen, 2000; Wypijewski, 2000).

5 The Bureau of Justice Statistics (1999) reports that as of 30 June 1998, the 10 states with the highest incarceration rates were Louisiana, Texas, Oklahoma, Mississippi, South Carolina, Nevada, Arizona, Alabama, Georgia, California, all in the South or the West (where many of the same characteristics can be found).

References

Allen, J. (2000) *Without sanctuary: lynching photography in America*. Santa Fe: Twin Palms Publishers.

Ayers, E.L. (1984) V*engenace and justice: crime and punishment in the 19th-century American South*. New York: Oxford University Press.

Brundage, W.F. (1993) *Lynching in the New South: Georgia and Virginia, 1880–1930*. Urbana, IL: University of Illinois Press.

Bureau of Justice Statistics (1999) *Prison and jail inmates at midyear 1998*. Washington, DC: US Department of Justice.

Burns, R.E. (1994 [1932]) *I am a fugitive from the Georgia chain gang!* Introduction by Alex Lichtenstein. Savannah: Beehive Press.

Butterfield, F. (1995) *All God's children: the Bosket family and the American tradition of violence*. New York: Alfred Knopf.

Cable, G.W. (1907 [1883]) *The silent South, together with the freedmen's case in equity and the convict lease system*. New York: Charles Scribner's Sons.

Christie, N. (1993) *Crime control as industry: towards gulags, western style?* London: Routledge.

Cole, D. (1999) *No equal justice: race and class in the American criminal justice system*. New York: New Press.

Featherstone, L. (2000) 'Prison labor', *Dissent* 47(Spring): 71–4.

Foucault, M. (1977) *Discipline and punish: the birth of the prison*, trans. Alan Sheridan. New York: Pantheon.

Fried, R. (1999) 'Chief Justice Rose Bird, 1936–1999', *Cal Law* 7 December.

Lafer, G. (1999) 'Captive labor: America's prisoners as corporate workforce', *The American Prospect* 46(Sept.–Oct.): 66–70.

Lichtenstein, A. (1993) 'Good roads and chain gangs in the progressive South: "the negro convict is a slave"', *Journal of Southern History* 59(Feb.): 85–110.

Lichtenstein, A. (1994) ' "Through the rugged gates of the penitentiary": convict labor and southern coal, 1870–1900', in R. Halpern and M. Stokes (eds) *Race and class in the American South since 1890*. Oxford: Berg Publishers.

Lichtenstein, A. (1995) 'Chain gangs, communism, and the "negro question": John Spivak's *Georgia nigger*', *Georgia Historical Quarterly* 79(Fall): 633–58.

Lichtenstein, A. (1996a) *Twice the work of free labor: the political economy of convict labor in the New South*. New York: Verso.

Lichtenstein, A. (1996b) 'Chain gang blues', *Dissent* 43(Fall): 3–7.

Lichtenstein, A. and Kroll, M. (1996) 'The fortress economy: the economic role of the US prison system', in E. Rosenblatt (ed.) *Criminal injustice: confronting the prison crisis*. Boston, MA: South End Press.

McKelway, A. (1909) 'Abolition of the convict lease system in Georgia', *Proceedings of the American Prison Association*. Indianapolis, IN: William H. Buford.

Mancini, M.J. (1996) *One dies, get another: convict leasing in the American South, 1866–1928*. Columbia, SC: University of South Carolina Press.

Myers, M. (1998) *Race, labor, and punishment in the New South*. Columbus, OH: Ohio State University Press.

Oshinsky, D.M. (1996) *'Worse than slavery: Parchman farm and the ordeal of Jim Crow justice*. New York: Free Press.

Parenti, C. (1999) *Lockdown America: police and prisons in the age of crisis*. New York: Verso.

Shapiro, K.A. (1998) *A New South rebellion: the battle against convict labor in the Tennessee coalfields, 1871–1896*. Chapel Hill, NC: University of North Carolina Press.

Steiner, J.F. and Brown, R.M. (1927) *The North Carolina chain gang: a study of county convict road work*. Chapel Hill, NC: University of North Carolina Press.

Tannenbaum, F. (1924) *Darker phases of the South*. London: G.P. Putnam's Sons.

Tonry, M. (1995) *Malign neglect: race, crime, and punishment in America*. New York: Oxford University Press.

Wallerstein, P. (1987) *From Slave South to New South: public policy in nineteenth-century Georgia*. Chapel Hill, NC: University of North Carolina Press.

Whitin, E.S. (1912) 'Convicts and road building', *Southern Good Roads* 5(June).

Woodward, C.V. (1951) *Origins of the New South, 1877–1913*. Baton Rouge, LA: Louisiana State University Press.

Wright, P. (1999) 'The cultural commodification of prisons', *Prison Legal News* 10(November): 1–5.

Wypijewski, J. (2000) 'Review of James Allen, *Without sanctuary*', *The Nation* 270(12).

Epilogue

The new iron cage

DAVID GARLAND

At the end of his classic work, *The protestant ethic and the spirit of capitalism*, Max Weber (1930/1985) described how the capitalist system came to outlive the spiritual vocation that originally gave it impetus and meaning. Weber says that the Puritan had *wanted* to work in a calling, and pursued capitalist enterprise as a way of escaping his anxieties and working out his ideals in the world. Those who came after were *compelled* to work in this way. Fate decreed that the capitalist institutions the Puritan built to pursue his vocation would become an iron cage, from which subsequent generations could not escape. Once the capitalist system of production and exchange was in place, once it had established its 'mechanical foundations', it no longer had need of the spiritual motivations that first gave it meaning. Subsequent generations were not driven to work by religious enthusiasm. They were forced to work by the dull compulsion of economic necessity.

Weber's point, more prosaically put, is that institutions have a way of taking on a life of their own, and outliving the meanings and motivations that led to them being set up in the first place. Once they become established, they form an environment to which everyone is forced to adapt, a context into which new generations are born. If they survive for long enough, institutions tend to form habits, to vest interests, and to channel thinking. They reproduce themselves and become part of the scheme of things, continuing long after the original reasons for their creation have faded.

It is quite possible that, given time, and in the absence of concerted opposition, mass imprisonment will become a new 'iron cage' in Weber's sense of the term. As the contributors to this issue show, its original causes lie in the history of the closing decades of the 20th century. These causes include:

- anxieties about crime and violence;
- the demand for public protection;
- the notion that concern for victims excludes concern for offenders;
- political populism married to a distrust of the criminal justice system;
- the discrediting of social solutions to the problem of order;
- a stern disregard for the plight of the undeserving poor.

But if these are the *originating* causes of mass imprisonment, its *perpetuating* causes may be quite different. Once established, the system begins to take on a life of its own, to give rise to adaptive behaviour, to serve a number of secondary functions. The most striking example of this is the emergence of a penal-industrial complex, with newly vested interests in commercial prison contracts, and the jobs and profits they bring. But we also learn how 'law and order' policies and tough sentencing laws function in the rhetoric of political exchange and the entertainment business of the media. And over the last two decades, mass imprisonment has come to form a central element in a new culture of crime control. It has created attitudes and assumptions that are hard to dislodge, and which are reinforced whenever high prison rates coincide with observed crime reductions. All of this makes one wonder how America could ever scale down its penal response. How will the new iron cage ever be dismantled?

At the beginning of the 21st century, the USA is experiencing an unprecedented economic boom, with low unemployment levels, rising standards of living, a federal surplus and healthy state budgets. Crime has been declining steadily and markedly since 1992. And yet there is every sign that the shift towards mass imprisonment continues. As the market in private security expands, the delivery of penal legislation speeds up, and the crime control culture reproduces itself, we face the real possibility of being locked into this state of affairs. After all, the new arrangements spawn institutional investments and produce definite benefits, particularly for the social groups who are at the greatest distance from them. They entail a way of allocating the costs of crime – unjust, unequal, but feasible nonetheless.

But they also involve serious social costs that will become increasingly apparent. These costs include:

- the allocation of state spending to imprisonment rather than education or social policy budgets;
- the reinforcement of criminogenic processes and the destruction of social capital, not just for inmates but for their families and neighbourhoods;
- the transfer of prison culture out into the community;
- the discrediting of law and legal authority among the groups most affected;
- the hardening of social and racial divisions.

The strategy of mass imprisonment might be a feasible solution to the problem of social order, but it is a deeply unattractive one. The marginalized, criminalized poor may lack political power and command little public sympathy, but in aggregate terms they have the negative capacity to make life unpleasant for everyone else. And, of course, the policies that we adopt towards such groups define 'us' as much as we define 'them'.

As Rusche and Kirchheimer (1968) pointed out long ago, the prison system is part of an institutional network for governing the poor. That we now choose to allocate social spending budgets to meet the rising costs of incarceration rather than to fund education or housing or income support, will strike many people as a scandalous waste and a betrayal of America's highest ideals – particularly as and when crime rates level off, and public opinion becomes less convinced that 'prison works'.

As David Greenberg points out in his article, the US prison population continues to grow, but there are signs that the social, fiscal and political costs of mass imprisonment are themselves becoming a topic of public concern. The sustained reduction in crime rates has made the issue of crime control slightly less urgent, slightly less prominent in political discourse. Some of the most conservative figures in crime policy are beginning to back away from the prospect of continued mass incarceration: former Attorney

General Edwin Meese has publicly complained about the passing of 'symbolic legislation' and has criticized the federal government's expanding role in crime control. Even John J. DiIulio Jr, who with James Q. Wilson has been one of the few academic voices supporting the prison boom, has been moved to declare that '2 million prisoners are enough' (DiIulio, 1999) and to admit that an increasing proportion of prison inmates are neither violent offenders nor 'career criminals'.

At a recent Democratic presidential debate at the Apollo Theater in Harlem, Al Gore and Bill Bradley were asked a question about race and imprisonment. Both candidates ducked the issue of mass imprisonment, and the need for it, confining themselves to some *pro forma* agonizing about the racial bias involved. But candidate Gore did say – with an intonation that made it sound like a political slogan in the making – 'we need to pursue *education* with as much energy as we pursue *incarceration*'. Perhaps this is the first hint that, even within an avowedly law and order administration, mass imprisonment is beginning to be viewed as part of the problem, and not part of the solution.

References

DiIulio, J.J. (1999) 'Two million prisoners are enough', *The Wall Street Journal* 12 March.

Rusche, G. and Kirchheimer, O. (1968) *Punishment and social structure.* New York: Russell & Russell.

Weber, M. (1930/1985) *The Protestant ethic and the spirit of capitalism.* Hemel Hempstead: Allen & Unwin.

Index

African Americans *see* black
  population
age, and crime, 161
Aid to Families with Dependent
  Children (AFDC), 35–6, 40, 73
Alaska, 36
alternative public space, 32–4
American exceptionalism, 53–5
American Indians, 46
American Law Institute, 155–9
American South, 21, 87–8, 171,
  173–6
Anderson, E., 97, 121–37, 138–9,
  141, 142
Anti-Drug Abuse Acts, 6
Arizona, 40
Asian population, 46
asylum seekers, 74
attitudes, influence on penal policy,
  11, 150–62
Austria, 57, 74
Ayers, E.L., 172, 173

Bates, S., 156
Beccaria, C., 159
Beck, A., 6, 7, 10, 72, 82, 160, 161,
  168
Beck, U., 25
Beckett, K., 6, 9, 15, 21, 22, 23,
  35–47, 56, 62, 63, 70–3, 151
Belgium, 62
Bennett, J.V., 156
Bennett, W., 6
Berry, M., 141
Bird, R., 171–2
black population, 2, 10, 35, 40–6
  passim, 60, 62, 82–114, 171,
  173–6
Blackburn, R., 64
Blair, T., 58
blaming, 16, 17, 21
Blumstein, A., 6, 7, 83, 161
Bourne, P., 152
Bradley, B., 181
Bridges, G.S., 41, 42
Britain, 34, 52, 57, 58–9, 76
  black population, 60
  crime rates, 56
  health and welfare services, 61,
    62–3
  homicide, 75
Brown, J., 168
Bruner, J., 139
Bulger, J., 56
Bureau of Justice Assistance, 6

bureaucratic institutions, and risk
  selection, 17–18, 24
burglary, 8
Bush, G., 6, 23, 55, 83
Butterfield, F., 35, 172

California, 40, 44, 99, 147, 148, 166
Canada, 52
capital punishment *see* death penalty
capitalism, 52–3, 74–5, 179
Caplow, T., 6, 15, 70, 151
Carroll, L., 41, 42, 96
causes of crime, 51
Cayton, H., 89, 90, 92, 93
chain gangs, 171, 175–6
Chambliss, W., 56
Chesterton, G.K., 144
China, 52
Chiricos, T.G., 42, 75
Chomsky, N., 138
Christie, N., 9, 28, 52, 173
church, and black population, 92, 93
Churchill, W., 32
cities, as sources of crime, 21–2
class, 9–10
  and black ghettos, 90–1
Clinton, B., 23, 55, 58, 83, 106, 168,
  169
'code of the street', 97, 121–2, 142
Cold War, 18–19
communicative rationality, 32
communitarianism, 25
community care, 61, 63
community corrections, 10
Conservative Party, 58
'convict code', 97, 142
convict leasing, 171, 174–5
corporatism, 61, 62
cost-benefit analysis, 10–11
courts, as institutions of social change,
  20
Cressey, D., 103
crime control, 7–8, 57–9
crime prevention, 71
  situational, 60
crime rates, 6, 7, 8, 42, 51, 56–7,
  60–1, 71, 75, 76–7
  Europe, 56–7, 76–7
criminal careers, 161
criminality, 100–1
  blackness and, 104–5
Crutchfield, R.D., 41, 42
cultural capital, 106
Curran, J., 29–30
Currie, E., 35, 51, 55

Curtis, R., 7–8

Danziger, S., 35, 38
death penalty, 10, 77, 171
declension, 54
Delaware, 40
Delone, M., 42, 75
Denton, N., 75, 94
deregulation, 52, 61, 62, 75, 77
deterrence, 38, 51, 71
DiIulio, J.J., 96, 181
disenfranchisement, 106–7
distrust, governmental, 148, 172
Dole, R., 24
Donziger, S., 35, 83
Douglas, M., 15, 16–20, 21, 22, 24
Downes, D., 51–66, 57, 58, 59, 60,
  73–5
Drake, St. Clair, 89, 90, 92, 93
drug markets, 7–8, 22
drug policies, 5–6, 15, 56, 64, 83,
  146, 165, 168, 169
drug use, 21, 56, 152–3
DuBois, W.E.B., 105
Dukakis, M., 23
Dumm, T., 53
Durkheim, E., 1, 53

economy/economic conditions, 9–10,
  42, 51, 61–4, 74, 75
  and the ghetto, 84–5, 91–2
  see also poverty
educational programs, 106
Ekland-Olson, S., 97
Elliott, L., 62
employment, 63, 72, 75
  see also unemployment
entertainment, demand for, 30–1
environmental pollution, 16, 18, 20,
  21, 23
environmentalism, 18, 19, 20
Esping-Anderson, G., 36, 84
Europe, 51–66 *passim*
  see also individual countries
European Convention on Human
  Rights, 59

fear of crime, 15–16, 20–4, 28, 58
Fee, J. Alger, 158–9
Finland, 52
Finley, M., 107, 142
Flood, G.F., 159
Florida, 160
Foucault, M., 1, 143, 151, 171
France, 52, 57, 62, 76

Frankel, M., 5, 154
freedom of movement, 60
  see also labor, mobility of

gangs, racially-based, 97–8
Garland, D., 1–3, 15, 24, 37, 38, 55, 57, 179–81
Geijer, L., 32
genetics, 100–1, 112n
Georgia, 40, 174
Gerbner, G., 29
Germany, 52, 57, 61, 62, 76
the ghetto, 83–4, 85, 88–90
  hyper-, 85, 90–5
Gilmore, G., 152, 153, 155
globalization, 24–5, 77–8
going straight, 121–37
Goldwater, B., 9
good time, 158
Gore, A., 181
Gottshchalk, P., 35, 38
government, distrust of, 148, 166, 172
Gray, J., 53
Greenberg, D., 42, 53, 70–8, 83, 180
Greenfeld, L., 168
Greenfield, J., 138
guns
  control of, 64
  supply of, 7
Gurr, T.R., 75, 76

Habermas, J., 32, 140
Hagan, J., 46
Hassine, V., 96, 99
Hattersley, R., 58
Hawaii, 36
Hawkins, G., 2, 42, 56, 64, 146
health sector, 61, 93
  Britain, 61, 63
Helms, R.E., 42, 71, 75
Herrnstein, R.J., 100–1, 140–1
Heymann, P., 169
Hills, J., 55, 59
Hispanic population, 2, 35, 46
homicide, 7, 56, 75, 76
homosexual relations, 59
Horton, W., 23
housing, 93, 94
Howard, M., 58

ideology, end of, 139–40
Illinois, 102
immigrant populations, 60, 74, 77
  see also minority populations
incapacitation, 38, 51
incomes
  inequality of, 9–10, 42, 51, 74, 75
  see also poverty
individualism, 9, 25, 54
inequality, social and economic, 9–10, 42, 51, 74, 75
information industries, 19
institutional frameworks, and risk selection, 16–19
International Victim Survey, 57
Internet, 99–100
Irwin, J., 95–6, 97, 103, 105

Italy, 57, 62

Jacobs, D., 42, 71, 75
Jacobs, J.B., 97, 165–9
Jim Crow system, 85, 87–8, 103, 176
Johnson, P., 151, 155
Johnson, R., 96, 97
Junger-Tas, J., 58
just deserts, 55
juvenile justice, 22
juveniles, 7

Kagan, D., 152–3
Katz, M., 38
Kennedy, R., 104
King, R., 55, 98
Kirchheimer, O., 37, 42, 180
KROM (Norwegian Association for Penal Reform), 33
Kross, A.M., 158
Kuhn, A., 52, 55, 58, 64, 74

labor, mobility of, 77, 78
Labour Party, 58–9, 62
Lawrence, S., 59
legitimation, of policy decisions, 32
Lettiere, M., 53, 55
Lichenstein, A., 171–6
life histories, 139
Louisiana, 40
Lynch, M., 70
lynching, 171

Madsen, D., 54
Maguire, M., 71, 77
Maine, 40
Mancini, M.J., 174, 175
marginality, social, 36–47
market institutions, and risk selection, 17, 24
Marshall, I., 59, 62
Marx, K., 53
Marxism, 74–5
Maryland, 102
Massey, D., 75, 94
Mathieson, T., 28–34, 52
Mauer, M., 2, 4–13, 28, 29, 62, 83, 103
media, 11–12, 29–31, 33
  see also press; television
Meese, E., 181
'Megan's Laws', 100, 146, 148
Melossi, D., 42, 53, 55, 104
mentally ill, 61, 63
Michalowski, R.J., 42, 70, 71
Michigan, 40, 102
Miller, J., 15, 55, 62, 83, 93, 94, 102, 138–44
Minnesota, 36, 40, 161
minority populations, 40, 41, 44–6, 60
  see also black populations
Mississippi, 36
Model Penal Code, 155–9, 168, 172
Morgan, R., 55, 57, 58, 59
Morris, N., 96, 98, 105
Murray, C., 55, 100, 140–1
Musto, D., 152, 153, 155

narrative, 140–1
National Advisory Commission on Criminal Justice Standards and Goals, 4–5
Nebraska, 40
Netherlands, 52, 56, 57, 62, 74, 76
Nevada, 40
New Deal, 18, 109n
New Hampshire, 40
New York, 102
Nixon, R., 8, 9, 23, 55
normalization, 55
North Dakota, 36, 40
Norwegian Association for Penal Reform (KROM), 33

Ohio, 102
Oklahoma, 40
Omnibus Budget Reconciliation Act (1981), 35
operational function of criminal law, 146–7, 172
organized crime threat, 28
Oshinsky, D.M., 103, 171, 174

Parenti, C., 55, 173
parole, 6, 22, 99–100, 158
partisan politics, 168–9
  and crime control policy, 57–9
  and incarceration rates, 42
  see also Republican Party
Pastore, A.L., 71, 77
Patterson, O., 86, 106
Pearson, M.A., 42, 70, 71
Pease, K., 42, 58, 168
Pennsylvania, 102
Petersilia, J., 99, 100
Pickens, W., 141
policy, 5–6, 8–13, 31–2, 37–9, 72–3, 146–9, 165–9, 171–6
  Britain, 57, 58–9
  influence of changing sensibilities on, 150–62
  see also welfare policy
policy regimes, 36, 39, 72
political participation, 106–7
politicization of crime, 9
politics
  of criminal punishment, 146–9
  structure of, 19–20
  see also partisan politics
Portugal, 57
positivism, 139–40
postindustrial economy, 19
Postman, N., 30
postmodernity, 25
postprison supervision, 99–100
  see also parole
poverty, 35, 38, 41, 41–2, 43, 44, 45, 51, 74, 77, 84
press, black, 93
preventive detention, 154
prisons
  as ghettos, 95–103
  as instrument for social purging, 98–9
  racial division in, 96–7
private punishment, 173–4

privatization, 61
probation, 6, 22, 157
property offenses, 8, 41, 43, 44, 45, 63, 76
prosecutorial sentence appeals, 154–5
public debate, 32–3
public opinion, 11, 152–3, 158–9

race and ethnicity, 10, 12, 44–6
    see also black populations; minority populations
race riots, 105–6, 113–14n
racial segregation, 10, 21
    see also the ghetto; Jim Crow system
Radzinowicz, L., 52
rape, 20–1, 168
Reagan, R., 6, 9, 23, 55, 83
recidivism, 63, 154, 160–1
reform strategies, 10–11, 12–13, 171
rehabilitation, 5, 37, 38, 46, 54, 55, 58, 111n
reparation, 59
Republican Party, 42, 43, 44, 45, 46
respect, in street culture, 122
responsibility, individual, 58
restitution, 10
restorative justice, 13, 59
retribution, 38, 171, 172
Rhode Island, 40
riots
    prison, 4, 105–6, 113–14n
    race, 105–6, 113–14n
risk and risk selection, 15–19, 23, 24, 25, 60–1
Robert (case study), 122–37, 138–9, 141
Rothman, D., 4, 37, 54, 55
Ruggiero, V., 57
Rusche, G., 37, 42, 108n, 180
Russia, 1, 28, 52
Rutherford, A., 32, 58

Scandinavia, 52, 57, 61, 62
    see also Sweden
schools, 93, 94–5
sectarian social organization, 22–4, 25
    and fear of crime, 21–2
    and risk selection, 18–19, 24
    and social change, 20
security-mindedness, 38, 60–1
segregation see class segregation; racial segregation
Sennett, R., 53

sentences
    appellate review of, 154–5
    lengthening of, 146, 165
    mitigation of, 157
    reconsideration of, 157
sentencing, 5–6, 12, 146, 148, 165–6, 168
    determinate, 2, 5–6, 12
    indeterminate, 5, 12, 38
    mandatory, 2, 6
    purposes of, 156–7
    'truth in', 2, 6, 12, 146, 148
service industries, 19
sex offenders, 100
Shapiro, K.A., 174, 175
Sharpe, J.A., 75, 76
Shils, E., 17
Simon, J., 6, 15–26, 28, 53, 57, 70, 74, 96, 151
single-issue politics, 19
situational crime prevention, 60
Skinner, Q., 140
slavery, 85, 86–7, 103, 106, 107, 176
social control, 38
social marginality, 36–47
social policy see welfare policy
social reform, 54
social stratification, 9–10
    in black ghettos, 90–1
socialism, 52
South Africa, 52
South Carolina, 40
Spain, 57
stigmatization, 99–101
Straw, J., 58, 59
street culture, 121–2
Sweden, 76
Switzerland, 74
Sykes, G., 96, 97, 103
symbolic function of criminal law, 146–7, 172

Tannenbaum, F., 171
Tappan, P.W., 156
taxation, 75
Taylor, I., 57, 75
television, 11–12, 20, 28–33
Texas, 36, 40
Thomas, W.I., 139
'three strikes' laws, 12, 111–12n, 146, 147, 148, 166
Tonry, M., 5, 35, 52, 53, 55, 56, 57, 60, 62, 83, 102, 150–62, 167–9, 171–2

'tough on crime' movement, 8–13
Travers, T., 62
treatment philosophy, 32

underclass, 84, 85
unemployment, 9, 24–5, 41, 42, 43, 45, 62, 71–2, 75, 77
urban population, 41, 43, 45
Useem, B., 71, 105
Utah, 40

Vermont, 40
victimization, 60–1
victims, interests of, and severity of sentences, 147, 165–6
vigilantism, 173
violent crime, 7, 20–1, 41, 43, 44, 45, 51, 56, 76
Voegelin, E., 139, 143
voting rights, 106–7

Wacquant, L., 60, 82–114, 138, 140, 141–3
Washington, 40, 44
Weber, M., 179
Wechsler, H., 156, 157, 158, 159
welfare policy, 35–47, 52, 61, 70, 72–3, 84, 106
welfare state, 2, 36, 38, 55, 61, 62, 77
welfarism, 37–8, 46, 62
West, V., 70, 71, 83
West Virginia, 40
Western, B., 9, 35–47, 62, 63, 70–3
white males, 2
Wideman, J.E., 104–5
Wildavsky, A., 15, 16–20, 21, 22, 24
Wilkins, L., 9, 42
Williamson, J., 86, 88
Wilson, J.Q., 15, 54, 100
Wilson, W.J., 62, 64, 89
women, black, 82
Woodward, C.V., 87, 174
Work Opportunity and Personal Responsibility Act (1996), 106

Yates, J., 41, 83
Young, J., 51, 55, 70

zero sum model of punishment, 147, 172
zero tolerance, 59
Zimring, F., 2, 42, 56, 64, 145–9, 165–6, 172
Znaniecki, F., 139